"*Sticky Karma* is a wild yet nuanced ride through our complex dance with COVID and into the mind of one very interesting man. Uncomfortable as it is to be taken back through the challenges of the virus, the re-grieving induced becomes healing as a result of Shainen's deep understanding and gentle ways.... It's like sitting next to an old pal in a pub and ordering another round because you don't want the night nor the stories to end."

–Earl Hipp, 2022 NYC Big Book Award-winning author of *Fighting Invisible Tigers*

"If you are thirsting for musings and observations that will resonate with you, that will leave you reassured that you aren't losing your mind in this age of cascading catastrophes, Lee's delicious writing will sate your soul. *Sticky Karma* is on my nightstand like a lighthouse on a rock, a beacon that I reach for when the waters of turmoil rise and I am in need of provocative comfort, profound humor, and an excellent read by a gifted author."

–David Fitzsimmons, nationally syndicated cartoonist

"No doubt, COVID-19 changed the way many people think and act. For Lee Shainen, add a near death event during the pandemic. Together, they changed his interest from writing what he once called 'fast food fiction' to looking inward. The result is *Sticky Karma*, a gentle ramble into streams of both past and present consciousness.... Shainen's self-deprecating humor, mixed with his new age spiritualism and midwestern roots, provide both chuckles and insight."

–John Hudak, publisher, *Tucson Lifestyle*

"*Sticky Karma* reminds us of the anxiety and uncertainty experienced with COVID's arrival. Like a jazz musician, in each chapter, Lee presents progressions on remembrance, introspection, and wonder. Always returning to themes of our evolving COVID fears, he takes us through riffs of reflection, inspiring readers to do the same, but without having to almost die!"

–Elliot Glicksman, comedian and founder of the Tucson Jazz Festival

"Weaving together current events, dazzling observations, and wondrous insights with his often tumultuous life events, Lee Shainen is the deeply affecting narrator of his own life story.... Witty and searing, Shainen invites us to explore his life's learning journey and—in ways that will astonish and move the reader—inspires us to do the same with our own."

–Lois Bridges, Executive Director, Bring Me a Book Foundation

"Profound and beautiful, *Sticky Karma* is a book worth savoring slowly. Written as a series of anecdotes and reflections interspersed with poetry, Shainen offers insights into creativity, aging, human interconnectedness, teaching, solitude, and the art of loving another human (and two cats). When reading Shainen's book, the pleasure lies in the witty, wise, and wonder-filled journey. As he reaches for meaning, we gain understanding into our own search, and discover the inconceivable gift we all share: the gift of a life lived interconnected with others who help us see what we cannot see on our own."

–Rodney Vance, international award-winning filmmaker and screenwriter

"I was among the legion of those who were entertained and uplifted by Lee Shainen's social media musings throughout the COVID crisis. *Sticky Karma*, the book that sprang from those posts, whips those musings into a disciplined, literate, funny, and heartwarming account of everyday life in the plague years."

–Tom Beal, former editor and columnist, *Arizona Daily Star*

"*Sticky Karma* is an introspective look at life disguised as one man's discussion with himself about the COVID pandemic. Using the pandemic as a jumping-off point, Lee leads us through the most impactful moments of his life, and in doing so, puts words to the thoughts, feelings and emotions the rest of us usually find too difficult to face. The breadth of Lee's experiences are truly dazzling, and hearing his unique take on these events, as filtered through his personality and inimitable perspective, take us on a humorous and touching ride not to be missed, all within a thinly veiled love letter to his wife. A must-read."

–Jeffrey Jay Levin, author of *Watching, Volume 1: The Garden Museum Heist*

Sticky Karma

Sticky Karma

Meditations on Meaning
and Madness in the
Time of COVID

Lee Shainen

Sticky Karma:
Meditations on Meaning and Madness in the Time of COVID

Copyright © 2023 Lee Shainen

For permissions, contact: editor@latahbooks.com

Cover design by Randy Harris and Kevin Breen
Book design by Kevin Breen
Interior illustrations by David Fitzsimmons

ISBN: 978-1-957607-11-5
Cataloging-in-Publication Data is available upon request

Manufactured in the United States of America

Published by Latah Books
www.latahbooks.com

Preface

Early in the COVID-19 pandemic, with growing concern about conditions in crowded hospitals, a tumor burst in my stomach, and I began bleeding out. Born in 1954, I'm not terribly old, yet no one in my family of origin seems to have lived as long as I have. Even my adoptive mother was dead at 47. It wasn't hard to imagine I had reached my expiration date.

I never liked hospitals and didn't want to go to one then, but too weak to stand, I tenderly said goodbye to my wife and agreed to an ambulance. While receiving blood transfusions to be able to survive surgery, I started to send out amends and words previously unsaid to others in my life. It felt like enlightenment, as in the lightening up of all that I had been carrying inside.

I spent ten days in the hospital and then months recovering. The world was in lockdown. I had the leisure to read through a lifetime of journals, letters, unfinished manuscripts, scribbled great notions, and to revise, edit, and write afresh. My thinking seemed to become clearer, and my writing more honest. Once eager to merge with others through their stories, I have finally found a place from where I can share my own. It is my first attempt, without the safety net of fiction, to tell the truth.

The writings that follow did not start with the intention of becoming this book. Only through encouragement and guidance did something long-brewing in me finally emerge. And perhaps under the influence of the precious scientist I live with, a double helix writing style of poetry in narrative and narrative in poetry developed to unify the realm.

Those who have been reading my musings will know that the events happened closely to the order presented. If it were fiction, some of it would have been too unbelievable for any editor to allow. Truth is indeed often stranger and, I might add, more demanding to write, as I had to locate records and verify how things actually unfolded. Memory is suspect. Often, I would have bet I knew the way a thing happened (since these are my stories), and often I would have been wrong.

And so I offer this: the distilled essence of a life story, and the meditations on meaning that emerged in two years of a pandemic as seen through the lens of a man who had to almost die before he could write what he had been carrying unspoken for forty years.

For my family
by birth, adoption, friendship,
love, marriage, and golf

Part One: 2020

January/February

Now that this body of mine not so quietly discourages much adventure, I notice, midst the loss, a habitual deliberateness in taking better care of both self and surroundings.

Hallelujah!

Like other youthful self-abusers who tackled and swallowed Life unfiltered, I never thought I'd live this long. Don't get me wrong, I'm not disappointed to find myself alive

... as a rising sun pokes holes in morning clouds. There is more than enough light to consider and combine fresh ingredients with eggs from a friend's brood. This preparation of food, slow and thoughtful, has become a sustaining meditation.

Just a few years ago, after twenty years of inching towards it, my wife and I finally moved in together. 2020 had long been a target for us. In May, Susan will join me in retirement. We bought a townhouse that can be locked up and left. Our plan is to become sunbirds who spend summers away from the desert heat.

Moments once searched for without are now often brewed within this home we are still co-creating. There is warmth in the morning light as I hand-wash dishes and place them in the dishwasher to dry. Standing at the sink, rocking chair memories emerge and merge with my view of sky and garden. There is no hurry, no haste, nowhere I need to be but here learning to love, sometimes even understand this slow journey of ours.

Today, watching the news: A continent is burning. Australia, high on our bucket list, is being devastated. Susan will tell you, I worry about everything, but also imagine people coming together when facing disaster.

I had a teacher who emphasized that everything we know and perceive is because of those who came before us. Our first task is to understand the past; next, to modify and apply that understanding as it pertains to our own times; then, pass along what's relevant and meaningful: a never-ending bucket brigade of knowledge over ignorance.

Actually, we have always been passing on buckets of what is most needed. It is in our deepest nature to work together and assist each other. When we don't, mistakes are made and repeated, suffering and inequality increase, and soon what holds a civilization together, deteriorates.

Yet there is enough of what is needed. Our problems come from the greed of some and the lack of motivation of many to overcome distribution difficulties. In our separation, we have forgotten we are meant to be in service with and for each other. We have become too distant from the next set of hands, even from those in the home next door. Fear seems more prevalent than trust. And there is so much pain, so many crises, it is truly overwhelming.

My instinct is to retreat. I don't know how to fix the whole. But my challenge to myself is to get back in that bucket line anyway, share what I have, and look into the eyes of a neighbor, or a stranger, and nod: "I'm here too."

Perhaps that is connected to why, whenever I'm walking along a road, I pick up every nail or rubber-puncturing object I see. Or am I selfishly improving my chances for good Tire Karma? Don't really know. But it is an easy thing to do that perhaps might spare another human the hassle, time, and aggravation of a flat. It's not specific or personal assistance, of course, and may even be presumptuous of me to assume that it may NOT be in so-and-so's best interest to be slowed down by some inconvenience.

I also get that no one will ever thank me for meddling in these complicated Karmachanics. In fact, it is the random, unknowable nature of the outcomes from this now habitual, anonymous behavior that appeal to me.

I might be interfering in the Grand Scheme of Things, but as a citizen in this particular Cosmos, I'm also voting for a reality where simple acts of thoughtful consideration shape our common ground.

For most of us, there are things that take a lifetime (if ever) to learn. If we're lucky, we survive our own mistakes and foolishness.

Once, faced with moving an old piano no one wanted, I had the notion to dismantle it for art parts and for ease of disposing the remainder. I had no clue how much tension was in the strings. Standing on a section of collapsed piano while leaning over to unscrew the iron plate below me, that tension explosively released, catapulting me across the room.

It was yet another stunning lesson in how little I know about what I find myself already doing anyway.

Well, even rounded mountains did not give up their hard edges all at once. Weathering winds, storms, and relentless time slowly carved and smoothed them. I feel that way about my belly, the six pack that once was. I paid dearly for this current softness. Oh sure, those jagged peaks were once exhilarating to attain, but such lofty altitudes do not long the best bedfellows make.

A couple of hours ago, umbrella-destroying winds picked up and some rain began. It woke me up. And then, my busy little brain remembered the new umbrella with solar-powered LED lights cranked open in the yard. Dang it! No way to go back to sleep now.

Naked, I went out into the wind and rain to close it, not thinking of how the cold water would then cascade off the umbrella and down my bare back. Nor did I think to grab a towel or something to wipe my wet feet before tracking back into the house.

I did, however, follow that brave excursion with crawling back into bed to my darling. Seems cold and wet, even if soft and round, also does not the best bedfellow make.

A couple of weeks ago, the World Health Organization announced a coronavirus in Wuhan, China. Now it's here. On February 6th, 2020, the first American died from what is being called COVID-19.

Also in the news: After a year in the dark, communication with Voyager 2 has been restored. I find myself contemplating the long-term planning of those involved, the good fortune and excellent timing behind the achievement.

(Stars align in many ways. I remember house-sitting for Brad Smith, an astronomer at the University of Arizona, and marveling at the screen saver on his computer: the known universe! One could shift perspective in it to see the view from anywhere. He was the leader for Voyager's imaging team. I only knew him because he married Diane, who was living with me when they met. I knew her because I impulsively approached her on campus once, connected, stayed in touch through letters for years, and then offered her a place to live when her first marriage ended.)

Entangled

I've heard about how particles
that once vibrated closely together
still react in unison
even when separated
by whatever distance

Perhaps, Everything That Is
originated from such a place,
and how why
even when asleep to each other
we dance still in dreams

Back in 1977, an alignment of planets that wouldn't happen again for another 175 years or so allowed the Voyager space probes to use the gravity of all four giant outer planets to propel their extraordinary exploratory journeys.

At the leisurely speed of no more than 38,610 mph, and traveling anywhere from 290-320 million miles a year, it still took years to first reach Jupiter, then Saturn. Six years after Saturn, Uranus. Another three years to Neptune. All of that time to travel through our tiny solar system.

Back on Earth, course adjustments were made and monitored, all the while receiving images and information that have transformed our understanding.

What we are collectively capable of doing is astounding.

Voyager 1 left our solar system in 2012, Voyager 2 in 2018; both are still transmitting! I have friends across town I hear from less.

Human-crafted objects, billions of miles from home, now in interstellar space, but still 40,000 years from an encounter with another star. OMG!

Hey, I just replaced the transmission in my truck after only 100,000 miles. That's not even halfway to the moon.

Sometimes reluctant to even leave my house, I find myself dreaming of escape velocity—the energy needed to break free from the confinement of old expectations into the weightless place where a body can slow forever, approaching—but never reaching—zero speed.

Nowadays, after being on call around the clock for decades, I have an old flip phone that is seldom on. I miss a lot of calls, but that's okay—I have little to say. Susan is still working, and I spend a fair amount of time alone.

However, I often wander around and eavesdrop. What are people talking about?

Yesterday, I was surprised by two loud and toothless guys sitting at a bar. There was no ignoring them. But I resisted any impulse to join in, which I considered quite the accomplishment. I just listened.

One had never finished high school. Both were veterans who liked guns and had trouble staying married. They had arguments with others that I thought could have been avoided.

But here's the thing: They listened to each other without talking over each other. They'd acknowledge what the other said, then added to the subject, rather than changing it.

They went back and forth in time together, enjoying every moment, while nursing, not guzzling, their beers.

I left them without ever having said a word and walked home with a grin. I didn't try to fix anything, just witnessed.

There are so many things wrong in the world, so much I can't imagine how it will ever be repaired, but there is something in the human spirit that can't help but to grow and evolve. It can spring forth from where least expected and not look like anything that came before.

There are now 60 confirmed cases of COVID-19 in the United States. It is worse in Italy.

March

The World Health Organization is now calling this virus a pandemic. It has our attention.

St. Patrick's Day parades have been canceled. The NBA, NHL, NCAA, MLB and more are all suspending games. The market is plummeting. Schools are closing. Shelter-in-place, stay-at-home orders for non-essential workers have been given in several states. A national emergency has been declared. It's getting real! Americans with no sports to watch, not going to work, and with no school for the kids? I sure wonder how this will affect families and relationships.

A virus is an equal opportunity agent, demanding our collective attention, a species' response. These mutant migrants care nothing for borders or walls, make no distinction of gender, have no preference for race.

Meanwhile, what to do in our various shelters while waiting for this kind of storm to pass?

Books are good company, for sure, but with a Shadow spreading across the globe, I wonder if it's not a time for self-reflection sparking a deeper truth-telling. There just might be something in softly sharing our honest, genuine light that disinfects and heals what truly ails us.

As kids in elementary school, we had drills where we'd all get under our desks. We were being prepared for the inevitable bomb to fall. As if ...

Seems like people always need to do something while waiting for oblivion. We buckle up in airplanes as a convenience for those who might have to sort through the wreckage of a crash. It increases the possibility for identification, not survival.

We carry guns or charms, wear masks or talismans for protection, luck, and prayer, live as we can, while waiting … for the attack, the accident, the asteroid, the moment that either ends or changes everything.

But waiting for a virus to come and go is not like anything else. In over-preparing, we take from others. In our withdrawal and not-doing, essential exchanges slow and halt. People suffer.

There are so many hands that need holding in this time of no touching. It's as if we are being asked to become something else, something still unknown, something (I hope) worth waiting for.

Finally living with Susan also means living with cats. I can be allergic. We keep two rooms cat-free, so I can take refuge when needed. Of course, the cats are aware of any slip, of a door left open, even for a moment, and get in.

Ever since learning how cats make sounds around humans that activate the same brain response in us as an infant's cry, I have felt resentful and manipulated. I now eye our cats suspiciously, wondering what else they're up to, while questioning what ways I've already changed my life for them.

Long ago, humans and felines made a pact: They could hang around our structures and eat our scraps in exchange for them taking care of rodents. Perhaps it was a good deal once, but nowadays they've moved indoors, send us out searching for the exact right food for them, and have mostly sub-contracted out their extermination duties.

I know, the dogs warned us about them. We just didn't listen.

If these are the trenches, the muddy fields where we are asked to do battle, can we not do that?
I imagine our grandparents shaking their heads in amazement at how little is asked of us.
Yet there are so many kinds of heroism, and the entire world, more than in any war before, is engaged in this struggle.
There are those on the frontlines gathering data, testing, working on vaccines, coordinating responses, and everywhere, providing care.
There are those still farming, packaging, transporting, and delivering food

and supplies.

There are those who keep our infrastructures and communities functioning: getting, giving, and doing all that is needed.

But not doing is also a gift. Retreat, a necessity. From there, we can ask the questions: What might my role be? How can I contribute?

There is almost always something to share, and to receive is what completes the blessing.

We become One together on the threshold of the unknown, connected in ways that would stun and astound the ancestors whose shoulders we stand upon, while we reach out, joining webbed hands and hearts across the globe.

Just yesterday, I moved my last few things from the Damian Community. I had an office and a locker that I kept while training others to take my place. An era had ended for me, but like milestones for so many others these days, there were no trumpets present (just a septic tank pumper), and thus there was no fanfare.

However, I got to come home to my life partner, the woman I have loved for a very long time. After so many years living separately, we are now figuring out how to live in the same place. I think our timing is pretty good.

I thought of some friends who have been recently dating. Who knew that would suddenly stop like in a game of musical chairs? Hold on to the last person you kissed? Stay single? How to date now? Whose germs do you trust?

So, for those both with or without a companion, I have a story:

Must have been somewhere around 1980 in Fairbanks, Alaska. I was there for the first time, at a party with friends and friends of friends. There was something strange in the air: crazy energy of both attraction and repulsion. I noticed people staring at each other, making faces, or obviously ignoring someone. There was a tension and a familiarity between people unlike anything I had ever been around.

It wasn't until later that night that I learned the answer: Everyone had, at one time or another, been partnered with almost everyone else. Why? Because of the very long, very cold, very dark winters where whatever daylight there might be would last for less than four hours.

People prepared a lot for winter: chopping wood, insulating their cabins, gathering supplies, and, most importantly, finding a mate before the lockdown of winter began. However, after months confined in small spaces together, many relationships became strained, and when spring finally came, people would burst from their cabins and often away from each other. That is, until the music of summer stopped again, and it was time to get ready for another winter, perhaps another mate. I wonder if something like that will happen here once people feel safe going out again.

From my window, I see neighbors, wearing masks and carrying chairs, walking aimlessly around, perhaps looking for someone to talk to. They remind me of an old Alaskan prospector who would keep a fellow at gunpoint just to have some company.

Hmm, I might have some stories to tell. Perhaps I'll grab a chair and wander out there with the others, looking for the truth of companionship.

On our evening walk yesterday, Susan and I came upon a man— approximately a contemporary, perhaps older—on the ground, bloodied, beside his fallen bicycle. We asked if he needed our help. He did. It required a fair bit of close physical contact in this time of no touching. But what is one to do?

The experience made me aware of the amazing courage, selfless compassion, and magnificent gift our healthcare workers are giving us all every single day. In a society now dividing between essential and non-essential workers, I was glad to be of use to someone.

It also got me thinking of something like a tag team wrestling approach to the Great Viral Unknown. Aren't there some things the rest of us can do? Imagine those on the frontlines being able to raise their hands (electronically, of course) when they need a break, and those of us on the sidelines jumping into the ring to spell them.

Sure, they'd have to walk us through each step, but they could do that from home. Seems only fair, right? Hey, it's either that or just turn everything over to the robots. (How soon might they be ready?)

The Day the Earth Stood Still! (Okay, not completely still, but significantly so.)

I wonder how far this peacefulness has spread? Might it be contagious as well? The headlines are almost absent of warfare and gunfire. People everywhere are helping each other. And there are so many more bicycles in motion, so many fewer cars. Can an atmosphere sigh in relief?

I know, people are scared. Many are suffering, dying. How to breathe into that without hyper-ventilating? But it's this disease of the lungs we fear, right? And the air is cleaner, easier to inhale. Does that matter? More than jobs? The market? The economy?

What about everywhere I wanted to go? Everything I thought I needed to do? Can we really leap from a life of "I want" to one of "We care"—from "I need" to "We share?" If the myth of self-reliance gives way to something more selfless and cooperative, could this be the dawning of that age everyone once sang about?

I find myself less interested in television and movies. Kind of surprising as I'm also looking for ways to fill the day. Maybe it was everything prior to this crisis that I needed escaping from, and now that IT'S REAL, I'm more fully present and wanting the truth, not the fiction.

Yet I feel as if there is more to do than what is actual. Some misplaced anxiety? Perhaps from doing so little? "I must be falling behind!" But, at what?

The end of March in the desert means preparing for summer. In the fleeting beauty of wildflowers, anticipation and dread can sneak in through my open senses. A tax deadline can be pushed back. The heat cannot. Yet the solution to the larger problem requires my absence, not my presence. These are uncharted islands we find ourselves cast upon.

Hard for me to admit, but as someone with a lifetime of autoimmune and respiratory illness, I am one of the most vulnerable. My island is small, loosely guarded, not as difficult to maintain as where I've been before.

There is an order that borders on the obsessive from where I pull on words, like threads, wondering where they will lead; sometimes unraveling my own mystery, but always searching the patterns that tie our lives together, for an answer that might never be found, to a question I've forgotten how to ask.

As the current occupant of a body once capable of remarkable endurance, I marvel at how quickly it now tires. If only someone had taken better care of this contraption. I am almost tempted to utilize this windfall of unscheduled days to do something about it. However, now that I am safely sitting again, my attention can turn from the unproductive "if only" to the holy "what is." And what is in front of me are two dismantled lamps.

My intention is to swap pieces to get at least one working again. Just last week, it would have been a simple trip to the hardware store for the exact right part. With hands only slightly less steady than just a year ago, night reading glasses back on for this daytime task, I puttered. I thought of all I've discarded in my endless campaigns against clutter and disorder. I thought of friends who have always stockpiled and wondered how validated they might be feeling.

I also remembered being in remote places in the world where there was no garbage, no waste; everything had a purpose. If not potential fuel, an object, no matter its original intention, could become whatever was currently needed. Value, it seems, can remain dormant for years without diminishing.

My mind is not as quick as it once was, my reflexes are not as fast, but I accomplished my goal of reassembling a functioning lamp.

In the time before becoming a father, with just a PO Box in Bisbee, I'd often wander in a Toyota Chinook with everything I then owned and imagined I'd need if things started to unravel: water, freeze-dried food, gold coins taped behind paneling, hammock, books, candles, notebooks, and pens.

One day, camped in a particularly isolated place, I had the realization that I would not want to survive a crumbling civilization. My journey to join others in taking care of what we have began then. The by-product of this decision was that it became okay for stuff to accumulate around me.

This morning in my garage, still with more than I'll ever use, but not with all I'll need, I feel more accepting of our different ways of living, grateful for what we each offer to share or exchange, while I learn to long for what I already have, even rejoice in what is missing, what I'll never have.

One cat sits by Susan. The other is on my lap. They probably see no difference in this day.

I'm often home to provide the desired rubbing and scratching. But perhaps the cats sense our unrest and worry and are offering themselves for our sakes today instead of napping elsewhere on their own.

There is plenty of food here for the cats, yet we have not stockpiled anything for ourselves.

Faith? Ignorance? For me, I'd rather fast than panic. For Susan, although she hasn't said as much, I think she is looking forward to finding out exactly what is in our freezer.

As for the cats, perhaps they will welcome more of our company ... at least for as long as their food supply lasts!

April

There is an added weight in even the simplest tasks,
and so these days of less can feel like more.
No one knocks at the door, yet everyone's reaching out:
sharing, joking, needing,
caring, hoping, bleeding.
It's enough just to tend to each other.
It's enough
to tend
to each other,
and ourselves,
without knowing
where we are going
only that wherever it is,
from home or hospital,
we are going together.

After waking up from a dream where Scarlett O'Hara, on her knees in the bathroom, vowed: "As God is my witness, I will never run out of toilet paper again!" I realized I should make a list. I like making lists. Okay, fine, at my age, I need to make lists. How about a Not-To-Do today list? Yeah, that could get too huge. But maybe, in the spirit of Scarlett and toilet paper, some reminders. For example, stay fit.

I watch our cats who do almost nothing besides eat and sleep yet can still leap up on countertops in a graceful bound. I noticed that in the short interval between a nap and the next meal, they stretch. So, I get down on all fours and imitate their moves. Which reminds me to put something else on the list:

Don't do anything stupid and hurt yourself, Lee! This is not a good time to be needing medical help.

Meanwhile, in this self-imposed traction, I can only be grateful for the foresight of having fully stocked our wine cabinet. And I didn't even need a list for that!

Even after showering, an odor from the mask I wore today lingers. It was my first outing wearing one. I was not alone. There were no smiles to see, only restless eyes and muffled sounds.

The guy at the register, noticing my Python (programming language version) t-shirt, became animated, mumbled something about the Ph.D. he's not using. At another time, we would have chatted, commiserated even, but spaced out at six-foot intervals behind me, a long line of the temporarily docile, masked marauders snaked down the aisle.

I waved "another time" to him in spontaneous sign language and made my way to the exit where a gal with a spray bottle asked if my rice was okay. Or at least that's what it sounded like to me through her mask. I stumbled a bit but nodded in the affirmative and kept moving while my brain translated. She must have said, "Have a nice day!"

"Yeah," I said to my truck as I unmasked myself in great relief, "I will."

But once home, I realized several items from the shopping list were not checked off. I could not imagine braving another trip. I remembered that I'm a senior now and decided to return the next day at 5 a.m. for the senior shopping hour.

What a sight! First, the shelves were full, including all the various paper products. It was almost normal except for the small, bent-over, alien couples in odd masks and strange protective wear mumbling to each other behind carts stacked higher than they were. Whatever was going to happen, they were in it together, in pairs, but horrified when others of their kind came anywhere near. Judging by the sheer amount of goods being purchased, I admired their life-expectancy optimism.

I learned I wasn't one of them when a surprised employee double-checked my I.D. to make sure I belonged there. She wondered where my packed cart was, as I only had the single reusable bag I'd brought along. I shrugged my shoulders, told her I had heard rumors of a Rave nearby, got distracted by all the cars parked here, and was curious about who shopped at 5 a.m.

Turns out, I've become one of those guys with a floppy hat, wearing old clothes, who roams the sandy bottom of the Rillito riverbed carrying a golf club. Hey, if this lockdown goes on for a long time, I'll be a helluva bunker player!

The other morning, while posing on the follow-through of a particularly good swing, I heard a raspy voice from above say, "Nice shot!"

I turned to see a head leaning over a property boundary wall. We chatted. She told me she's a caregiver, taking a break, enjoying the plane-free sky, imagining breathing cleaner air. A bit ironic, as she's smoking, but I just nodded and agreed.

We shared a few pleasantries and uncertainties before she concluded by saying, "One thing's for sure, nothing will ever be the same."

I agreed again and tipped my floppy hat as we wished each other well in whatever is to come.

I walked away from this viral-free exchange with a slight, yet limping, increase in vitality. Can one both simultaneously trudge and revel in anticipatory grief and jubilation? I don't know. I've never known so little.

I can almost feel/hear an invisible teacher nod and whisper: "Finally, Grasshopper, finally. You are ready to be here NOW."

However, my newfound enlightenment was immediately challenged. Returning home, on the unpaved side of the Rillito, I was faced with a large guy stretched out across the path, sleeping, sunning. His cart full of stuff blocked any way around him.

I would have to step over him to get by. I hesitated. He looked rough, like he'd been living outdoors for some time. To turn back and find another way occurred to me, but I didn't have the energy for it. Nor did I want to wake him.

Was I offended? Perhaps a bit annoyed, with a leery type of fear as well. Still, I stepped over his legs and had taken a few steps before his head rose and I heard, "Good morning."

I was surprised. Pleasantly.

I can dream of being someone who might think, feel, or act differently than I did, but I also know that I'm unlikely to ever fully let go of either my fears or my judgments.

I was almost home when a scraggly-looking guy and a dog were making their way up and out of the wash right where I needed to pass. Some hunger in his eyes made me pause.

On any other day, I probably would have avoided him. Today, we chatted for a while, sharing the little we actually knew about what was going on in the world, but affirming something with which I had so recently struggled. There is a way. There is always a way to get past our fears and judgments to connect with another.

There is no one to pay for what comes forth from this closet retreat,
no guide to thank for the rooftop vision quest.
And yet there is a terrible price exacted from so very many
that can never be repaid.

We must do what we can.
Listen to all the voices claiming to know the way
until they merge into the one that uses no words.

These many weeks of isolation have chipped at,
diminished the resistance of a lifetime.
I glimpse what I cannot grasp.
If I could name it, I would.
But even that is elusive.
It is what I had hoped meditation could provide,
minus the effort of no effort.

There is a stillness found even in movement,
a quieting of want and need.
Is it surrender or is it acceptance?
I cannot say, but the ground itself welcomes me
down into her even as the sky lifts me up.
Perhaps there is nowhere else to be,
nothing left to do.

I catch myself chasing the perfection of nothing to do, wondering if my hunger for unplanned days will finally now be sated? A chore not done can distract more than the one in process.

Repetition and habit are useful but empty companions.

Even before the shutdown, I had already been driving less, staying home more. Some of my friends and I whisper in shared guilt how okay we really are.

If it weren't for the suffering of others, this release from all we've expected of ourselves and our lives might feel like a blessing.

At a past street fair, Susan bought me a shirt with a Chinese symbol and the word Contentment on it. It also says:

to hold onto
and
to let go of
everything
all
at once

This morning, I feel like Dorothy discovering that the answer I was looking for was with me all the time.

Perhaps today will be the day Susan and I will finish the project of hanging photographs and paintings we began years ago.

With Susan soon retiring, it's now her turn to empty an office and bring stuff home.

Soon, everything we own will be, for the first time, in one place. It's okay. We have long been on a slow path of intimacy, selecting and consolidating our things accordingly along the way.

Mainly that meant me getting rid of almost everything of mine (other than my reclining massage chair), which gave us the opportunity to scour the state to find unique and artsy furniture.

We first met in 1991 at St. Francis in the Foothills. I was a youth minister and she, an adult volunteer. We were also involved in what was called a Base Community Group where the members imagined being on belay, supporting each other's ascent toward personal goals. It gave us a shared vocabulary for working things out.

We've had just one tiff during our current isolation, but it wasn't about differing decorating aesthetics. It was about conflicting notions of acceptable alcohol consumption during any given quarantined day. I saw no reason for a limit. We weren't driving. She saw a bigger picture that included my health. It's hard to argue about that with one who hopes to have a long life together.

Strangely, some old photos helped me be more understanding. They're a couple of black and whites of her at 20 years old. In them, a very soft, shyly beautiful face looks down and away from the camera. I see someone there who wouldn't be confronting me unless it was deeply important to her, someone I would not want to push away by my brusque behavior.

I didn't know her then, but even from forty years past, these photos inform me there is still more to learn of the gentle and sensitive spirit with whom my life is joined. I can drink—in moderation—to that!

The pandemic has taken at least 165,000 worldwide, over 40,000 in the United States. And yet there are protests against wearing masks and against staying home. On the bright side, gas prices are going down.

There is a tray on my desk where time-sensitive reminders—coupons and mailings—for various projects gather. Sorting through, tossing most as no longer relevant, I felt a sad relief, an empty dizziness, as my attention and anxiety clashed over what to do next.

Last night, watching an early *Madam Secretary*, Chief of Staff Nadine (being empathetic to a loss in Press Secretary Daisy's life) quoted Søren Kierkegaard: "The most painful state of being is remembering the future, particularly the one you'll never have."

Is that it? Is that what's going on? Is an imagined future, both personal and collective, disappearing? What connections to goals and dreams are being severed? What will be restored? Replaced?

It's too soon to know, to fully grieve what's passing or to embrace what's emerging.

But how to approach this time? May I, as a male, suggest the metaphor of pregnancy as something that changes everything and can't be rushed? It's when we hope for the best, prepare as we can, but ultimately must surrender.

The outer life slows. Meditation helps the inner life. And now I'm stretching away from my own experience, but was close enough to a birth to witness: Let go. Breathe. Accept the pain. Something miraculous is happening. Cross your fingers now. The time for counting fingers has not yet arrived.

On one of our isolation-sanity walks, a gal shouted from the other side of the street, "Glad you've got your shirt on!"

Susan and I looked at each other quizzically, perhaps each wondering if we had just stumbled into one of the other's past lovers. Since neither of us showed any signs of comprehending, we asked, "What?!"

Turned out some shirtless guy rode his bicycle past us. We hadn't noticed. This woman, however, was offended.

I thought of that moment this morning while navigating a morning walk hauling garbage bags. Susan had been making a case for carrying them with us to collect the ubiquitous refuse and debris along the undeveloped pathway on the south side of the Rillito.

I had long resisted. After decades of attending to all the needs of an eight-acre chunk of earth, I did not want that hyper-vigilant awareness to kick in again, and for an even larger area! Being a caretaker, for me, was like being an alcoholic. I had to quit it.

Eventually, Susan won out. We agreed to begin doing this practice on Sundays as a walking worship of sorts.

The odd thing is people who saw us out there usually shared welcoming greetings or smiles, but some seemed offended, as if what we were doing was somehow in their way. We never know what's going on inside of each other.

I know I can be disgusted by the choices and actions of others. I imagined I might overreact if I saw someone mindlessly littering where we had been working to keep clean. However, it was me almost having to carry Susan away from a guy who had just thrown an empty bottle down into the wash. What is the middle way between a turned cheek and a confrontation?

19

On the very next morning, at Valley of the Moon where I volunteer for watering and light landscaping, something was different for me. I had brought a hand spade and some gloves to dig around some plants that needed more water retention. While placing rocks to finish this small project, I noticed the absence of any urgency or impatience. I had let go of any sense of time, of needing to do anything or be anywhere else. It was an old, familiar, and welcome feeling, but it came with a sense of ownership, of responsibility. These fallout sensations were the very things I had been consciously, even loudly, avoiding since leaving the community. How lovely.

So, today, I can name the struggle, the tug of war, between the part of me that has finally learned, and has come to fiercely defend, his boundaries, with the part of me that flourishes in service to something other than myself. Perhaps, with enough coaxing, the two may one day become dance partners in this ever-unfolding journey of discovery.

While wondering about different ways to fill a day, I have begun to consider the previously unthinkable. I've been eyeing the box! The one marked, TBSBNG. It's up on a closet shelf. The one box that has survived, unscathed and untouched through every move, every cleansing, every purge.

I have long known that there was no way to simply "just go through it" because there is no criteria for what to keep or what to get rid of. Thus, it earned its TBSBNG status: To Be Sorted By Next Generation. And, yes, I know that really means to be thrown away by somebody else.

It is where the random photos that never found an album home have gone, all the love letters, early journals, odd mementos and awards, first attempts at poetry, and the rest of the once meaningful scraps of a long life. In other words, a nostalgic emotional minefield!

So, has sheltering-in-place brought me to this? Entire days could be lost! Life decisions questioned! I could be set adrift in endless currents of beautiful, painful, and magical moments. As Kurt Vonnegut cautioned, I could become unstuck in time!

Then, I thought of what that first physician, Hippocrates, prescribed, "Desperate times call for desperate measures." But do I dare?

Instead, I chose to get out the ladder and go up on the roof to inspect its condition. I worry about things. It would be getting warmer soon, so I took a look at the HVAC, cleaned the fins, contemplated a professional coil service.

I also did some sweeping, strategic caulking, and applied crack and joint sealant to a small area of concern and was glad to see that past compulsive care made it unnecessary for any large-scale roof coating this year.

Once in motion, it was no big deal to do some touch-up trim painting out on our 2nd-floor balcony. Cleaned that tile flooring, table, and chairs up there, so we can savor sunsets while the weather allows.

If we're going to be home all the time, we might as well enjoy it.

None of it will keep us any safer from what is looming, but I'm taking my own advice: doing what's right in front of me, tending to my surroundings, and nursing the mind that just might let me sleep better tonight.

Maybe tomorrow I'll consider that box on the shelf.

With little to see in the dim and muted first gray light of day, and with coffee already brewing, my mind is visiting a place far away. I catch myself thinking we should get back there again soon. Then, just as quickly, I start wondering if travel will ever be the same. If anything will.

If we shake hands again, will we look into each other's eyes and hold on just a little bit longer?

What about hugs? Will we be tempted to get lost in each other's arms and not let go?

Or will we forever be suspicious, keep a safe distance, have virtual lunches, engagements, and lives?

Will those who are single now feel the same as those currently living with another?

Will we all want to trade places, believing that what we most desire is elsewhere, rather than where it has always been, only unseen, unfelt, without a love of self?

I remember wanting a break from work, from others, from everything. I remember traveling far for some long-desired taste of solitude, for time to myself: to reflect, to heal, to create.

There is still an empty journal, an unread book, a sketch pad, an instrument—all ready to help share what's inside, just below the uncertainty.

If I move even one eyelash in that direction, let another synapse follow, some muscles speak—a listening journey can begin. A stretch can turn into a walk, can become a dance, transmuting even this fear into something light.

May

Anxiety floats like a virus
attaching itself willy-nilly
to every looming task and challenge.
So far, there is no vaccination
nor successful treatment
for this restless roaming worry either.
Even though a lifetime of problems solved
and obstacles overcome
suggest attention need only be
on the very next step ...
and the breath we can't help but trust
and be grateful for.

There's already talk of a second wave. Intensive care units are filling around the country. Nursing home deaths are rising. Brazil is getting hammered by the virus. Every trip from home feels like playing a game of Russian Roulette. Will I be next?

There are long lines of people in cars, some in luxury vehicles, waiting to get food. (Would edible toilet paper help?) And now there's talk of "murder hornets" in the United States. Are we living in biblical times?

This morning I took a peek in the TBSBNG box. Nothing like time with old photos and letters to activate dormant memories. Like many who had the luxury to do so, I was once always imagining loving somebody. And I wrote letters, like a peacock showing what he had to offer, sending invitations to others to join me. I think my love of language came from the association of writing with longing, as my vocabulary and creativity grew to meet the need of expressing such passion.

In my early thirties, I took a year off from loving others to learn how to love myself. It had occurred to me that to get the best from myself, I had to date me to receive what I had always given away. Turned out, that began a path that led to the love I had longed for outside of myself as well.

These writings of mine today are like those love letters, only now public. Have I moved only from seduction to exhibitionism? Perhaps, but today I find myself also reading and imagining listening to those who came before me, while considering those who will follow. If there is something I understand and can articulate, I feel compelled to do so.

Snapshot of this moment's domestic blissfulness:

Susan is baking muffins; cats are chasing invisible things; the local radio station is playing fun covers; I am burning up pen and paper; and cool morning air fills our house.

We've committed to a longer walk than usual and another day without starting a vehicle.

It's again a day with more meals planned than we could possibly consume and, of course, appropriate costume changes throughout the day.

We will debate what else should be on our list: Lee will nap; Susan will practice guitar, play piano, do crossword puzzles, study Spanish, prepare her next Toastmaster speech, have some kind of Zoom meeting, make her own lists, attempt to wrap up various retirement-related paperwork, consider how to spend what's left in a flex-spending account, hunt for insurance, and then roam around the stacks of things that have come home from her work office, while engaging in a half dozen or so online Scrabble matches.

Lee will get up from his nap, stretch and scratch, ask how he could help, and then find a place to hide in the garage until it's time for the next meal.

We used to finish each other's sentences. Now, a simple gesture is an entire paragraph. Today, we looked at each other and, without a word being said, knew it was time to write a group letter. Quarantine is like that.

Every family has someone who sends those newsy letters. We have already been writing and posting musical parodies from our captivity, so why not a group letter?

Of course, we're not really writing to anybody. That's the point. It's all about us. However, to be so self-indulgent, without a significant drop in social standing, there must be an announcement of some kind. So, here's ours:

Dear Friends,

We're having a baby!

Not really! That was just a dig at Lee's beer belly. The real occasion is Susan's retirement! She's using up some vacation time now, but Friday was her last day of actual work.

Her work retirement party was a Zoom lunch. Plans for celebrating with others have been postponed, but she did go out with a bang.

Friday was this year's Women in Data Science regional conference. 300 registered. 30 presenters. All in our kitchen!

Susan was last year's ambassador, and on the planning committee this year, wrangling this event into something virtual.

Lee, as a well-trained Houseboy, catered, and, otherwise, stayed out of the way.

Could it have gone better? Perhaps. Could it have been worse? Well, there's this: Just hours after the closing remarks and visiting the various Happy Hour chat rooms, our router went dark. Turns out the in-line power converter blew. Lee, eventually, managed to splice in an old one to get things running again, but that was a near disaster. Timing is everything.

That same night, while finishing some bubbly and playing Codenames, we went around opening up windows to let the cool night air in.

At some point, and for some reason, Lee started counting cats and noticed one missing. They are indoor cats, whose official veterinary names are seldom used, but are affectionately known around here as The Bean and The Bear. The Bean (or Beanie) could not be found.

We hadn't realized there wasn't a screen in one of the windows we opened, and she had exited through it. Anything could have happened. She could have given chase to some critter and wound up far away, but she had stayed in the yard. And quickly returned inside once discovered.

We'll never hear her side of the story, what the sudden expanse of space and sensory stimulus must have been like, but we were, again, grateful for what didn't happen, and for what we call good timing.

We do know that even in hardship we are blessed, thankful for our lives and for the people in them. There is something in our connectedness that helps watch over each other. It's not perfect, but it's something. And, we look forward to the moment when, perhaps like what our cat recently experienced, we can burst forth into the larger world and be amazed at everything!

With so much appreciation and anticipation,

Susan and Lee

As of this writing, there have been no responses in the mail, but Susan's phone has been ringing.

Can both joy and despair be in the air?
Something heavy, something light
jock and bob for my attention.
Is it a choice?

A premonition of death derails me
and I forget why I started this writing ...
From dinosaurs to Caesars, everything empties
back into from where it emerged.

Do I wish to have lived and loved better?
Seems like there was always something, like a mosquito,
getting in the way of my perfect moments.
Cultivated, manipulated, forever waited upon,
such moments, touched or tasted, never possessed.
Oh, to have known earlier that it is our imperfections
that allow each other in.
Did ever your wanting
keep you from seeing
what might have brought you joy?

I've overreacted and underachieved,
overthought while ignoring the truth in this body
blessed with gifts both well-used and not.
I know the feeling of playing golf under par,
imagining and making impossible shots for both money
and, quickly fleeting, small glory.
I have remembered, at times, when to speak
and when to listen. Have been the student
and the teacher. And almost always the lover of words
and what they can reveal.
Was blessed to have helped bring a life into this world
and to learn everything of love and commitment
through having a son while still having a father.
Through it all, I grew enough to say "I do" to love
and life with one woman.

Yes, there is something in the air today.
I hope it stays.
I hope it leaves.
I hope to not hope,
and to just be.

As a teacher, I stood between those who knew and those who didn't—a bridge of sorts. I was never particularly well-informed on any one subject, but if I understood something, I could usually find the passageways that would lead to another's understanding of it.

Luckily, I married a scientist, who often gives me puzzled looks, corrects my thinking, or digs deeper to uncover more.

I was just reading yet another piece about the division in this country, and it got me thinking about when I was new to teaching. At first, I was thankful for the smartest and most-prepared students because they made my lesson plans work. Then, I started being more concerned about those who were the least successful, or the least interested, and tried to find ways to get them more involved.

Eventually, I learned that the wisdom of Buddha applied to the classroom—the middle way. If my attention was there on the majority of the students, the two ends of the spectrum had a place to meet. Otherwise, there was no chance of having a successful class experience.

I doubt I'll ever go back into a classroom again, and yet here I am still slowly sorting through boxes of notes, hand-outs, syllabi, and other potential course material.

Always reluctant to discard something that may be of use one day, I just tore up the notes for the best presentation I ever gave. It only took me a quarter of a century to do so. First, I had to let go of ever doing the presentation again. One sentence, on its very own index card, stayed with me: "I was fortunate enough to not be able to carry out the plans I had made for myself." Such emphasis and certainty got my attention today. What did I think I knew?

I was addressing a conference on adolescents in treatment centers and how to encourage their continuing recovery. I was making a case for allowing the creative and responsive unknown into the rigidity of a treatment plan. I then gave examples from both my own life and from the teens whose art and writings I was sharing at that gathering.

Something about all of this clicked with me now, but I needed to re-examine the premise and how it had indeed played out in my life. Sure enough, over and over again, I could point to where I thought I was going, and to where I wound up instead.

Of course, there is no way to know where the path not taken would have led, but I can affirm, again, that something other than my best thinking determined what happened.

For example, when I first graduated from the University of Arizona, I was hanging out in the old mining town of Bisbee and using some of my construction background to get by. I had the idea to buy rundown homes, renovate, then sell them.

In Tucson one day, I noticed a gathering of garbage trucks and asked someone what was going on. I was told it was a test for potential garbagemen. This cracked me up. I parked my car, got in line, and, just for the heck of it, took the test. Weeks later, I was notified I was the top candidate. I took the job.

That led to my writing "What Is Your Garbageman Saying to You? The Secret Language of the Alleys"—published in the *Tucson Citizen*.

With a job that finished early in the day, I enrolled in a master's program. During the first week of class, the aristocratic, white-haired Charles Davis yelled my name from halfway down the hallway. Turned out, some instructor had broken his contract, and Dr. Davis was looking for someone to teach a class. I had never thought about teaching, ever.

I said yes.

Months later, I was invited to the first ever Southern Arizona Writing Project and, all of a sudden, became immersed in the reimagining of teaching writing. I became a research assistant for SAWP. My creativity was flowing like never before, inspired by being in the company of so many brilliant minds.

But my love life was quite confused. I had been rooming with one woman, Cindy, who I wanted more than she wanted me. And there was someone exciting, Judith, who I met at a restaurant where she was waiting tables, but who I thought too young for me. Plus, there was a kindred soul from SAWP who I enjoyed being with, but she was married. Nothing seemed right. Time for me to run away again.

After receiving my degree, I went off to Alaska but found myself still thinking about Cindy. Not understanding my own intense feelings for her, I came back to Tucson where she again confirmed her lack of interest in me as a romantic partner.

Too Love

We watch the airplane cut the sky like a razor.
The cloudy stream of blood trails behind, then disappears.
The scream fills the air and is everywhere
and yet we can't help but see its beauty.

We climb for the sun
and a black-eyed sinister caterpillar Cupid
grows out of a rock and laughs at the curse of our union
but sill we climb for the sun.

Near the top, a rock sticks its purple cactus tongue
out at me, and I don't know what to say to that,
so I wait for her.

Then together we get lost inside a Japanese picture frame.
She feels at ease between the thorny trees
contemplating serenity instead of obscenity.

But we tumble down and apart
bouncing off rocks and each other
until the sparks from our friction
set the mountains ablaze.

Yes, I tamper with the earth like a child
and then cry for its forgiveness
and, ever patient, the earth tries to teach me
to be impeccable
but only half of me listens;
half of me keeps going back to her.

She's happy lying lizard on a rock.
I follow the cow express to an eagle's nest
and lie in my words
offer them to the wind.

I'd give them all just to believe.
I want to believe, me, what I say, what I think,
what I am.
I lie in my words
and crave the snake's venom
for its clarity.

At a bar, drinking off rejection, I met a guy who had recently perfected a compact method for separating gold. I had the notion of being his representative up in Alaska. To prepare, I went to one of Tucson's old bookstores, with narrow aisles and books stacked high, for some research material.

However, once I found the aisle with books about gold and mining, there was some tramp parked on the floor reading. I walked around for a while, but he seemed to be there for the duration. I approached and asked if I could squeeze by to get a book. He looked up, and I immediately recognized the face of the actor, Lee Marvin. He inquired about my gold curiosity, then invited me to join him on the floor where he gave me a mining tutorial, including which books to read.

I walked away grinning and sure that I must be on the right path. A famous Lee had just confirmed it.

I sold my VW convertible (My Darling Clementine) and bought a Toyota Chinook to haul the equipment and to live out of once in Alaska.

However, prior to leaving, I went on a hike with Judith in the Huachuca Mountains where we met and chatted with a forest ranger, Duane Bennett. I suspect the conversation might never have happened without Judith being there. She was quite attractive.

During the conversation, Duane asked me if I might be interested in being a fire lookout. I had been reading Ed Abbey and already had file cabinets full of my own scribblings that I had hoped to compile into something.

In 1982, I became a fire lookout for the Sierra Vista Ranger District, assigned to Red Mountain, above the small town of Patagonia.

I parked the Chinook, loaded the double-stacked cardboard filing cabinet, a box of paperbacks, and a manual typewriter into my open-air, sand-colored, 1946 Willys CJ-2A Jeep and made my way up the rugged and steep road towards a turning point in my life.

38 years later, I'm still sorting paper. Discarding much of it now, but sharing the distillation best as I can.

Before sunrise, this simple rule:
one cup of coffee, as companion.
The practice of savoring goes well
with the waiting of writing.
Pen moving across paper
is first a signal of readiness

for anything that wants out.
I marvel at those who know themselves so well;
talk, even walk, with such certainty.
I am a question, a discussion.
At best, a process punctuated with reflection,
saved only by some quickness
born of fear, sharpened by learning.
Without knowing you better,
I offer the gift I myself would want,
act like the neighbor I wish I had,
reach out to the friend I only remember,
and whisper to every lover
the world has ever known,
"Where are you now?"

It's Mother's Day. I should say Mothers' Day. I had two: the one who birthed me, and the one who raised me and died when I was 15. The path that led me to finally search for my birth mother began up in the fire lookout. I'll get to that. But today I'm thinking of my adoptive mom.

She used to freeze everything. Freezing food, maybe even feelings, was our family's way to ensure some kind of security. Besides the stand-alone fridge/freezer combo in the kitchen, there were two separate freezers in the basement, plus another fridge with freezer behind the bar. Yes, I grew up in a home with a bar. In fact, after she died, I moved into the basement with the bar, a fireplace, and a big brass bed I had found at a yard sale and then restored myself.

At 16, I was driving her 1967 Cadillac convertible with frozen feelings and a strange freedom.

The few Yiddish words I know come from her and her family. Farblondzhet would be the word she'd use to describe how I was then. Spelled in a variety of ways, the basic meaning is to be wandering without any idea where you are; to have gone astray; befuddled and bewildered; lost and confused. All that in one word. Being farblondzhet was what I finally faced in the tower on Red Mountain.

Return
Follow the tracks of those
who've been here the longest.
Understand the origin of a trail.
Remember relying on your own senses.
It has been a while.
Even our first roads were built
on the long wisdom of use.
We moved and turned as the land did,
never losing connection.
Until we did.
Now the problems we face
are immense and many.
If there are answers to be found,
no GPS will lead us to them.
A willingness to go back and search
for where we lost our way
is as true in love
as it is in the wilderness.
Might it be true for living
on the one planet
we need for everything?

You know how it is when something small is what finally allows a larger release to happen?

Crystalized grief becomes fluid, and in the flow of tears, all that was lost is remembered.

I can hold onto things with the best of them, yet also be one who lets go of much—a pack rat minimalist of sorts. It takes all kinds, right?

So many objects around my home are memories in condensate, moments preserved in some physical form, like my father's Mr. Coffee maker from 1972. (The one Joe DiMaggio's ads convinced him to buy.) Somehow, it has survived all of life's upgrades, purges, and moves, even entropy, until yesterday.

It helped that I mostly use a single cup French press. (I live with one of those tea-beings.) But every Saturday would begin with a pot from Mr. Coffee at my side, while I listened to Hawaiian music on KXCI, and prepared the more elaborate weekend breakfast. Until yesterday ...

I won't attempt any more resuscitations. Mr. Coffee served me and my family long and well. It's time to let the maker meet its maker.

Mr. Coffee's parting gift was a surge of memories of those who passed from my life: my mom when I was still in high school; my dad in 2002; my sister, just last December. I am the last of the family who once resided at that house on Fitch Ave where Mr. Coffee first arrived.

Perhaps I can hold onto and find some use for the coffee pot that came with Mr. Coffee.

I wonder how much life can still be compacted into, and loss poured from, one container?

I still keep track of the days of the week. The repeating seven-day rhythm provides some useful order. The date itself, however, has lost much meaning outside of paying monthly bills.

Desert seasonal reminders are not all flowery and gentle, so I know it's early May and any outdoor activity is best done in the morning before the heat arrives and the wind picks up.

I remember to shave, but, admittedly, it's sporadic. Most other grooming goes on as it has. My hair has often been long, so I'm okay with its growing unruliness. I have lots of hats.

One odd thing: Without deciding it, I've been wearing the same shoes for all excursions. That is not how it ever was before. I have different shoes for everything, like golf shoes for walking and golf shoes for riding in a cart. I have indoor and outdoor OOFOS, for goodness sake, plus shoes for easy hikes or rocky ones. The list goes on: three pairs of slip-on dress shoes in different colors and styles, plus two kinds of work boots, flip-flops, water sandals, trail runners, and hip basketball shoes. All unworn of late.

Has the practical unraveled the fashionable? Should I be concerned about my current footwear apathy?

Like others, Susan and I walk and talk a lot; share some worries; are more creative in the kitchen; have become more comfortable with virtual gatherings; rely, gratefully, on wine, books, movies, music, and AC as needed. And we sort through and organize life's collections, losing ourselves for hours in nostalgia, curiosity, and an emerging efficiency.

Personally, I wrestle with a misplaced sense of urgency as I hover and bounce between dread and hope. When nothing else will do, there is still just one breath to take at a time.

Looking around at our quarantine tidiness, I suspect it's as organized as it will ever be without moving into an RV. Even old to-do lists, with long copied and recopied items, have vanished. I don't need to remember places we want to visit or dine anymore. And we certainly won't be browsing book, music, or antique stores anytime soon.

But if everything has a place and everything is in its place, what next? I almost don't want to touch anything, disturb this order achieved.

I wonder perhaps if it's time to awaken the slumbering, inner slob? He might be the more comfortable one being indoors so much—wouldn't worry about making a mess, breaking things, or using them up.

Of course, to avoid conflict, Susan would need to simultaneously unleash her own draggle-tail. Hey, maybe the cats would clean up after us for a change!

Besides, I've heard dirt is good for the immune system. I wonder what the HOA would think of a mud-wrestling pit?

Maybe Susan and I can talk about that on our next walk!

"When This Is Over."
I hear that often.
I say it too.
A plan, a prayer, a proclamation
for those things we now can't do.
And with every absence, an illumination,
revealing to ourselves what was false,
what was true.
I, for one, will hug more.
What about you?
When this is over, I hope

you won't have to remind me
to be kind.
Or to be grateful for being alive.
But will I remember
those who did not survive?
Those who carried on in the face of Fear?
Those who cared for all we hold most dear?
When this is over
will we finally see and agree
that jobs can come and go,
but healthcare should be free?
And now that we know
how simple a day can be
will we rush to fill it again
unnecessarily?
What about the sky and the air we breathe?
For those unborn, what kind of world will we leave?
When this is over …
When this is over.

Susan has a small but precise list of trespassing insects that can be killed. She relocates all others. The cats and I, left to our devices, would approach their presence in our environment differently.

However, in any attempt at cooperative and enlightened co-housing, the most sensitive becomes the touchstone conscience. So it goes.

Our species isn't quite ready to organize itself with the most sensitive in mind. We can't even agree to wear masks to protect our own elders. But I'm watching a lot of news these days, and it sure seems we need to do something soon.

With that in mind, it seems like I should say something about Saint Judy now.

These days, admiration, respect, and trust for any one individual is quite rare, especially for those frequently in the public eye. Now, imagine someone being a steadfast, calm, reasonable, intelligent, questioning force for over forty years! That is truly what being a news anchor means.

I salute Judy Carline Woodruff and the *PBS NewsHour* for their nightly, responsible, thoughtful, and thorough coverage and inspiration.

Judy will be 74 this year. Who knows what keeps her going? I'm just grateful she keeps showing up and showing us the way. It helps so much during these hard times especially.

Growing up with Walter Cronkite and *The Huntley-Brinkley Report*, I trusted the news as an accurate, unbiased, well-researched source of information. Propaganda was something that came from places like the then Soviet Union. It was laughable and sad to hear the blatant lies and misinformation spewing from government-controlled media. We were lucky to have what we did.

During the Reagan era, I joined a group of Citizen Diplomats trying to promote a sister city program between us and the U.S.S.R. The belief was that if and when the people would lead, the governments would follow. It was a direct response to the president calling them "the evil empire." We traveled there even though our government advised against it.

One of our stops was in Kyiv where a few of us had connected with a group of Ukrainian intellectuals. Spending time with them was not part of our official itinerary, but it led to a most enlightening evening.

At some point in the various discussions (they all spoke some English), the topic of propaganda came up. I said something about my faith in our news, and how our government couldn't stop whistle blowers, Watergate coverage, or the leak of the Pentagon Papers.

Natasha, a dark-haired, cigarette-smoking poet took me to task. She pulled out publications from all over the world, identifying their funding, their prejudices, and their various purposes. She chided me for not recognizing or understanding how something similar worked in the United States. Then, together, the group of them went through headlines, like a board game, quickly assessing the story not being told because of the one being emphasized. I was astounded at what sophisticated readers they were. I also felt both naive and lazy in comparison.

I was thinking of them and that night recently while scrolling through various news feeds and not knowing what was real or what was bogus anymore. Misinformation, blatant lies, and extremely biased opinions, passing as news, are everywhere.

There's no need to list all the ways things have gone wrong with blowhard broadcasting, the dangers from what we are losing with diminished reporting, and the difficulty in knowing what to read and how to interpret. But I'd like to talk to Natasha and her pals again, share a bottle or two, and hear their version of "And that's the way it is."

Meanwhile, I truly wish us all "Good luck and good night."

Anti-lockdown protests have been happening around the country. In Arizona this weekend, hundreds showed up at the state capitol, and Operation Gridlock in Michigan last month had 20,000 people jamming the streets around their capitol. There are over 30,000 confirmed cases of the virus in Michigan and yet people are gathering, asserting their right to protest, demanding for everything to re-open, even as they spread the very virus causing the problem.

One alert black cat sits at the table with me, listening to the birds noisily speculate on what kind of day is in store. The cat has eaten, so is more tolerant, only curious of the commotion.

We indoor creatures do wonder at all the fuss, have forgotten how long a night can be, how welcome the light's return.

Something crawls under the screen door, and the cat pounces. There is a limit to everything. Yet her sister could care less, has already gone back to sleep.

In an odd twist of mind, I start to think of those protesting the lockdowns, even strain to compare their behavior, and mine, with these two cats. Certainly, some instincts serve; some do not. And even siblings can see the world in remarkably different ways.

I am lucky to be comfortable in this increased home-based life, which is, honestly, more tedious than difficult. I don't understand what motivates others to show their teeth, what makes them act as they do. But I am more like the cat that naps.

I do know that complete agreement, thankfully, is not the prerequisite for our survival. However, finding common ground and cooperating is what will allow our civilization to work for all. It's not impossible. These two cats, as different as can be, do, from time to time, share the same perch and each other's warmth in the chill of morning.

On the verge
between impermanence and preservation.
Precarious habitats I call home,
like this body I owe
all the pleasures, all the pains
I've ever known.
That which keeps us must too be kept
in the endless chore of life.

Can't shake a sluggishness—
I bumble more
nod off easily.
Please, no drool!
Not yet ...

I understand those who want to get on with it.
I really do.
There has never been a decision
that has ever worked for us all.
But might it be possible
for those so eager to go
to take care, consider us,
the most vulnerable,
as you move, safe and slow?

Checking out the truck for a trip up the mountain, I noticed the oil change sticker, dated 2/27, then compared it to the current mileage. A whopping five hundred miles in three months! Could have done that in a busy week, once upon a time.

It struck me as a micro-view of the shutdown and its ripple effect, both positive and negative. For me, each mile not driven represented stress that didn't happen, but each trip in the prior reality also included the exchange of money for goods or services. (No es bueno para la economia!) There's less car exhaust, of course, but then there's all of the plastic being used for take-outs; and grocery stores aren't allowing reusable bags. Back and forth, up and down, the consequences are far from clear.

Susan and I picked a day in the middle of the week for this outing, thinking it might be less crowded. Nope. The rhythm of weekdays and weekends is no longer the same. With school out and no summer camps, families are roaming any open recreational area, seeking relief from the heat and from being home together.

We just pulled off to the side of a forest road, carried our chairs and picnic lunch to a spot where we couldn't see or hear anyone else. It was good enough.

After lunch, we donned our CamelBaks, grabbed our hiking poles, and went exploring. It had been a while since we walked at high altitude, and I certainly felt it. Noticed that old inner talk about getting back in shape and laughed at myself. When will that fantasy ever finally go away?

Can't help but wonder if it's also a fantasy for us to think that we can all return to our previous way of life. I know I'll personally be better off by accepting what no longer makes sense for this body to do, and to find what is appropriate today.

We stopped at a rock overhang with a beautiful view of the canyon below and distant mountain ranges. We found two Ponderosa pines spaced enough to hang our parachute hammock and then sunk into the cool breeze and shaded comfort of the moment.

Twenty years ago, we thought about buying a cabin up here, but one day at the 4th Avenue Street Fair, we saw these hammocks and bought one instead. Lightweight, packed up small, we've been carrying it on trips, all over, ever since. We paid about $40 for it. It was the hammock life we wanted, not the expense and hassle of a second home. The return on that particular investment has been immeasurable.

I think something similar is occurring in the reordering of our economies. Working and shopping from home, for example, is changing not only personal and family lives, but even how cities will function and be organized going forward. Value itself is being reevaluated.

Let's face it, with 40 million people unemployed, there's a hole in our bucket. Those at the bottom feel the leak first. Those on the top, not so much. But it's hard to imagine anyone not seeing it as a problem. Dear Henry? But with what shall we fix it, Dear Liza, Dear Liza?

In any volcanic event, what has been going on beneath the surface is unseen prior to the explosion. Yes, some hot spots are monitored, but none can be controlled. The question is what will be the final trigger, the breaking point that forces the magma up and out?

Months of locking down have left tens of millions without jobs, without insurance, last in line for assistance, and ready to erupt. And then one brutal, heartless image, seen by all, pressed deep into the oldest, most painful wound of all, and ignited the inevitable fires, again.

On May 26, we witnessed a police officer with a knee on a black man's neck. He kept it there for 9 minutes and 29 seconds. George Floyd died. His last words, "I can't breathe" have become the chant of millions.

Minneapolis is burning. Protests and unrest are erupting in thousands of cities around the world.

There are curfews being enforced in hundreds of U.S. cities. This is being called the largest protest in our history.

June

Extinction Event Haiku and Commentary

I am only here
Even my mind stays at home
What is there to say?

Remember reading a morning paper from a pile touched by others, with a
cup of coffee, in a favorite breakfast spot? You know, back in the days of travel
and restaurants ... and hugs.

I knew and forgot so many names, shared all kinds of words and smiles with
those both familiar and strange.

We just didn't know how good we had it, huh?

As I write from home, potent drops of memory, distilled by a process I do not
understand, seep into this moment, flavoring this confinement, what I share in
this electronic journal,

this fragile connection, my lifeline to you and what remains of a life
I did not always know how to hold, or love,
but believed in.
And still do,
even with the smoke in my tearing eyes.

Memorial Day holiday gatherings have sent cases soaring again. Over 100,000 new cases and around 1,000 deaths every day just in the United States.

In Arizona, as beds are filling, hospitals have implemented emergency plans.

And the Black Lives Matter protests continue.

I received my first ZUI (Zooming Under the Influence). In my defense, the discussion had been about how we are living in the End Times and how it all started when the Chicago Cubs won the World Series in 2016. One guy was certain we were all doomed back then, and that it was only a matter of time.

It's all so odd. I can feel both more and less connected because of electronic devices. I know things now about people I never did before because of their phones and social media. Much of it is empty and useless, but sometimes my heart is opened, and I will reach out directly to someone.

Often, though, ordinary conversation dries quickly. It's not just the physical distance kept from each other, but from avoiding topics political and loud opinions regarding what is not understood.

Sometimes it is a challenge to find something positive to say, and arguing seems pointless.

Many have abandoned social media in frustration and/or disgust. I wonder, though, where else can we all meet? Isn't something like this what we once only dreamed about? Can't we make an effort to utilize it better?

Yes, there are bad actors passing misinformation, contributing to the divisiveness tearing us apart. But there will always be such forces. We have to make choices in how we approach it and what we can glean from it.

My commitment is to check out everything myself before passing it on. And my personal intent is to share what's real in my life in the most thoughtful way I can. I post about myself what I would like to know about others. Anything from others that makes me think, feel, or laugh is welcome.

Recently, I have seen police kneeling in solidarity with protestors; Whites protecting Blacks; Blacks protecting police; and a global response to this moment that is truly astounding. These images are transformational.

Everything is being revealed, including the twisted ugly and the breathtakingly beautiful. I might not want to talk about it all, but I don't want to miss it.

Besides being connected through our devices, I am always intrigued by nonverbal communication and the mediums that intertwine us. Perhaps it's a hunger for the invisible, for discovering we are more than what we can think or speak.

I have an example from this morning, but I'll start with yesterday when a friend sent a link to a radio station in Laurel Canyon to me and only one other mutual friend. This in itself was highly unusual. We have several other friends in common. What motivated him to send it on that day and to those two specific people?

I know, doesn't sound very strange yet. However, Susan and I recently received a Netflix movie in the mail, *Echo in the Canyon*, and watched it the night before. Enjoyed it too. I had an extra smile or two thinking what a coincidence to be watching the history of music made in Laurel Canyon on the same day as my friend's sending.

Still, nothing earth-shattering. But this morning, the first email I opened was from the second recipient of that sending. He had just read the message about the Laurel Canyon music. His response? Last night, after about a year since it was recommended to him, he decided to watch *Echo in the Canyon* and was wondering if either of us had seen it.

That's the Unseen World at work. Mystifying. Inexplicable. Profound or trivial, and whether we understand it or not, it just is. For some, calling it Chance allows them to continue as before. For me, it's a reminder that whenever this small mind of mine can't imagine how things might work out, such moments tell me that there is more going on than I'll ever know, and, somehow, I find that comforting.

We recently listened to a Chautauqua Institution lecture (the original TED talk) on aging from Arthur Brooks. Lo and behold, we are indeed aging!

It's been a few weeks, and yet I'm still thinking about a few things he said. First, he made the distinction between fluid and crystalized intelligence. Both types are present throughout life, but fluid, which is the more creative, flowing, and innovative, begins to decline in midlife. Whereas crystalized intelligence, which is the accumulation of facts and experience, continues to grow throughout life. It's what we call wisdom and is well-suited for mentoring and instructing. (Okay, so teaching was a good choice for a long, productive career.)

Using art as a metaphor, he then talked about how as we develop in life it's like adding to a canvas, but that when we reach a certain stage, it's more helpful to think of a sculpting process, rather than a painting one. We come to a time in life where removing the unnecessary pieces to find the art within is what is most appropriate. I get that! That's the confirmation and affirmation I walked away with from his lecture.

It hasn't been easy extricating myself from a lifetime of obligations and expectations, but as I have, I've begun to experience a different kind of creativity. There is still some fluidity in linking to the past, uncovering crystal connections and bringing them into the light of the present.

It is a solitary activity I've long desired.

His final caution also hit home. He talked about the enormous organism that is a Quaking Aspen grove: thousands of trees sharing one root system. It was his reminder that we are in this together.

Our shared roots are visibly intertwining on social media. As I watch more protestors around the globe shouting enough is enough to racism, I'm struck by how what happens here still matters.

The flawed foundation of the American Dream has long been known, but it was once a powerful and inspiring dream, calling to people for centuries and from everywhere.

When I was 16, in Israel, my friend Jay and I met two gals of a similar age in the lobby of the King David hotel in Jerusalem. We hung out some together, but not much. In fact, I remember trying to avoid them, especially after learning they were looking to get married and come to America.

Dorith, an artist, gave me a drawing of us meant to persuade me of how we belonged together. I kept it, and thus remember her still, all these years later.

As I got older, I learned to travel with desired goods, like blue jeans, which were once the gold standard for international barter. I think Hollywood, probably more than anything after Americans being liberators in World War II, best promoted and marketed an irresistible image of us to the world.

Of course, English is widely spoken, and people from every country had relatives or knew someone who was living a better life in the U.S.A. We were where the action was, or where the opportunities to get a piece of that action were best found.

So, even though those days are mostly gone, it seems there is still a beacon that many hope will mean something again. And so our struggles are taken on by others around the world. Not because they want to be here or be us anymore, but because we are all joined on this planet, and success here benefits everyone, everywhere.

It's time to resurrect the dream, but with the nightmare finally addressed and put to rest.

"When did you know that the color of your skin mattered?"

I read that a few days ago on a friend's page and have seen similar questions since. I've been reading the various responses but haven't been able to comment.

The other night I heard Jimmy Fallon apologize for doing a blackface comedy skit back when he was on *SNL*. He also talked to anti-racist activist, Jane Elliot, about her social experiment using blue and brown eyes to separate students in a class. She made up reasons why those with brown eyes were superior to those with blue eyes. Her objective was to show how prejudice was something learned.

After a restless night's sleep, I started to dig around inside, looking for my own hidden and silent prejudices.

My story begins with a sick mother who needed help raising her children. Along came Rose, a black nanny, who for many years was the one who cared for me and my sister. She may have been hired by my parents, but she was our boss. In those early years, the roles people played in our lives were what mattered most.

Certainly, everything changed as the civil rights movement got going. Color was an issue seen on the nightly news. The coverage, and my family's and their friends' comments and reactions were what first delineated, in my awareness, an us and a them.

Whatever was happening out there did not show up in our Jewish neighborhood until the integration of our schools began. In Rogers Park, on the north side of Chicago, prior to 1968, I didn't know any black kids, but that changed for me at Mather High School.

Some of my friends might correct me, but there were no problems that I can remember. In fact, with the help of sports, music, and marijuana, we hung out together, perhaps found even more common ground because of Vietnam, the Draft lottery, and then protesting both. It was the time when the term "brother" emerged, and it was applied liberally across racial divides.

I was also involved in a few programs that were about connecting with and helping inner-city kids. One was a camp program where teenagers from north-side schools were counselors for kids from poorer areas. The other was a tutoring program at the west-side Marillac House. In a turn of events, we were bussed there on Saturday mornings, where each of us paired with a younger, black student. It was a huge commitment. Saturday mornings for a teenager were meant for sleeping in, right?

Here's the heartbreaking part, and where I found my concealed shame. Our presence mattered. It wasn't just about getting someone through a math class, or turning them on to a great book, but rather it was a human bonding. We were providing some kind of desired attention and care. And when one of us didn't show up, an eager child watching the empty bus would wait and wonder until the hurtful realization sunk in.

I couldn't take it. I did not want anyone to need me like that, and so I quit. And when I did, I shut something down inside of me. I never talked about it, never mentioned until this writing that I was one who had left someone waiting for me.

I know race is a huge part of it, but what I saw, what I turned away from, was need, born of poverty and the resultant broken families. We don't just have racism in our country; we have a class system that effectively divides and separates people.

In 1983, I spent three months in Africa, where I was never so white, never felt so conspicuous. There was no blending in. However, I almost never experienced any hostility and was welcomed just about everywhere I went.

On my return to the states, I landed in Chicago, and in parts of the city where I was born and raised, the welcoming experience I had in central Africa was just not possible.

That's the painful wound, not from race but from what was done by one to another; the refusal to acknowledge and make amends; and the prison of poverty that remains.

As a people, all of us—we—the people must commit to heal and reinvent how we live in this land together. We can begin by doing what we do best: go to war! We don't have to take a penny from the military, but simply charge the Pentagon to fight the war on poverty.

How memory and storytelling work: When the movie *The Help* came out, I didn't want to see it but stated no particular reason. Eventually, Susan put it in our Netflix queue. Reluctantly, I watched it with her. That's when I first (and emotionally) remembered how significant a black nanny had been in my early life.

A couple of days ago, in response to all that has been being going on regarding race and to a particular question about skin color awareness, I wrote about Rose. And I thought again about my mom, often in the hospital, who died when I was 15.

And then, I remembered Billy. A black man who worked as a janitor at Temple Beth-El. In the afternoons, after school, for a variety of reasons, I'd be there with just him, following him around as he worked. He sang. He even danced with a mop or a broom or a polishing machine. I loved being with him.

Perhaps he gave me advice, but, if so, I don't recall any of it. Mostly, he demonstrated a way of being, an attitude of joyful presence that attracted me in my youth. Smiles and laughter, his and mine, filled those afternoons.

It wasn't until I wrote about Rose that I realized how when I was a teenager losing my mother, I turned to the only black person then in my life for comfort.

There was a time when my dad was the president of the temple and active in their Men's Club. I learned later that he had helped Billy out a few times, but one night, years after any of us were still involved with Beth-El, I answered the telephone, and it was Billy. He was drunk. I didn't know how to talk with him. I think that hurt him, but he had called for my dad, and I quickly turned the phone over to him.

After that, I heard only my father's end of the conversation but understood that for whatever reason, there would be no more assistance to Billy. I was numb. My dad didn't want to talk about it. I didn't pursue it, and that was the last time we heard from or spoke of Billy.

This week, I wish I could go back and say what I could not have said until today, and tell both my father and Billy what those afternoons of song, dance, and joking meant to me.

There are so many debts in a life. And some that can only be repaid by kindness to those who have no idea why they are receiving a payment of gratitude meant for another. But it's a gift given, along with a blessing, passed on and on as long as it has been and will be needed.

What if there were a way of rebooting a civilization? What would it look like? Would we shut everything down, send everyone home, and wait for the green light to come? And then, would we just return to what we were doing before?

Or perhaps look around, check in with others and ask, "Might we do things differently this time?"

Maybe with acknowledgment of wrongs and amends made—apologies offered and forgiveness given—that might be possible today.

As someone who used to go home with strangers, hopped a freight train along the West Coast, jumped out of airplanes, hitchhiked around different countries, free-climbed mountain peaks, and rode a Kawasaki Enduro through the desert like a Kamikaze eager for dying glory, I've actually become quite a boring guy.

Can't speak for others who lived through the Sixties & Seventies and survived everything since, but I'm still here because I've not the reckless spirit I did back then. Still, who would have ever guessed that a shopping trip or a backyard gathering (with appropriately distanced friends) would become the new daring behavior?

Many who have hungered for some time at home have had their fill. And there is much to take to the streets these days as we sense we have finally arrived at the tipping point—where we will either emerge into the dream long-imagined or descend into the chaos long-feared.

But here's the thing: If we're not being careful with and respectful of others, no matter what we say we're protesting for or against, we're choosing the path I, for one, do not want to travel. Not even the younger, crazier version of myself would want to go where that leads.

Just a little while ago, I watched a couple walking along the Rillito jump, extremely startled. I imagined only a rattlesnake could produce such a dramatic reaction. They walked away backwards from it, animated and gesturing, their suddenly rapid heartbeats almost palpable from a distance. The surprising presence of a merchant of Death is not something one takes likely, nor ever forgets.

Later, on their return, although the snake was now gone, they moved faster and more alert through that same area. It helps to be able to see what endangers us, but it's what we can't see that can be most troubling. Yeah, like a virus.

When in Africa, I was duly impressed with and properly respectful of the large predators, but it was the Putsi and Tumbo flies laying eggs on my clothes drying in the sun that would then hatch and burrow into my skin, or the various worms, jiggers, and ectoparasites that would get into my feet, and the entire microbial universe in the water that would make its way into my stomach and gut that truly terrified me. So, yes, I have a profound distaste and aversion for knowingly exposing myself to anything that could bring me again to my knees.

We are so remarkably fragile, and neither our faith, nor our needs, nor our beliefs can spare any of us from this aggressive invisible world. Therefore, I am quite alarmed by the conflicts that are arising across our country.

This is not the time to assert the rights of individuals to be stupid and to risk the lives of others. That is not what is being asked of us. It is a time to let the rattlesnake cross the path and to be grateful if it did not strike you nor your loved ones.

We all know Hans Christian Andersen's telling about a princess and a pea; however, there is an 11th-century tale from India illustrating a similar situation. In other words, something long-noted in human behavior is marked and perhaps mocked.

In the days of those earlier tales, the stories portrayed a test for royalty, what we could call privilege today. An obvious theme is that those who don't have to work hard with their hands and bodies are overly sensitive and bothered by what others wouldn't even notice.

Recently, I saw a meme with side-by-side photos: in one a black child is holding a sign saying, "Please don't kill me"; and in the other a white woman has a sign saying, "We want haircuts!" That's what brought to mind the Princess and the Pea.

On a morning bike ride, I noticed how quickly and efficiently people adjusted trajectories to avoid each other. In the random way thoughts occur, I started thinking of the attraction and repulsion of magnetism.

Back in my college days, I had a physics professor who introduced me to the Earth's wobble and to periodic polar reversals. Both concepts intrigued me. I've learned recently that the axis is shifting as a result of ice melting in Greenland. Seems water weight is an issue even for a planet (but don't you worry about it).

However, the magnetic poles' movement might be another matter. You know magnetic north, right? The north the arrow points to on a compass. That one is moving quickly, and towards Siberia of all places. Up to 34 miles per year! In comparison, tectonic plate movement is measured in centimeters per year.

What does that mean? Well, since no one knows for sure, let me take a stab at it. I read a paper that described it as the North Pole's "extreme restlessness." Huh?! That got my attention. Seems that at different times in our planet's history, the poles would reverse, sometimes frequently. Rapid swaps have been connected to extinction events, like the Kotlinian Crisis (for those who want to look something up).

Hey, I'm not suggesting anything here. This is indeed something where there is absolutely nothing to do. And, better yet, human activity can't be blamed for it. But if the poles do flip, the disruption to our magnetic field might be catastrophic for technology, especially satellite-based communications, and increased radiation reaching the earth's surface might not be so good for living things.

Again, I wouldn't be writing this just to alarm. A reversal process like this could go on for centuries. Whew! But back to the bike ride where this began. Our human poles have already shifted. Avoiding each other is now almost automatic. What else might we be capable of changing in our time of extreme restlessness?

The older and more comfortable I get, the more my attention is drawn to whatever interrupts my well-deserved quiet order. For a lot of old men, it's the call to pee we must heed. You know how it is when you have to pee but you want to finish what you're doing first? For me, it's usually while doing dishes. That old warm water effect. So, here's my latest awareness challenge to myself: Instead of seeing how long I can hold it, see how quickly I can respond to my body and go pee. My thinking is to "eliminate" the feeling of urgency and replace it with both relief and being more present.

Speaking of relief, I notice that not only does every trip to a well-stocked grocery store bring such a sense, but so do things like timely garbage pick-ups and ongoing utility and internet service.

Back when I traveled without an itinerary, I got stuck for a while in Kigali, Rwanda. I was a guest of an American diplomat and so was in a more upscale part of the hybrid sprawling city and mega-village. The power grid, however, was inadequate for the size of it all and would rotate around the area, giving energy for only a few hours at a time.

Guess what? It was okay. People adapted. Some even welcomed their time with electricity rather than complain about their time without it. Imagine that! Our expectations are truly what define our attitude and thus our well-being.

There is no doubt that my every return from a remote or undeveloped part of the world was accompanied by some relief to be back where things like sanitation and utilities were a given. It is in part how I've come to measure a society: its commitment and ability to provide ongoing basic services. Other than issues around healthcare and regarding homelessness, I'd say we have historically measured up.

However, today our infrastructure is in need of great repair. Meanwhile, we're printing trillions of dollars to stay afloat. Perhaps it's time to resurrect ideas like the CCC and WPA and overhaul our roads and bridges, create more pedestrian and cyclist greenways around our cities. Giving people meaningful work to do might accomplish more than just taking care of our country. It might bring more of us together again. Now, wouldn't that be a relief?!

Years ago, I had a therapist, Alice, who shared about a time in her life when she needed a reason to keep on living. Her guidance came in one word, curiosity.

At the time, I didn't think it particularly enlightening, but her utter sincerity embedded the moment in my memory.

A couple of weeks ago, I wrote a haiku asking myself to stop see-sawing between anger and despair and to become the fulcrum instead. But what did that mean? What, pray tell, was the fulcrum?

Today, I realized it was curiosity. That's the place between emotional extremes, between hope and hopelessness, where one can be to witness these storms and to meet our uncertain future.

So, if I were someone who would display a bumper sticker, mine would read: "Surrender to Curiosity!" Thanks for that, Alice. I'm a slow learner, but I often did and do still listen.

Anyone else have arguments or conflicts that aren't necessary, or even really happening, except in your own mind? If so, does it ever feel good? Well, for me it doesn't.

Had a tailgater today. Watched the list of potential reactions scroll down in my head. You know, from slowing down all the way to giving the finger.

I decided to try something different. First, I imagined it was someone wanting to get closer to me, for a peek (at my hair perhaps), or to give me a blessing.

So, I waved. And then, I couldn't help but laugh.

I think he did too.

At least, that's the story I'm telling and choosing to remember.

Our beloved Santa Catalina Mountains are burning. I'm not complaining. Really. Just want to share some misery. And, yes, it's another inconvenienced privileged guy speaking—blah, blah, blah—but as the virus spreads quicker in Arizona, a terrible fire accelerates through our beautiful sky island summer oasis, and then with temperatures soaring into the hundreds, our power went out yesterday!

Okay, not even for two hours, but long enough to get a sense of life without electronic refuge or air-conditioned relief.

I thought of the firefighters and the homeless out in that heat, which kept me from whining much about missing the golf tournament I wanted to watch. Yeah, I know, but when I was able to get back online, the first thing I looked up was how many people were displaced worldwide. I was startled by the number: over 70 million! The U.N. reports 37,000 people a day are forced to flee their homes because of conflict and persecution. Every day!! That is staggering. Mind blowing.

Yes, there are folks around here who are packed and ready to evacuate ahead of this fire. Some already have, but they all have somewhere to go and a support system in motion ready to address their needs. I wonder how much we all have to suffer before we develop both the empathy and the collective will to fully take care of each other.

My empathy for firefighters comes from having been at the apocalyptic front, cutting line ahead of a fire's inferno. The otherworldly orange-yellow glow of a landscape, sunlit through smoke-filled air, would hypnotize me into a trance-like state. The fire, sucking up all the available oxygen, would hiss, "Shhhut your eyes, Lee. Go to sleeeeppp …"

And I know the jolting terror of hearing the shout from the radio, warning that the fire had jumped line and was now coming up from behind our position. You don't try to outrun a fire going uphill. In fast-burning brush, the best option is often to turn towards the fire, find it in yourself to burst through the flames to a spot already burned, and then wait.

It was the hardest work I ever did, and it is absolutely work for the young. I've been watching the air tankers dropping slurry, but even with binoculars can't see the hot, back-breaking, lung-aching tasks being done by those crews on difficult-to-reach rocky ground. I salute them. And thank them. And for them, and for all the homeowners in the area, I pray that the winds hold off … at least until they can bring some rain with them.

Yet I Yeti
Like a cat waiting to pounce upon the right words, I sit with pen in hand.
Yet my eyes keep wandering, inspecting clouds for signs of the rain
we're more than ready for here.
Yet life goes on for most, doesn't it?
There are always those suffering so much more,
while others live seemingly unaffected, above it all.
Let it go. Everything in its time.

As for me, I can't hold anything, or anyone (not even myself)
in my own mind for long.
A dry wind blows, there's dust and smoke,
yet I do hold on to a glimmer of hope.
(Why am I thinking of Yeti?)

When I was much younger,
I looked long for something I thought
could only come from a woman.
So few are immune to the whispers of imagination
or the urges of reproduction.

Yet, like the whistling swooshing sound
of the elusive Yeti,
something unknown is out there,
and
something will be born.

Will it be an abomination from our collective unconscious
or the lovechild from consciousness joined?

I don't know,
but for now, let it rain,
and I'll meet you,
meet you in the falling rain …
yeah, I'll meet you in the falling rain.

Tens of thousands of acres are burning in the mountain forest we would be seeking refuge from the summer heat in. I think of the images from earlier this year when 27.2 million acres were scorched in Australia. How much will this Bighorn Fire take from us?

In the news, besides the relentless updates on the virus, there are reports of enormous swarms of locusts devouring India. More and more, it feels as if we are living in biblical times.

And still life goes on. I need to go to the dentist. I've canceled previous appointments for fear of being somewhere with no mask and mouth wide open, but at some point one must resume normal care. Plus, I need some of the clarity that often comes with it.

The dentist's chair is not just about my teeth for me. It has become the interface between realities for me. Let me explain.

In youth, as the young are wont to do, I quested for insight, tested the boundaries of perception. I learned whatever I learned, and in doing so found I could then accept, even embrace, the refuge and challenge of ordinary life.

From time to time, I still like to get a tune-up for this mind/body vehicle, an alignment between inner values and outer behavior. Oddly enough, the best place nowadays for that is no longer the desert nor a mountain top, but rather in a dentist's chair.

Hear me out. The historical vision quest meant temporarily leaving one plane to gain a new vantage point and understanding of the one left. But how to bring back and keep that awareness was always an issue. With the help of nitrous oxide and headphones, I found I could make a similar journey while maintaining the interface between planes. Go as deep as I could but keep track of the progress and expectations of the teeth cleaning, perhaps even anticipate the "open" and "close" instructions.

Instead of the effort and danger of a psychedelic rock climb, I could relax into whatever pain or discomfort and surrender control while continuing to appropriately interact with the hygienist even as the realizations of how everything that ever existed is connected return.

The experience in that chair can become a nexus of science and spirituality, a crossroad of consciousness where I'd remember my family's ceramic foundation and how my Uncle Marty left his father's Acorn Tile Company to branch into dental porcelain.

There was the time, as a small child, I accidentally (note the "dental" even in this) slipped my mother's Pontiac out of park, and it rolled down the driveway. I jumped into the back seat pretending to be asleep while the car made its way backwards into the car of our neighbor, a dentist, who lived across the street.

Many years later, he literally extracted a tooth in retribution.

Nowadays, I might bring my own music to the dentist's chair, but this morning I chose the random messaging from turning the dial of a radio.

After my hygienist assured me of how safe dental offices around town have been, and we caught up a bit, I got in position. As the gas started flowing, I kid you not, "Magic Carpet Ride" was playing. I started to laugh. I shared why with her. I wanted to somehow include her in the experience, and I certainly didn't want her lowering the flow.

She said something about the sound of my laugh as I recalled tiptoeing into a darkened house late at night only to find it rocking with laughter. I'd follow the sounds to their source, my father watching something on television by himself and laughing hilariously. I never could understand it then. How could he be laughing by himself? My teenage mind could not comprehend it. Laughter was a social act, a result of group dynamics.

The gas was doing its thing, and my mind was bringing up moments from my teens like when Pamela's mother came into the kitchen one morning only to find a blurry-eyed congregation around the table. Her mom accused everyone of being high. Pamela immediately denied this as she got up from the table and promptly walked into the wall. Everyone around the table fell to the floor laughing, including Pamela. Only her mom didn't see the humor in it.

Laughter separated those who knew from those who didn't. It was the barometer of any given moment. But it was something I could not imagine doing alone.

So, as a child, I could not understand my father's laugh. He liked to hear and tell jokes. And there was always laughter wherever he was. I could walk into the most crowded room and find my father right away just from the sound of his laugh.

And what a laugh it was! The sound itself was a thing to be heard. Quite distinctive, it took place over several octaves as he would throw his head back and let loose. The incredible abandon of his laughter rattled my sense of what was proper. One simply didn't risk such displays. I was often embarrassed.

"Everything looks good, Lee," the hygienist interrupted. She mentioned that Father's Day was this week, and I responded that I was just thinking of my dad.

As I was driving home, wondering if having my mouth open for so long let in anything undesirable, I thought about how my dad was seldom ill. I don't think he ever spent two consecutive days home sick in bed. Was there a connection between health and laughter?

Years ago, when dealing with persistent back pain, I read about Norman Cousin's experience with laughter as medicine. I started to see how perhaps my own disconnect with my feelings and the honest expression of them might be at the root of my own physical suffering.

My dad had always been showing me the way. He knew something I am still struggling with. He trusted people. He believed in them. He shared who he was with them and expressed his joy of living in laughter. It was his gift, and a gift he gave to me.

Now, if I could only get out of my own way and open it more often.

With smoke billowing up from the mountains behind her, she sat under a royal blue canopy on this hot June morning outside of St. Francis in the Foothills as a seemingly endless procession of cars, many with hand-crafted and lovingly made signs, inched by to say farewell to Helen "Robbie" Dick.

She's 96. Has been in Tucson for 66 years, but is leaving now with her son for California, and hospice. I have never known anyone in this life like her. From the long line of vehicles around me, I'm not alone in my amazement, appreciation, and love for Robbie. She is a wonder, an indomitable phenomenon. Ask anyone who knows her, and the first thing they will say is the world is a better place because of her. Ask her, and she will tell you all that still needs to be done.

I met her on a Citizen Diplomacy trip to the Soviet Union in 1985. It was my first and only one. She and her husband Jim were on at least fifteen, leading many of them. She has been a tireless activist for just about everything, including the most relentless registerer of voters the world has ever known.

She was also my neighbor, and partner, in the Damian Community for 30 years. We've sat in countless meetings together, many unpleasant. We did not always agree, but I always respected her commitment, her enthusiasm, and her ideals.

In our last years as next door neighbors, I started doing more things for her. From her place, we had an internet hub that served several. I even became her surrogate to deal with CenturyLink. She trusted me with much. And, as someone whose own mother died when I was 15, she filled something of that long-absent role for me.

When Jim died, I wrote her this note: "Dear Robbie, I've often thought of Damian as an orchestra where no one knew for sure what instrument he or she wanted to play, and where no one could agree on what music we should all play together. In the last days of Jim's life, his blessings allowed each of us to pick up our right instrument, while his love became the music."

Today, I would add that the band director, the stage manager, the ticket taker, and the entire marketing and promotion department were positions all held by you, Robbie. I'm grateful that you let me work the lights, from time to time.

Another long day in June. Looking for inspiration in notebooks, I found an unfinished golf story about a tournament from earlier this year: a partnered ladder match play event.

For several years, my partner has been my friend, Pam. We call ourselves "Pam & Egg" for how one of us would rise to the needs of any given hole in a match, especially when the other was faltering.

In the first tournament we played together, we wound up in an epic match that lasted 6 1/2 hours with us finally winning the endurance test on the 24th hole. It was Pam's brilliant 2nd shot from a tough position to an elevated green that closed the match.

In front of me now are the notes from our shortest match, one that we closed out on the 13th hole. Instead of writing about it, and while wondering if we'd ever have the chance to do something like that again, I asked her if she wanted to meet to play 9.

Her house was in the danger zone from the Bighorn Fire. She was living under an evacuation watch. We had been texting about fire behavior, tapping into my long-ago experience with the Forest Service.

During the hardest times, I've always found that golf was the best way to take my mind off a problem and bring my attention to something else. I imagined Pam could use a break from worry.

We met on the 10th tee, and with the smoke above us, played golf. We talked some of worldly matters, but mostly just let golf displace everything for a while.

Golf has regained popularity in this pandemic in part for that reason. Many have been looking for something to do outdoors with others and have found a welcome refuge on golf courses. The bonus is how the preparation for golf, and the golf swing itself, focuses one entirely in the moment.

Forgetting about the fire for a bit, Pam mentioned she hadn't had a birdie in a long time. Then, on the 15th hole, a par 4 for me, a par 5 for Pam, her second shot finished pin high on the green, giving her a chance for eagle.

Did she make it?

With so many unanswered questions facing us all, I'll leave it there. After all, aren't we all writing our own versions of reality these days?

There are many things I'd like to know, questions I have for those who have passed.

And there are legends of lost treasures, of shipwrecks unfound, all around the globe. Even today, with every instrument imagined, so many secrets elude us.

I had a friend whose death I never believed. I knew there was more to the story, even playing detective for a while until I became entangled in stories not mine to know.

When I was young enough to not be seen as a threat, I saw the jar of gold and silver my father kept hidden near his brown, leather World War II diary. When home alone, I played with the heavy coins and read of air battles above Italy. I learned in those pages of my father's fear, and of flak and shrapnel tearing through the body next to his.

Many years later, I accompanied him to a reunion of those who survived. I never heard anyone speak of the terror, but as the end of their natural lives approached, they gathered more often, toasting perhaps the fate avoided, saying farewell to those who shared what remained unspoken.

After he died, it was left to me to settle his affairs. I never found the treasure I knew he once had, but I did find the tattered old diary. However, the pages that revealed so much more of my father than I had ever witnessed had all been torn out.

I'll never know why he could no longer bear to have such truth exist. I only know his story as it lives in me, and what I myself choose to conceal or reveal.

For every word salvaged from all these worn papers carried with me forever, I now discard a thousand. It's not just sentences and ideas falling away, not just the stuff of living downsized, but longing and belonging, that fascination with association: so, membership and magazine; that club, those clothes; my teams, my dreams; a need to drive, a desire to meet; long telephone calls, love letters, photographs, secrets, and old address books …

Even as I write these thoughts, something of me is disappearing. I seem to be erasing myself.

Long ago, in self-serious, dramatic fashion, I announced my departure from this world, got rid of most everything I owned, and wandered off into the mountains in search of enlightenment. I didn't expect to come back. I won't say what I found, other than a reason to return and live a more ordinary life.

The fire lookout tower was where I began to reassemble myself. I'm almost ready to talk about that experience.

But today, I'm questioning my behavior. Is this now an age and era appropriate to once again find that elusive, shimmering path? Or is it a descent into becoming some crusty recluse?

I'm noticing an increased lack of patience for anything, or anyone, that wastes my time. As if time were more precious than ever before. As if there were something urgent needing to be done, waiting for me, for you, for all of us to begin.

For the 23,929th Time

Dreams of death and a damaged child rustled my sleep.
A twisted Elmo in a fiery glow hovered over my bed
while a long line of elders exited a horror show.
Battling and trying to trick the kid,
needing to grieve, while caring for this difficult orphan
who, for all I knew, could have been myself,
a cosmic friend babbled conspiracy theories
and, even asleep, I felt my impatience.

I'm up now, writing in the dark,
unable to read a word of this night-toxin bloodletting.
Even before caffeine, I look to uncover, discover,
a lifeline to grasp.
Have you ever counted the sun risings of your life?
The thousands, the tens of thousands of times you've been given
another chance to start again, make a different choice,
perhaps not try to fit in where you wanted only to belong,
or speak words your heart had no say in?

Perhaps today I'll let more of what comes from silence
inform my way towards a setting sun.
Maybe find a feeling from a day lived, in my own body,
reflected in the slow burst of color at day's end.
In my dream, I told the child either the bed by the window
or the hammock under the porch would be okay for a restful sleep.
I asked of him one thing,
"Would you caress a fear tonight for me?"

July

Regret

There is this thing, like desire, that sits as a boulder
near the bottom of my life.
I cannot remove it, nor do anything with it,
yet my life, like some persistent sapling, has grown around it.
Without moving it, I have branched in different ways,
become stout and dense, a formidable yet gnarled tree
in a desert oasis.
From time to time, I stoop to gaze at this white quartz-veined,
orange lichen-covered granite at my base
and see there still some promise of beauty,
some revelation of insight and wisdom
I know not how to mine.
I dust off its surface instead
with an old rag, once a favorite shirt, though seldom worn,
its life worn thin and through on a hanger in a closet.

I've been reading about "crisis fatigue"—exhaustion, anger, despair, and anxiety—the cocktail of a chronic stress with no clear endpoint in sight. Drug overdoses around the country are increasing, so are shootings.

4th of July will mean more gatherings, more opportunities for this virus to be passed around.

People want to travel this summer, yet many countries remain closed to visitors. Strict policies in South Korea and New Zealand seem to be working against the virus. Isn't it too soon to think we can go back to normal?

In Florida, despite rising cases, Disney World is planning on re-opening.

Theme parks in Japan are discouraging screaming on roller coasters to prevent the spread of COVID-19 with this motto: "Please scream inside your heart."

Yes, I think we can all do that.

Thinking of summers and escaping the heat, I remember how I would look forward to camp season in Wisconsin. My favorite time to be there was for preparation prior to the arrival of campers. A small team of guys would arrive a few weeks before opening to set the camp up.

We each had our own cabin but would join the founders, Ma & Pa Jordan, for her home-cooked meals and his homespun wit and wisdom in their home on the property.

He was a retired educator, and for years would randomly, and without explanation, ask, "Have you seen Josephine?" Most of us would shrug a no, and he would scratch his head and move off, presumably, to continue his search.

Eventually, he and I started writing letters to each other, and I learned that Josephine was a beloved mule from his childhood. He wasn't senile; he was odd and funny. I enjoyed being welcomed in their home and having them both in my life.

And I relished the zaniness of guys in the Northwoods, figuring things out, working together, and, especially, the rainy days when we were confined to a cabin, smoking, drinking, and playing cards. We often played partnered games, like euchre, which fueled the banter and the hilarity.

There is something of the shared solitude and corny intimacy of those cabin'd days in the present electronic lockdown.

Lately, Susan and I have been playing games and sharing activities that are more collaborative than competitive, so we've become a bit more lyrical and less hysterical than before, but are still amusing ourselves.

Susan's middle name is Jo. I sometimes call her Josephine. Pa's not around anymore, but I think he'd smile if he knew I had found my own Josephine.

In Tucson, the first drops of rain have fallen. There is relief and celebration. Firefighters rejoice and rest.

Still, close to 120,000 acres have burned. The loss is devastating. How much wildlife was lost? Where have all the survivors gone? And, more selfishly, where will we go to escape the heat?

Susan and I have no interest in traveling during this pandemic. We will find ways to stay busy in our two-story dwelling. Retreating to different floors doesn't offer quite the same distancing we once had when living next door to each other, but much is simpler in our lives these days.

I will wake up earlier, often long before first light, have coffee and write in the company of cats.

Susan will stay up later, perhaps working on a puzzle or playing an online game of Scrabble.

We used to practice living together by picking remote getaways with kitchens. We'd bring our own food and drink, various projects, music, books, and relax into days and nights together. We'd cook together, or take turns preparing a meal, drink wine in the evenings, go for walks during the day, talk, or be silent. It was all okay, and not unlike how we've been living here these past months, but at a fraction of the cost.

I've come to dread going anywhere, and mostly only get in a car to go shopping for food or something truly needed. Each trip feels like maneuvering through some tense video game, with a deep sigh of relief at returning safely home.

I feel as if I'm wrapped tighter and tighter in talisman and precaution, especially in response to others cutting loose.

There are already those we'll never see again, and those we suspect we never will. The only remedy I have for this growing sadness is to keep speaking the ancient words of grateful love to the people in my life, as if chanting back the darkness, and blessing our way into the light.

My empty calendar reminds me of when, as a teenager, I seldom made plans. Didn't want to be caught in an obligation only to find out later I had missed a happening.

I learned early that the best things couldn't be planned, only discovered.

I was part of a group that would randomly meet at one park or another on Chicago's north side and then roamed together the night streets, ever on the lookout for what might be unfolding.

More often than not, we were rewarded for being open to spontaneity. Surprise, I think, was the chalice we sought.

Nowadays, in the virtual, pandemic present, we can go from an educational talk to a happy hour to a concert to whatever else kind of gathering, effortlessly, from home, and all in an evening. It may not lead to many surprises, but it sure is versatile and convenient. And, worth repeating, without the risk of drunk driving!

Certainly, we miss restaurant get-togethers and culinary-accented travels with friends or just the two of us, but the real surprise today is what we are creating in our own kitchen, and without any meat.

I am an omnivore opportunist, but Susan is a long-time vegetarian. If I did eat meat, it was never at home. That was part of our agreement for living together. So, without planning to cease the consumption of meat, it's now been almost three months since I've had a bite. I now refer to myself as the "accidental vegetarian."

Surprise, surprise. I don't miss meat. In fact, I'm not only feeling better, I'm dressing better. And I certainly must be taller, with the other interesting side effect of both thinking and storing information in Fibonacci sequences.

SeriousLee, with all the coverage regarding conditions at meat processing plants on top of the problems of CAFOs (concentrated animal feeding operations), I'm unsure about ever going back to my previous diet.

However, Susan has been closely following progress with lab-grown meat. It seems all kinds of possibilities are being imagined these days. A future is emerging, even as the failures and mistakes of how we've been living are exposed.

Every day, I think there's nothing left for me to say, and then I find myself further below the surface of the life I was previously living, brushing through the seaweed, and peeking under shells.

Recently, I started writing the story of where my time in the lookout tower led me. Here's the first line: "My birth mother tried to drown me."

Why tell a story like that?! Isn't it enough to have survived, to be alive, and to have been able to still thrive?

But here's what I can't avoid anymore: an awareness of my resting place consciousness, the place I return to if not engaged in a task. My inner screen saver keeps resetting to it: I don't belong here.

Sure, I can type in a new command, breathe my way into a place more universal, but my story is my story. And not belonging is my personal trigger.

Even when watching a movie, any scene where someone is sneaking around where they should not be makes me uncomfortable. Oh sure, I've rushed into many a situation where others would not, but that was just the way a youth rebelled against his programming and constraints.

My early morning writing at this time in my life is me diving in with the equipment and training from a lifetime's work. I don't expect to change anything really, other than getting to know my own underwater terrain better, and perhaps catching its influence before it bubbles up.

Creative Source

It showed up again—wild, vibrant, alive.
Long pursued, ever elusive,
like a promise of rare revelation.
But to chase it is to fail
For it can't be caught,
never tamed, nor ever bought.
Yet, somehow, thirty years of living
restrained, in service to the necessary,
forged the only saddle it will accept.
When ready, it saddles itself, with me already in place,
and I am lifted and carried, dazzled by the breadth
of its windy power.
Between the challenge of holding on
and the jubilation of letting go,
I forget as much as I remember.

On my way home from a morning walk, I came up behind a crouched figure working intently on an irrigation line. Turned out to be a 71-year-old neighbor fixing someone else's problem. I was properly awed by both his flexibility and his goodness. There are many ways to age.

What I didn't say to him, nor was ever planning to reveal, was that just yesterday I anonymously fixed a neighborhood gate. Those who know me have long heard my maintenance stories and emergency dramas, which, again, for the record, I no longer willingly participate in. I don't want to be known as that fix-it guy anymore, and have some attitude about it. I'm retired, done with all of that.

Yet even the thought of having crossed this worker's Finish Line is almost as enervating as imagining being back in the race. Perhaps that is why I choose to do these secretive mendings.

Seeing Stewart this morning got me thinking about my furtive ways, about what else I withhold, and what kind of community I might be able to participate in more cooperatively today. I've always been an all-or-nothing, take-charge guy, and I still wonder about my ability to set boundaries. Perhaps the next time I see him, I'll ask Stewart how he manages his. Everybody needs an inspiring elder or two.

I've heard neighborhood reports of people "stealing" showers and breaking into unoccupied spaces for somewhere to sleep. I'm both concerned and upset about what is unraveling and how little is being provided for those in need.

Arizona tops the world in the recent spread of the virus with 105,000 confirmed cases, and in Tucson threatening signs of hate are turning up around town. (Here's an inflammatory cocktail recipe: mix the most heavily armed nation in the world with tens of millions of eviction notices.)

In Phoenix, there's a push to find temporary housing for the homeless who are infected with the virus. The Circle the City program currently has 136 rooms available at the Phoenix Inn. However, the U.S. Department of Housing & Urban Development estimated in 2019 that there were 7,419 homeless in the Phoenix area.

This morning, I heard yelling and investigated. Wearing a dark, large-brimmed hat, a guy on a bicycle was going up and down the streets shouting,

"What did Obama know?!"

I'm not sure if it was an angry accusation or a conspiracy chant, but there was a touch of Fellini in the moment. And, I must admit, I don't really want to be in this movie.

Looking for omens? Well, there's the appearance of a great comet. First seen on March 27, 2020 and named NEOWISE, I'm thinking it should have been called "Pandemic."

Long considered mythological messengers, comet sightings have been associated with the death of kings, famine, and war. The long orbit of this celestial visitor means it was last here 6,800 years ago.

Let's take a peek at the sketch pad from Creation to learn what was going on its last visit. Around that time, a change had begun in the fragile human animal. It's known as the Neolithic Y chromosome bottleneck. The genetic diversity of the Y chromosome was starting to collapse. In terms of our ancestral gene pool, it was as if there were only one man for every 17 women.

Since it was only observed on the genes of the Y chromosome, a social, not an environmental cause, was the most probable culprit. One theory is that it was the beginning of the accumulation of wealth and power which concentrated reproduction into fewer male hands.

Susan and I talk about things like this. Well, actually, I tend to ask questions that she answers or points me towards something to read. She just retired as the Deputy Director for Research Cyberinfrastructure at the University of Arizona. She spent most of her career using supercomputers to help researchers with genomics projects. More recently, her team had a hand in an Air Force Research Lab-funded effort to map space junk, and rubbed shoulders with personnel from the Event Horizon Telescope that captured the first image of a black hole. She knows things I can't begin to understand. However, that doesn't stop me from speculating.

When I think of that time in history, with humans living in clans on a wild and dangerous planet, the many were subservient and dependent upon the few. As the world was tamed and our numbers grew, people rebelled from previous controls and began to move towards more independent thinking and living.

Recently, we watched *Hamilton*, and I wondered about the phenomenon of its popularity. Of course, it was a cool and hip way to energize and celebrate our nation's story, but maybe it was also a premonition of what's changing and a nostalgia for what may be the ending of our current notions of independence.

Last week, on the 4th of July, I noted the widespread use of the term, interdependence, and thought perhaps that might be the next stage of our development.

With the world population approaching 8 billion, and with human influence upsetting the balance of the entire ecosystem, perhaps what now needs to emerge is the collective realization that we are each a unique independent being, dependent upon one another, and, together, responsible for the care of everything on the planet that cares for us.

As someone who grew up reading science fiction, I hope humanity gets it together and eventually reaches an interstellar era where we won't have to wait for comets to come to us because we will be visiting them. One can only hope the Y chromosome will last long enough to seed the stars with a more enlightened human seed.

Serenity

One voice campaigns for an empty schedule;
another clamors for doing it all.

Somewhere in between everything and nothing
if one can juggle the needs of living
while balancing the unexpected with the desired
there is an absence, filled with ease,
sprinkled with acceptance, joined by breath and dream.

Where if one can sit while moving still,
a great truth is revealed: inner peace is possible.

Fleeting, for sure,
yet with eyes closed, one can relax in this pursuit,
feeling first the pull, then the surrendering

into the gravity of serenity.

You might not even notice when
what you thought must be chased
was now carrying you.

I have been writing letters of late, often without much response. It's okay. What's the sound of millions holding their breath, waiting and wondering what will come next?

With the chalkboard of future plans erased, Susan and I now carve and craft daily routines like laboratory researchers, focused on cultivating optimal domestic rhythms.

Recently, in our ongoing attempt to catch up on all we have missed in our busier years, we watched the 2003 Joni Mitchell documentary: *A Woman of Heart and Mind*. It inspired another letter:

Dear Joni,

It's summer in the desert and the heat builds beyond what one can bear. I've been living here for two score and seven years more but still mistake the hot dry, anxious dread for something wrong with me before the monsoons explode and explain everything.

Speaking of explanations, you said it in Wild Things Run Fast: "My child's a stranger / I bore her / But I could not raise her." I wish I had heard that when it came out in 1982, which was when I realized it was time for me to learn of my origins and to face how one story can fuel and influence all of the rest.

Your music, however, accompanied me on many of my journeys, but I never knew about your decision or of the tearful reunion 32 years after giving up your daughter.

My own adopted ears perked up at this and wanted to know more. I read that you lost interest in songwriting after being reunited with your daughter. It was as if the separation of mother and daughter birthed the songwriter who then offered to the world what she could not say to her own child.

I was 29 when I first met my birth mother, who had not been reaching out to me in song, or in any other way; had not, in fact, wanted to be found. Too bad. I needed the direct experience of her existence, even of her rejection, to finally put an end to a restless searching, a skittish wanderlust, that kept me from having anything like love for long.

So, on behalf of every adopted, abandoned, or orphaned child, thank you, Joni. Thank you for being a mother without her child who kept caring, kept feeling the loss and the pain, but let art work it and work it until you healed your way into the lives of your daughter and grandchild, becoming and being everything you were meant to be, every step of the way.

Namaste!

A friend recently asked if I were using social media as an ongoing obituary. Hadn't thought of it that way, but it got me thinking. Rather than abandoning social media in frustration or disappointment, what if more of us used it consciously and purposefully?

I must admit that originally, when my son Ryan got me involved, it was interesting and fun to reconnect with so many people from my life, but that enthusiasm faded. There were always reasons why we had lost touch in the first place.

However, even though Ryan lives in Tucson, I would miss some of the things he's doing without being electronically connected. Before the pandemic, we'd get together for a meal or to watch sports almost every week. Now he coaches tennis and is around groups of kids, so we're more likely to see each other from the safety of a family Zoom call.

When we entered the Great Viral Unknown, my inner, slightly mawkish camp counselor attempted to be a morale booster of sorts. What I write serves me, helps me make sense, even does some alchemy with mood and attitude. If more people took the time to report the truth from where they are, we'd have a more accurate perspective of how things were truly going.

When I was in a lookout tower, there was a device called an Osborne fire finder. When smoke was spotted, I'd line up the sight to get an azimuth reading, in degrees, on a spherical coordinate system. That was useful, but to know the precise location, triangulation from other towers was needed.

I would like to see something like that happening with social media today: more of us sharing truth from our unique viewpoints. Perhaps if enough of us did just that, those loud but false voices would lose traction and be more easily ignored.

With the above in mind, notes for myself:
- Study the voices both inside and outside of me.
- Learn to distinguish which are trustworthy.
- Be patient with all the rest.
- Remember, emotions are for my own information.
- They have nothing to do with right or wrong.
- My job is to question and understand what they're about.
- BEFORE responding to whatever is going on outside of me.

Speaking of family Zoom calls, Ryan joined me and Susan to connect with my brother and his family in Sweden. How wonderful to see everyone. There's a story to be told about them that in a strange way started late at night early in 1969. I was sitting at my family's glass-topped dining room table, working on what turned out to be my first published story, scratching my head and then becoming fascinated by dandruff falling and swirling like fake snow in a globe.

That image became part of the surprise ending in a tale of a boy conversing with a man ice fishing on the Wisconsin lake, Lac La Belle. I named the boy Glen. At the time, I didn't know anyone with that name. But my wife's father, who died in 1987, was a Glen. Twenty-some years ago, I learned I had a brother, born and raised in Sweden, who's a Glen as well.

Coincidence? Sure. But what does that really mean? My experience tells me that by trusting intuition and allowing my mind to play with associations, I sometimes stumble upon the underlying fabric everything is woven into and upon. So I pay attention when patterns emerge, even though knowing the price of awareness is often responsibility.

Recently, I received an amend from someone I hoped not to see again. Then, a friend request from another who won't stay lost, as I'd prefer, in the forgotten past.

Yesterday, I played golf with a lady I had just met only to learn that the very reason she lives in Tucson is because of a connection to the one person I've lost my temper with in the past few years. Darn Sticky Karma!

There is no escape. And there's more, including a vivid dream of an international mural project. Drawings of hearts were placed in cities everywhere, and people would come and write their personal notes of forgiveness in them.

I get it! I don't like it, but if I want to live in a world where healing genuinely occurs (more than its opposite), I can't exclude anyone from that process, no matter my preference nor what may be revealed about me.

Even we of the reclusive sects are getting antsy, eager to escape from what is increasingly hard to avoid. (Has the Procrastination Society issued a statement yet regarding putting things off during a climate of excess time and fewer excuses?)

I suspect I'm not alone when I feel as if there's something more I should be doing. The varying degrees of lockdown are an incubator for some, a pressure cooker for others. We're all on the verge of hatching, or exploding, something.

As citizens of this country, we do have one thing in common: we are all equally unwanted in other countries. Ha! The bully, loudmouth, and know-it-all, as well as the artist, wanderer, and romantic—the beautiful and the ugly American alike—unwelcome!

We are in this pot, melting or not, forced to face ourselves and each other, and figure it out. Wow! If it weren't so terrifying and exhausting, it could be considered quite exciting, even exhilarating.

For whatever reasons of encouragement (or lack of imagination), I've received a lot of pens as gifts over the years. Engraved desk stands, gold-plated, customized, vintage, chrome, and elaborately displayed cases. I've regifted some, saved most, but without using. Until now. During the last months, rather than getting refills for old favorites, I've been burning through the collectibles.

For my morning scribbling, I need scrap paper. It frees me to play and doodle. Nice notebooks or quality paper intimidate and paralyze my process. However, the pen … oh, the joys of using a really good pen. Why did I wait so long?

Last night, I remembered and then went searching for a Pierre Cardin boxed set. Had to move a suitcase in doing so, which gave me pause. It seemed an odd and foreign thing, an artifact from a lost civilization. I mean, the only traveling we do nowadays is on PBS. Hey, the food still "looks" good, and there are no hassles, no bugs!

Speaking of illusions, my beard and my fingernails seem to be growing faster. Anyone else? And why is that?

Another curiosity: In the first months of this viral change of life, we drank a lot of wine, but our consumption has been steadily going down. Never would have guessed that would happen. It's as if we've been, consciously and unconsciously, inching towards a new way of sustainable living, utilizing the gifts we've already been granted, and caring more for each other and these bodies that carry us. Imagine that! Good can truly come out of most anything.

I start to scratch out something on scrap paper: "Rain reversed rhythm revealed a seam. Slipping through, something spontaneous occurred." The thought dries up. I turn to a news page and read how divorce lawyers and couples counselors are getting swamped with calls. Seems all the additional together time is not working for everyone.

I think I shall scribble something for Susan: "2/3 Yours Forever! There were one hundred poems of longing before arriving at the only question that needed asking."

Then a haiku came:

All these words of mine
do not connect me to you,
yet here I am.

In our waking hours, we have come to share most everything, but ...

Something locked remains.
We may never understand
this spark we carry.

Don't tell her (she already has so much of me), but the unlived past and the frustrated future still run campaigns, pitch pilots, in my dreams. Okay, so I don't really tell her everything.

It seems our vows don't extend into every alternate reality. However, I'm often the first one up, wondering why she is sleeping so long, hoping she wakes up, from wherever she's been, glad to be back with me.

Your tea is waiting,
a day never seen before,
and me, loving you.

I had a frustrating Monday dealing with our phone provider and a billing issue: automated menus, waiting to loud crappy music, then being put on hold, then disconnected, over and over again. It was an exasperating waste of time. I barely use a phone and was ready to just scrap it altogether, once and for all. I even snapped at Susan, then had to go for a walk in the heat (like back-burning to fight a fire) to get through it. I was more upset for letting it get to me, and for how I spoke to Susan, than for their incompetence.

This morning, I had an early tee time for 9 holes. A fellow walker, Jane, who I sometimes play with, had gone off before me. Thinking I'd catch up, I launched my tee shot fairly quickly, barely looking at its flight.

When I got to my ball, it was in the middle of the fairway, and Jane was just leaving the green. 160 uphill yards away, I hit a favorite hybrid solid and on a good line. Not being able to see the surface of the green from below, I imagined it probably went long.

Pushing my cart up that hill, I went straight to the deep rough behind the green to see where my ball might be hiding. Couldn't find it. I walked around the green to see if it had kicked into a bunker somehow. Then, I saw my ball mark and went to repair it.

On my way there, I passed the hole, and there it was! It had gone in the hole! A 2! I've been playing golf for over fifty years, and this was only the second time I had an eagle on a par 4.

To put that in perspective, on par 3s I've had three holes-in-one, which are considered quite rare and often lead to rounds of drinks, newspaper notifications, and even prizes.

Yet no one was there to witness it. I laughed and shook my head about that. And I remembered yesterday and felt moved to forgive myself. It was appropriate that this amazing moment of grace and redemption was a solitary one.

Other golfers might want to hear what happened next, but there is more to this story than just golf. But first the rest of the golf:

The 2nd hole is a short par 3 with a quick and sloping green. My iron shot was high and landed soft. I made the fast, breaking putt for a birdie. Nice start, Lee.

On the tee at the 3rd, Jane saw me from the fairway and waved. She signaled she'd wait for me at the next hole. Already at three under par, I was conservative off the tee on this dogleg right, par 4. My approach to the green was short and right, leaving a difficult pitch over a bunker to a green sloped towards Tucson. I finessed a 60-degree flop shot and made another good putt to save par.

Then I met up with Jane on the 4th and told her of my opening holes. She kidded that perhaps I should keep playing alone. I said it was already good enough for me and that I was ready to return to earth, which this hole had often facilitated. However, I proceeded to par it, and after four holes was three under par.

On the 5th tee, I made the mistake of thinking about how my current score was at only 12 strokes and then promptly drove my ball into a tree. It was a relief in a way. Jane and I chatted about a variety of things under a cloudy sky as I made my way to a bogey, followed by a par, then another bogey, and another par.

By the time we reached the 9th tee, the sun was out, the humidity was up, and we were both tiring. Some voice reminded me that one last par would still give me a subpar nine. Another voice countered with what a shot in the water would do to my score. I ignored them both, ended with a bogey and at even par for the morning, with myself, and hopefully soon, with Susan.

However, in my excitement about the golf, I forgot to drink any water. Within hours, I had a severe dehydration headache. I seldom take aspirin or NSAIDs since the combination had once caused some internal bleeding, but I took several to get some relief.

August

Amends

If this were the last time we spoke, or joked, would it be okay?
Was there something we forgot to say?
Once upon a time, when we were young and brash, and acted without
thinking, did we cross a line, leave a hurt unspoken, a heart broken?
Do you know I never meant you harm?
I believe that about you, with me.
Like you, I struggled between wanting and being
and couldn't see or feel you any better than I could myself.
We might have missed each other in the dark.
But now without the longing that moved me from there to here,
I can hear you.
Is there anything left to say?
Something forgotten that needs the light of day?

Like a wolf pack picking out the old and feeble, I hunt for a well-worn t-shirt for my morning chores, but I'm the one feeling weak. I have to sit down often and quit before finishing some yard work.

I don't say anything to Susan about it, but the Ibuprofen seems to have triggered some bleeding again.

My plan is to take it easy, let it heal itself, and not do anything that might force me to go to a hospital in a pandemic.

I watched some of the funeral for John Lewis. Obama delivered a powerful eulogy to a bipartisan invitation-only crowd. President Clinton called John Lewis a man "on a mission that was bigger than personal ambition." President Bush talked about both working together and disagreeing: "… in the America

John Lewis fought for, and the America I believe in, differences of opinion are inevitable elements and evidence of democracy in action."

I meditated on such a life of service, courage, and dedication and wondered at his perseverance. And I tearfully rejoiced at the respectful tribute from three former presidents acknowledging another's long battle for what he believed in.

By Saturday, I am extremely weak and confess to Susan what's been going on. I convince her to be patient, reminding her that it happened before and stopped by itself.

By Sunday, I can barely walk. Without being overly dramatic, I start preparing some papers and instructions, just in case. The only news I've heard about hospitals is that they're overcrowded with coronavirus patients and short of staff and ventilators. If whatever is going on in my body doesn't get me, what chance will I have if exposed to the virus, weak as I am?

On Sunday, I have to get up in the middle of the night to pee. I don't make it back to bed. I'm done. I can't put Susan through anymore of this. Before I agree to a 911 call, though, I ask her to help me get back in bed and to be with me.

We talk about our life together. We share our love and gratitude for each other. Not knowing if this will be the last time, we hold each other. I am as present as I can be.

Lifted by your words
Heart and mind want to share more
Body speaks in tears

And then she makes the call, helps me get dressed and gather a few things to take with me. I go down the stairs on my butt, one step at a time, and she helps me to a glide chair to wait.

What is loving
but listening with your skin
while minds move inside the other
until their words are your words

discovering, exclaiming, everything forgotten,
longed for,
remembered?

A fire truck arrives before an ambulance. The fire captain surprises me by agreeing with my assessment of the risk at hospitals right now.

"What would you do if you were me?" I ask him.

He shrugs his shoulders, suggesting he doesn't have a clue.

When the EMTs arrive, my line of questioning changes to which hospital might be the least crowded. One guy has a clear opinion that Tucson Medical Center, although not the closest, would be best. So, off we go.

August 2nd, 4 a.m., lights flashing, I watch the streetlights passing above me, feel the turns of the ambulance. I am lucid and in no pain. If one is to die in the most peaceful manner, internal bleeding is the way to go.

Now that I have surrendered control, put myself in the hands of others, my attitude has changed. I'm not worried. I've said goodbye to Susan. I'm chatty, even funny, with the technician riding next to me.

Once, with what turned out to be a false alarm heart attack, I spent a night at TMC on a gurney in a corridor, waiting for a bed and ignored for way too long. I didn't expect things to be much better during a pandemic.

The cheery technician I was buddying around with and who had recommended TMC stayed with me until I was in my own ER room. It took no time at all. Where was everybody?

The admitting nurse, checking my blood pressure, was puzzled. "How are you even conscious?" I learned how close to dying I actually was; a few hours was the nurse's estimate.

Blood transfusions began immediately, as did being wheeled around for various tests. I talked to everyone who came near me and learned that this section of the hospital was empty. All those infected by the virus were placed in a different wing. Even the staff from that section of the hospital worked only there. And everyone was wearing masks, of course.

A doctor performed an endoscopy and showed me the brightly colored photos of a tumor that had burst in my stomach. I wouldn't be going anywhere soon. I was admitted and brought to room #801, my first time away from home since the pandemic began.

Immediately, a veteran nurse of 18 years who I came to call Proud Mary let me know who was boss on her floor. She also wondered at the lowest blood count she had ever seen and how we were even having this conversation. I liked her, felt like I was in good hands.

My first challenge was the bathroom. There were bathroom "hats" that captured and separated waste. One does not flush. Every bit was inspected, measured, and charted. Hygiene, order, and control all had to go for me to survive. I didn't like that.

I had my old flip phone and my Apple laptop with me and nothing to do until I was strong enough for surgery. No visitors were allowed in the hospital, which suited me. Susan would be my conduit. We used FaceTime, so she was with me daily.

I found myself remembering being a child
far below my mother's hospital window.
Back then, children weren't allowed to visit.
I've always been a reluctant visitor
and this the first time admitted as a patient.
I had come as far as I could on my own.

I talked of love on the phone with Ryan, and with his mom, Lorie. Her words stayed with me: "I'm not ready for you to not be here."

Was I ready to not be here? I didn't know.

I was hooked up to two drips and had various monitoring wires, so typing wasn't easy, but what else was there to do? I used my laptop to write letters, make amends, say everything that needed to be said.

I spoke to a friend from childhood, Ira. Our moms died when we were young, and, in many ways, we helped shape each other through our countless adventures.

My cousin Gary, twelve years older but born on the same day, called. We always remember each other's birthday but seldom speak. We grew up in the same neighborhood. Our mothers were the oldest and closest to each other of four sisters and two brothers, and he, or his sister Barbara, were sometimes stuck with taking care of me and my sister. I think there's really nothing for us to clean up from the past, just connecting at a critical time, reminding me of bonds I didn't know how to take care of.

But later, my talk with Gary triggered a powerful memory: I was 15 when I witnessed my grandparents, howling and wailing, having to be half-carried, half-dragged away from my mother's closed casket. Shouldn't I have been screaming and tearing at hair and clothes with them? But I was paralyzed by their hysterical release and grief. It was like nothing I had ever seen, nor felt. My quiet tears fell without words and more when I was alone. Was there something wrong with me?

I had always been a stiff recipient of slobbering kisses and constrictor squeezes. I can still feel the scratching from my grandfather's stubble mixed with a whiff of beer. Only now do I try to imagine how this Bear Hug of a man might have suffered in the solitude of his last years.

And I remember a night after the funeral when my father, with me and my sister in tow, stopped at Gary and Barbara's parents' house for some spontaneous reason.

Inside, my mother's entire family were gathered for a meal. We had not been invited. That was the sting that had initially separated me from them. It wasn't, as my first inclination suggested, that I didn't know how to preserve childhood bonds.

Over and over, I'd emerge from some resting place in my hospital bed with new honesty and clarity to write another email.

What else can I do?
Besides see the cloudy sky
And smile at nurses

On a gurney, pushed down the near-empty corridors of TMC for yet another test by a young woman named Annabelle, I learned she was new to her job. And she liked it. I had to be near death to come to a hospital during a pandemic, and she had rushed in eagerly. Thank goodness, we are all so different!

With no visitors stressing and roaming around, there was less activity than ever. I had never experienced such easy normalcy and good cheer in a hospital. Between news coverage and my own morbid imagination, I thought I'd be rolling into a crowded, war zone-like scene. Instead, there were more smiles than anxiety.

And something was going on inside me. Even with masks on, I was making more eye contact, remembering people's names, getting into random and funny conversations that weren't about passing time or wanting to be liked or to get better service.

I was seeing others as fellow passengers on the same vessel, each with a unique perspective. Of course, being in a hospital with so few other patients was surreal, but I think my state of being was as much about letting go of the psychic suitcase full of stuff I had been carrying around.

By telling so many truths, I seemed to have lost my impatience with others, even those who were clearly incompetent or ill-suited for hospital work. It was as if having finally articulated all that a lifetime of interactions with others accumulated, I was more available, more capable of having non-judgmental attention on what was happening around me—even when left alone, perhaps forgotten, on a gurney in some corridor.

I felt liberated and present.

Room #801 was mine alone. It had a window that looked out into a courtyard. One tree mystified me. I've lived in the desert for decades and didn't know its name. I asked everyone who came in.

It seemed staff were drawn to whatever was going on with me. Some lingered and chatted longer than what I'd thought plausible. One tech explained to me why it should be okay with her man for her to be friends with a former lover. Her logic was irrefutable. I didn't interfere, just allowed.

Finally, RN Erin took a picture of the tree and sent it to her mother who identified it as a yellow crape myrtle. I was grateful.

I had a few rules that soon others would repeat for me:

- lights off unless needed
- shades always open
- door always closed

If only you'd try
My hospital bed yoga
So much to release

Feeling healed in significant ways, I was disappointed to hear from the surgeon that there was no chance of a ruptured tumor fixing itself. It had to be removed. My New Age Psychedelic Philosophy of Life & Death suggested otherwise, but my surgery was scheduled for the 5th of August.

The night before the surgery, I imagined checking myself out of the hospital and taking my chances back at home. It was a long restless night.

I knew the sunrise had come through the coloring of pine needles and the eager flight of carpenter bees. Watching this one grand towering pine, sensing its roots beneath my hospital bed, imagining all it has endured, I felt an urgency (perhaps learned from my father) leave me.

Acceptance came over me. Surgery it would be.

On the morning of the planned surgery, a sensitive knot bunched up in my right calf. I was wheeled over for an ultrasound. Three days in bed had resulted in a deep vein thrombosis.

We consider postponing the surgery, but the plan is to proceed with it and then begin treatment for the DVT.

Okay, I'm going to be cut open. Nothing else for me to do but go under and those trained for this to take over.

This is a day I might have missed
if not for the expert care of others.
When it comes to gratitude,
the causal chain is unending.
And yet I still carry this odd notion
of separateness

as if anything could exist apart
from the dazzling interconnectedness
of all things.
Years ago I learned the term
"Creative Source"
to transcend a childhood understanding
of the divine.
Of course, I can't begin to grasp the entirety,
but with just a little effort
I can accept my place within it.

There is a parade of specialists now involved in my care. The surgeon says it went well—he only had to remove about one-third of my stomach.

(A team of "hospitalists" stopped by often for reasons I never understood. One doctor, a urologist, impressed me by saying he wasn't needed and didn't want to charge unnecessarily, while another stuck his head in every day for a second and billed for every one of them.)

My oncologist and I get along in a profound way, often talking for considerable lengths of time on a variety of topics. He says my tumor is called a GIST (gastrointestinal stromal tumor), a rare form of cancer, little understood, slow-growing, and solitary. "Just like me," I pipe in. He laughs.

Alone, I think of my tumor as where I've stored everything I was unable to process along the way: every hurt, pain, and frustration; every disappointment and indignation; all concentrated in this one mass. In went rage and outrage and any hate I could not release or transform.

Perhaps it grew in my stomach because of some old hunger and longing born from a mother's abandonment. Whatever! It finally burst. Now it's gone. I don't think I'll need to grow another one. I have the life and the love I want. And these past days at the hospital have only confirmed that I'm better at speaking my truth, deflecting the words and behavior of others, while reining in my own reactions in an unpredictable world.

One Lee had to die
For surgery to begin
New Lee emerges!

85

Oh, but the pain of having my stomach split open! And now a catheter plus an NG tube going down through my nose to drain my stomach. I have never been so helpless, so unable to do anything on my own.

Green lollipop sponge
My connection with water
Memory of food

Very few positions are comfortable or even possible with these tubes and wires everywhere. A morphine drip along with muscle relaxers help somewhat.

One night a tall exotic African nurse shows up. Though foggy, I think I spoke Swahili to her. And then I'm back above the crater of Nyiragongo, looking down into the steaming volcano. The ascent began the previous morning and ended in rain. I tried to sleep in a smoke-filled hut with our guide, but without much success. Some bug had drained my already hurting body. I was spent. I couldn't imagine how I would ever get back down the mountain and through the jungle to civilization. I contemplated a fiery ending in the lava pool far below.

Back in the present, Nurse Nathan answered the call for help. An alarm had gone off, signaling another malfunction with a leaking IV tube. He was a most attentive and careful problem solver. I enjoyed his company. This time, however, dealing with a failed vein, he had to call an IV specialist.

Luis arrived with equipment to find a working vein. He talked nonstop with a New York accent, but his expertise was most welcome.

I learned to reset some machines and how to keep things flowing myself, but dang it, when would they stop poking me and drawing blood?!

In the morning, from my side of the window, I looked out at the old red brick and wood overhangs and thought of the havoc those carpenter bees must be doing. It's not easy for me to surrender the anticipation of problems, even those of others, not even from this hospital bed.

Lila, an elderly fireball, came around to move me and clean me up. Even as she demonstrated how helpless I was, she lectured me on how I needed to get up and start moving.

The very next day, Lila gave me a sponge, some towels, a change of gown and socks, and some medicated ointment to apply all on my own. She gave me tough-love mothering and encouragement daily, then helped me rearrange my little room so I could easily move from sitting at a desk facing the lovely courtyard back to collapsing into bed.

The energetic and helpful unit manager, Jennie, brought me pen and paper and worked out a plan to get things from Susan to me.

The smiling, laughing, caring faces of Stephanie, Amy, Erin, Audra, and Crystal popped in and out of my room. I was around more people in the hospital than at any other time during the pandemic.

RN Robert made it his personal mission to get that horrible tube out of my nose before he went on vacation. Bless him! Courtney, an aide, celebrated that moment as if we were related.

Each accomplishment of mine was met by cheers from staff. And instead of being ignored when I needed them or interrupted when I was finally able to sleep, the nurses allowed me to create my own schedule for things like those ubiquitous blood draws.

As the pain subsided, I sat and wrote with the sweet view of roses, palm, and pine trees. How nice of Medicare to pay for a spa vacation in this time of no travel—one of the few places where people actually touch each other. Some even bathe me.

The counter by the window became my stand-up desk where I witnessed the current visitation policy in practice. Folks were taken to a window where they would press their faces to the glass to catch a glimpse of a loved one inside while using their phones to speak.

I saw Susan on my laptop screen, which seemed just right for me, but perhaps we were supposed to suffer more for each other.

As I watched family members approach windows, I thought of how we look for things in others that cannot be found there.

Yet all around, the ceaseless beauty,
the wonder of creation, patiently continues.

I never opened the book Susan packed for me to read, seldom turned on the TV (except to watch some of the PGA Championship). The moment—with those around me in it—was enough.

When called for, I utilized some of my old skillsets to take charge of my care, including confronting the surgeon about his people skills. I had some anger as fuel, but never actually got emotional, just assertive and clear.

Perhaps that was what made me popular with other doctors and staff. I really don't know, but when my room started to become a hangout for those on break, the surgeon had a sign posted on the door saying no admittance without his authorization. It was mostly ignored.

However, I did thank him for the great job he did with my stomach.

While sipping my own apple juice and water mix (haven't had a meal in a week) someone from billing stopped by. I attempted to negotiate a discount on blood transfusions, since they kept coming to take it back through endless blood draws. I don't ever want to be stuck with a needle again!

A dietician arrived with a list of instructions for my reduced stomach and my surgical recovery:
- eat small meals throughout the day
- do not drink liquids with meals
- drink liquids 45 minutes before meals and wait 1 hour after meals
- avoid sugars and alcohol
- eating foods high in fiber will slow digestion
- eating food with more fat will slow digestion
- do not eat very hot or cold foods
- chew foods well and eat slowly
- rest after eating to decrease movement of food through digestive system

So, slow it will be. The same lesson I must learn over and over, in loving as well as in a golf swing. I get it. Now please, just give me something to eat!

Anyone who came into my room asked, "Any gas?"
I said, "Pull my finger."
I'm told I can't be discharged until I have a bowel movement.
Lila tells me to get out of bed and walk up and down the corridors. I do.

After gratitude
Surrender into service
As if a garden

The big moment finally comes. I proudly show off my creation. How things have changed. And so, 10 days after being admitted, I'm freed of all devices, allowed to take a real shower, and get ready to be discharged.

When Susan arrives to get me, I'm in a wheelchair, bearded, skinny, and weak, but our reunion is so joyful.

I know I won't remember everyone who helped save my life and kept me going, but I left with faith in how the good in people truly outweighs the bad, and with the realization that those who want to help others are seldom the ones who want to be in charge of them.

Once home, I will surely lose the near-death clarity I've had and will again be challenged by daily living. However, now there is an 8-inch scar that starts at my belly button. All I will need to do is rub it, like a magic lamp or a C-section, and I suspect I will remember enough.

Being home, the first question was could I get up and down the stairs or would we have to convert a couch into a bed. I could manage it, and most things, by moving slow and sure.

A friend asks about the new Lee. I tell him I had reached my expiration date and now whatever is left is bonus time. However, this emerging life form seems to look, move, and speak like an old man. He has access to my former records and history but from a greater distance. What has been lost? What has changed?

Obviously, I must be more careful in this body, move it and exercise it as if practicing ceremonies to hold back the darkness.

Dozing off is no longer a choice; it just happens. My love of food and drink will be expressed more sparingly.

I suppose the bar stool personality, appropriated from my father, will be retired. Like him, I could swell up on attention, reducing the available oxygen for others. Susan would seldom assert herself into such loudmouth banter. As a result, people might mistake her quiet, miss her penetrating insight, her quick wit, her breadth of experience, knowledge, and talent.

We've often kidded about becoming more like each other as we age. Now, with my shrunken stomach at least our eating patterns are becoming similar, but let's face it, I'll never match her discipline, her accomplishments, and her capabilities.

During these past weeks, she has become our voice, and I am more than okay with that. I only hope she doesn't take over my bar stool!

Read "very low risk"
From my medical report
No treatment needed!

Even as we celebrated this news, we learned that the matriarch of Damian Community, Robbie, had died. I'm glad I was able to say goodbye in July before she left for California with her son.

In the hospital, when experiencing how I was lightening and becoming more present with sharing what was previously unspoken, I thought about how her husband, Jim, had died.

At home in his own bed, he'd invited everyone in the community, one by one, to be with him. He'd imparted some insight or truth, a customized blessing for each of us. In his last days, he became a wild-haired, blazing-eyed prophet, and I was amazed.

When my own father was dying, I took the night shift at the hospital to be with him, perhaps be there when his own life's distilled meaning might be imparted. It didn't happen.

But Jim had shown me the way I wanted to go. I realized I had done an electronic version of his deathbed farewells, but without dying. I wonder where this path leads.

And now, I imagine Robbie campaigning from the next level. Is that her scratchy, urgent voice telling me to get out of bed?

"Wake up! Wake up where you are. There is a dream unfolding. And every act is a vote."

Okay, Robbie. I can't do much with this body, but I can add my voice to others.

Shuffling around the block at sunrise, followed by backyard chair yoga—it's good to still be in a body.

Yesterday, I heard from someone dear, learned her partner of 43 years has only weeks to live—his path from learning his fate to entering hospice mere days. He is aware of the blessing, grateful for the life lived. Her preparation the more difficult.

My days have never been this empty, my concentration this meager. My heart shows me the way. It is with them. And many others. Does it matter how they vote?

And what shall we do to save our civilization? We can't expect others to do what we ourselves will not. I won't pretend to know more than I do, but I have some suggestions:

- Reach out across your own aisle.
- Be of the party that leads in this dance.
- Reach out to someone in your sphere who does not agree with you.
- Find what you share in common and nurture it.
- It's not our minds that must change as much as it is our behavior.
- Every hand joined in cooperation is one less armed in tribalism.

Thinking about Robbie, how I thought for sure she'd make it to 100, I happen to watch a PBS program about a woman from Thatcher, AZ who had 127 living descendants before she died. She had long ago given up remembering their names. Blood, however, doesn't forget.

Back when Lincoln was president, a sentry fell asleep on duty. The punishment was death. The mother pleaded to the president who deliberated on whether one could better serve the country dead than living. In this case, Lincoln figured being executed wouldn't teach the young man much, so he granted clemency. A bloodline, blessed, continued.

I remember when Reagan was shot, how nearly fatal it was. I later learned Mother Teresa visited him afterwards, whispered to him how his suffering would make him great. Well, he certainly became more cautious. We all did, but never like now.

Insects use prolific reproduction, adapting and mutating rapidly, as a survival strategy. We need a different way. Yet there are answers in our blood. As one who recently lost most of his, had days of transfusions—precious gifts from others—I wonder at the secrets and stories now flowing through me.

These random thoughts might not even be my own. Is that the kind of surrender asked of us, perhaps the truth we can learn from insects: "Not my will, but ours, be done."

Do you remember how it once felt to be part of something greater than yourself?
What if this were the moment you've been waiting for all your life?
A time to don your hard hat, soften your heart, and lend a hand.
You might have a neighbor who is hungry; a friend who needs help; a community, steeped in collective wisdom, itching to get going on reimagining how we might do it better ... this time.
Can you put aside your own dreams of a self for something shared?
No one knows what rough waters must be navigated, what storms are coming, but I like our chances more together than apart.

As if the pandemic, various lockdowns, and travel bans weren't enough, it's a hundred and hell degrees in Tucson!

Only a week ago, I was still trapped in a hospital bed, wired, tubed, and dripped into submission, but now I feel almost as confined by the heat.

Before my surgery, I thought of this challenging time as being in a quarantine incubator rather than a pressure cooker, hoping to hatch something new rather than just explode.

Well, if there were a shell around me, it has cracked. I am cracked. Cut open, excised, sewn, and stapled. Even food won't lie to me now. Or I to food. There are no disguises left. Just this small pocket of breathable air I share with two cats and one dear woman who cares more for me than I ever dared hope for—on a planet headed who knows where?

Yet we speed and spin unperturbed through the radiation and frozen terror of airless space with nothing but a precious thin atmosphere to keep us safe. It's as if we somehow know that everything will be okay.

The surgeon cautioned another month before resuming normal activity. "A month?!" I'm already skin and bones. Must I lose everything before I can begin again?

I weigh as little now as when I was a tall, skinny kid embarrassed by any attention on his bony knees and stick legs.

There was a time I avoided trips to the beach and wore long pants in summer while privately exercising, drinking protein shakes, and weighing myself expectantly.

There isn't a scale in our home today. I only know what the doctor, my wife, and the mirror tell me. However, there are some old pants I'm anxious to try on again. I might even measure my waist—for entertainment. And there are some outfits of Susan's I've had my eye on for a while.

You know, this could be the start of a whole new phase of our life together!

It's been a month since I last drove my truck, three weeks since they cut me open to remove the bleeding alien from my stomach. I wonder now what will come first: my recovery or the economy's?

In my weakness, I feel aligned with what is ... willing to take the next small step.

Four of us—two human, two feline—share this space. We spend a lot of time together these days, more than ever before. It's been okay.

Sometimes, each on our own chair, we all sit around the kitchen table. If playing cards, we partner fairly, mixing species. It's quite the little family.

For solitude, I retreat to a den. One cat crawls behind the stereo near the fireplace. The other has figured out how to get into a drawer from behind an armoire. Susan will move from the kitchen table to her office (now the home of her crossword puzzles), but mainly she shuts us out with earbuds.

In other words, we can be together or alone according to the desires of each. I wonder, though, how will we ever leave the cats for weeks at a time again?

For so many reasons, I can't picture us going anywhere anytime soon.

There are fires across the West: 650 fires in California alone. 10 million acres and 10 thousand structures have burned.

On the Line

Drained, even of thought, sitting, empty
in waiting perhaps
midst stories of horror unfolding around us.
So many lining up behind one team or the other
discarding truth for a toxic loyalty

Where can we meet to face real problems side by side?

A 2,000-year-old redwood burns and surrenders to this onslaught,
awakening the Messiah, who takes a peek, turns and punches
the snooze button, again

We are left to figure out what every firefighter already knows:
first, help those who need assistance to safety
then, take your place where it matters most

do what you can
watch each other's back
trust in what can be done together
and pray for better weather.

September

Sunrise, like a broken egg yolk, spread yellow across the sky.
Agitated by a distant siren, the color coagulated in clouds
and dripped slowly down to roof and treetops.
The desert burners, not yet on, don't fry the color from the sky.
Just a hint of wind to stir this morning.
Sunrise egg in a shake, uncooked, on a plate.
Another day has arrived, like a short order chef at an understaffed health spa.
"What are you having today?"
"Silence please ... perhaps a side of laughter if you've got any."

There's talk of vaccines later this year, but 200,000 of our fellow citizens are already dead from this virus.

I am still alive. 30 pounds lighter than before but recovering and more ambulatory all the time.

When in the hospital, the news did not matter to me. I had my own problems. I've been resisting turning on the news again, but my attention needs something other than this hobbled body to attend to—que no?

I find myself going down the rabbit hole I've long avoided: my old journals.

For about ten years, from my late twenties through most of my thirties, I journaled everything. It was an attempt at self-therapy, an integration of intent with actual experience, and a movement towards understanding consciousness through obsessive micro-introspection. I never read the pages after they were first turned. It was all about the clarity received in the recording.

This slow recovery during a pandemic amidst a Tucson summer can motivate a guy to search for peculiar indoor activities, even awaken a curiosity about the distant past. I've been delving.

And I've been learning things.

First, as someone who today recalls so few, I was astounded by the details of the dreams remembered and interpreted. The unconscious mind is always working on healing. All we have to do is pay attention. Once upon a time, I did.

What else stood out were how some of the people named, who seemed so important at the time, I could not even begin to picture today. Maybe they were actors with matching stories who—as if by some law of attraction—appeared at a significant moment to play out a certain role to bring what was unseen into the light. I suspect we then blessed and released each other and went our separate ways.

Finally, memory itself was exposed. Prior to reading these thorough accounts, I would have sworn some things happened in a particular order, and I would have been wrong! Little by little, for whatever psychological or narrative reasons, we are always editing and rearranging our history to match a more current notion of self. It's a good thing to know. Perhaps it might spare me an argument or two going forward.

Like emotions, memories are for my own information—self-flagellation or amusement—and do not represent the truth. I can live with that. But like with much of what I've uncovered during lockdown, the bulk of it will be tossed.

The job I'm giving myself this month is to salvage the journal juju worth saving and to turn it into something to share. In a sense, I'm collaborating with some younger selves.

Check-in Countdown:
> 5 - weeks ago was the last time I played golf or had a drink.
> 4 - weeks ago I woke up from surgery and began this slow recovery.
> 3 - weeks ago I came home.
> 2 - weeks ago I began walking around the neighborhood.
> 1 - week ago I resumed chipping and putting.

And this week I went back to my volunteer watering at Valley of the Moon.

Hope to get back on my bicycle next week, perhaps fall off the wagon (but not the bike!) the week after that. Small steps back toward whatever normal might be waiting out there.

(Has anybody found any normal yet?)

Appreciating yesterday's balance,
when a muddled moon dropped like a coin
into an unseen slot
signaled the sun to peek out
between its cloudy sheets.
How often wonder eludes these lazy eyes.
How seldom the radiant noted
even as the way is illuminated
every night and day.

In Memoriam: *Under Patient Siege.*

Another unfinished novel has found its way to the shredder.

It was to be the story of one soul, followed over many lifetimes, in many places.

The title refers to the interior fortress against the self-knowledge and self-realization that would bring enlightenment and end the cycle of reincarnation.

Meanwhile, the truth, infinitely patient and resourceful, constantly flowing, relentlessly pushing against those fortress walls, was the protagonist of the novel.

It also refers to all the different ways life itself can appear to lay siege to an individual. Other people can become instruments laying siege: those who court us, sue us, or just move in next door. They can be rivals, lovers, friends, enemies, partners, or competitors. They can be actively knocking at your door, or simply be somewhere in your ken. Their presence might be a threat, a nudge, a caress, or a promise.

Altogether they exert the force that pushes on the walls our psyche has built to control its construct of a self. We let some people in; we keep some others out. We change as a result of both decisions.

Even our homes, our privacy, are under siege. It is a war with moves and countermoves. All the phishing, all the scams. We now pay others to protect our identities from being stolen, our computers from being hacked, while we equip our homes with steel gates and alarms.

As a result of these habits of self-protection, we unfortunately keep out what is most essential for our growth and ultimate liberation.

Once upon a time, I thought it a tale I could tell.

Today, reading through the folders and the almost foreign handwriting of some other me, I realized this is yet another project that will never be completed.

So, in relinquishing this unfinished manuscript, I hope to reclaim the energy infused in it and to then focus it on something this Lee can actually write to completion.

I can drive again, but the stick shift and clutch in my 2009 Ford Ranger are more work than ever before.

For many years, I had either a convertible, a motorcycle, or an open-air jeep. I never wanted to be contained in a vehicle or indoors. Now, I'm indoors more than out and often drive with the windows closed.

The first almost-new vehicle I ever bought was a 1991 Nissan Pathfinder, a purchase motivated by the birth of Ryan. It was time for a safer and more reliable set of wheels.

Early on, I had some reason to be driving it on the Pinal Parkway. I remember looking out the open window, imagining a climbing route up some desert mountain, the way I used to picture doing it as a kid from the backseat on family trips.

Suddenly, I saw how driving a 4x4 Pathfinder with all the bells and whistles was no different than my father driving his Cadillacs. Funny how such a moment of realization can break in and change an experience. Just like that, I was a bit older, and my father more relatable.

I was no longer the boy, nor the young man who would climb every peak he thought a worthwhile challenge. I was in the saddle of life. I could still get to a mountaintop, but there was now much to hold me back.

I spent much of the past thirty years involved with the Damian community. It wasn't always easy, and to be honest, it was often difficult and disappointing, even ugly.

I had forgotten this message to myself, but reflecting upon it today, I can say I did indeed become both a more efficient and fair person—but not a more friendly one. And that is sad. I am just now admitting this to myself: I have a wounded heart.

The Pathfinder is long gone. I can't even consider an ascent to mountain peaks. Getting up the stairs in our two-story home is often accomplishment enough.

I have not succeeded at all that I have attempted. And there is a heaviness in my failures. But there is a higher place I visited when close to dying where some healing tears, laughter, and truth-telling brought me.

I know gravity will always beckon, and one day I will fall back into the earth, but like that much younger self looking out a car window and plotting a path to a distant peak, I can now see myself coming back down, slowly—gliding, resting, soaring—air all around—with a clear conscience—heart and mind joining spirit—everywhere!

On a journey, everything backlit with myth,
moving like a cat, changing like a cloud,
I remember dissolving into a vibrating truth
while the sunshine talked of love
and water fountains asked if I were thirsty
(it really can be that easy).
Translucent toy tugboats floated by in the park pond
refracting light in a cascade of color and flame.
One can get trapped in visions of beauty,
skate through life in armor shining like mirrors
dreaming of others.
Once, a part of me longed for what it could not have.
Unlike with anything else,
you can look for love where you are
not where you lost it.

I was raised with the mantra: "If you don't have anything nice to say ..."
So, that's it, I'm done describing these apocalyptic morning skies!

Susan, however, in sweatshirt, gardens midst whatever it is.

100

I'm in the kitchen manipulating potatoes, peppers, and onions into something edible. It's Saturday. Yes, I do like some days better than others. Hope I'm not offending the other six siblings, but that's just the way it is.

Okay, wait a second. Someone stuck a thumb in red paint, smudged the sky, trying to fool us into thinking that's our sun up there. This is freaking Arizona! What kind of toothless, cold spot in the sky is that?!

Or could that be the moon dressing up as the sun? Come on, it's nowhere near Halloween. It only feels like we're in some kind of horror show.

I wonder if while we were sleeping, we all got uploaded into some end times video game …

I need that nicer thing to say right now.

"Uh, well, sure is a delightful temperature this morning."

How Suffering Shows:
the crumpled sheets of restless sleep; the time it takes to answer or return
a call; the number of dents felt and battle cries heard in your vehicle; the
pointless openings of a refrigerator door; the unexpected slamming of
another, exposing more than you can carry alone.
I know, it's not easy.
There are no magic words,
just others who care more than you remember right now,
each willing to hold one piece of this burden.
Only in weightlessness
is gravity relinquished.

I seem to be asleep more than I am awake in this recovery of mine. Any activity tires me.

My "scorched journal" search and destroy mission fits my current state of mind and body and so continues. I've been mining, extracting, and shredding as I revisit the musings, the dreams, and the written anguish from the years of wrestling matches between my desires and my frustrations.

The sad news is that the one fire lookout journal I hoped to find seems to be lost. Did I, like my father with his war diary, obliterate the records of the most raw and vulnerable experiences? I don't remember doing that.

I find myself re-reading one entry from another Forest Service notebook about a bad day that turned wonderful. It involved being in motion in nature, a sensation I sorely miss today.

"… running down a steep slope in the Huachuca Mountains, I startled a bunch of javelina. I was moving so quickly and quietly that I wound up smack in the middle of them before they could disperse. I jumped, yelled, and chased them around like a crazy man, laughing, excited to be in such a place.

Then, I stopped, sat down—beaming now smiles of peace—and sang to them. I'd like to say they came back and gathered round to listen, but instead in the stillness I heard the vibrato cacophony of frogs singing back.

I got up and moved towards them. They became silent. I sat nearby. After a while, they determined I was not a threat and resumed blowing up their throat pouches and vibrating. A small one, out of the water, sounded tinny and meek, looked at me and then scurried back to the water as if more embarrassed than scared.

A female showed up and the pitch became more frantic. Two of the males jumped, winding up on top of each other on top of her, all stacked up like a frog sandwich, the mating version of the leapfrog game. The top one eventually fell off, but the other one rode her wherever she went and was still on her when I finally left. It wasn't inspiring as a model for the passion of procreation, but certainly for its persistence."

I made a note to myself to remember to laugh, sing, and be crazy even in the face of the long, sharp teeth of unpredictable and aggressive creatures. A virus and a tumor have joined that list.

With bamboo blowing, I remember how
I used to tell students to just write.
Sit, know a poem must come,
like waiting for a piss to flow.
There's an urge, a pressure,
but no valve to switch,
just patience and pencil moving.
Be aware of the sound, the feel of lead on paper.
Sensual, sensing, connecting thought
through arm to paper.
I am what writing shapes me to be,

but when too aware of fingers,
compressed around this wooden stick,
I return to this mortal, vulnerable body
hosting mind.

Sometimes I want to be a thought, a breeze,
not having to tend to body.
Sometimes I'd prefer to be a body
relishing in flesh and movement.
Once it felt like a choice:
to be the lover or the writer.
Go to bed with a beautiful woman.
Wake up with a book written.
One act, the pleasure in the making.
The other, in the completion.
If I were to name it,
it would have to be
LoveWrite

For the longest time, I'd sit down to work on a piece of fiction, get stuck, and out would pop some silly letter instead.

Prior to having Susan in my life, most of those letters had a confused seductive reason for being. I once thought of putting together a collection of them. So, I made copies of the best of them, carried them around for years, but making them public always seemed too hazardous of a notion. The shredder is their appropriate destination.

However, in my last reading of them, I realized what they really represented: the search for my birth mother before I knew I was searching.

When I took the job as a fire lookout, there was the writer's romantic attraction to seclusion and the promise of creative productivity. But there was another story coming to the surface that I was not prepared for.

Relationships were not working out the way I wanted, and I had come to see I was the common denominator in all that went wrong. Cindy was the most perplexing. Why did I want someone who didn't want me?

On Red Mountain, I stopped. I stopped fantasizing about pursuing anyone, and I stopped writing letters. It was finally time to know myself.

Always scanning the skies and landscape below for signs of smoke, clouds became visiting entertainers to me, mimes, with or without a message. I made up stories about them.

When the monsoons arrived, following the same invisible tracks every afternoon, I'd watch how they painted swaths of desert green as if directed by an unseen muralist. Was the thin line between wet bounty and dry deprivation marked by chance or caprice?

Nothing prepared me for the intense lightning strikes that rocked the tower. Dancing purple, silver, and even green, rock-shattering bolts—sometimes as thick as crazed redwoods—seemed to threaten the existence of everything. My shivering insignificance was never more apparent.

Star-filled nights punctuated by meteors were healing. I participated without understanding in all they revealed of immensity and timelessness. They filled me with patience and granted respite from restless days.

I was never alone. White-throated swifts and rough-winged swallows buzzed, dove, raced around me with a quick joy of movement I could only dream of having. Turkey vultures suggested an easier way to be, soaring with only the slightest motions on thermals high above, waiting for any scent of death rising up.

Another oddity of dwelling up high was the unexpected attractant of the propane tank. Lady bugs were drawn to it. They would dot the sky in their migration, land on and around the tank, covering and crawling over everything like a colorful living blanket. I'd let them tattoo my arms and then laugh in the merging.

And I walked a lot, every sunrise and sunset, immersed in the habitat of the Patagonia Mountains. I learned to meditate in stillness and in motion through juggling on the helicopter pad. I let the floaters in my eyes become windows into another way of seeing.

Underneath the tower, in a windowless room where the metal cabinets for the various transmitters hummed, was also where some supplies were stored. The first time I opened the steel door, I was stunned. Tens of thousands of daddy long-legs on every surface.

The sudden light would get them vibrating and pulsating, causing a drum-like tapping from all directions. It was bizarre! The sound and sensation was unlike anything I had ever experienced. I was strangely moved by their uncanny gathering. They became the dancers, drummers, and chorus that encouraged me to look at what I had so long avoided.

And, after months of solitude from the ways of other humans, something in me finally turned around, looked into a dark place, and faced what had been pushing me all along: being abandoned by the one who birthed me.

When fire season was over, and with Judith's help, I returned to Chicago to begin the search for my true story.

I really do want to finally put the rest of that tale on paper, but today is Susan's birthday and our anniversary. People ask us why we decided to get married on her birthday. Okay, it was my idea as a guarantee I'd never forget either date. However, part of the deal was that we would celebrate the entire month and Susan would decide where we'd go and what we'd do.

It has led to many great adventures and memories.

Of course, like everything else, this September is not like previous ones. Still, just yesterday we did take our first trip up the mountain in months. We had a picnic, soaked up some sun, walked among the pines, enjoyed a cool breeze and the company of countless birds. Perhaps they were all forced into these small, unburned areas by the recent fires.

That's the image that stayed with me. Midst devastation, life seeks, finds, and gathers in safe places. And yet it wasn't a chaotic scene. My untrained eyes couldn't detect unusual stress or strain in this crowded cohabitation. Have all these birds adapted that quickly?

All around the planet, humans and animals are being displaced and will continue to be pushed from their homelands. Sharing sanctuary is possible, but for how many and for how long?

Susan reminds me of our bet. We made it 19 years ago after encountering (but not sampling) a $2,000 bottle of wine. Under exactly what circumstances would we ever pay that much for a few drinks? Well, one scenario would be because we knew the end was coming.

My bet was that civilization had about 20 years left before it started unraveling. She did not see such an end in sight. And so we made a bet for that wine or a bottle of equivalent cost. The terms were a bit hazy about exactly what constituted a winner or a loser, but today, with a year left, the virus still spreading, forests burning, enormous storms wreaking havoc, and the growing social and political divide, we are fine-tuning the terms of what unraveling or continuing mean.

A faraway friend urges a different dream, as if we collectively choose this reality. Might we? It's possible, isn't it?

We talk a bit about starting a Dream Tree, a place to share alternatives to the way we are living. There probably already is such a thing, but what would allow such a tree to yield fruit for all?

One thing I know: it's so much easier to destroy than to create (other than reproduction that is).

When I was a kid playing with matches, I burned down a patch of weeds, brush, and trees growing in a vacant lot. It was not intentional, but even the play of a small child can lead to destruction. I learned my lesson. I hope I paid back that karmic debt fighting fires with the Forest Service.

Back then, I ran to hide and denied responsibility. As an adult, I went in the other direction, joining others cutting line without the need to point fingers or assign blame.

But how are we all responsible for the fires today? There's so much to look at: our food and energy consumption; who and what we support; how we use or save resources; and, of course, our dreams for ourselves and our offspring.

Somehow, the "pursuit of happiness" transformed into doing as we please with minimum inconvenience. Here's the math problem with that: multiply everything each one of us does, needs, or wants by 7.8 billion.

I think I'm winning the bet with Susan, but now that what I feared seems to be happening, I don't want to be right.

This thought in search of words,
these words looking for something to say.
Still, we trod on
without her

now without him
yet getting nowhere
wearing patterns in smallness.
September
was once a month of celebration
for us.
We could light candles,
send cards ahead,
feed these bodies carefully,
even cheerfully, at home
as if the very mechanism of self
were being retooled
for a future, lurking
around the next blind corner
and we were hungry
for a change.

Watching PBS or dreaming are my current preferred ways to travel these days. However, this week I got back on a bicycle and am enjoying moving faster than my cautious shuffle step. Just a wee breeze and air rushing through my hair brought back a memory of gliding once down the backstreets of the French Quarter.

I had been driving for hours and needed to move my body, surprised by a strange vitality. Each step felt light and springy as if on the verge of flight. With every stride, I'd be airborne longer, covering more distance, landing softer, and then bounding back up higher.

My spirits rose as well, accompanied by ebullient laughter and effervescent energy. There were other people on the streets, but no one knew me, no one expected me. It was this place between places, between relationships, between forms. It was an experiential taste of a transcendent freedom.

Of course, it didn't last long, but it was simultaneously the most present, the most detached, and the most in love with life I had ever been.

At first, I thought it odd to be thinking of that today, but being so recently in a hospital, and near death, was also a place between places. There, in surrendering and accepting my fate, I felt an even deeper liberation. And now, in these first days of almost actually speeding about, under the power of my own locomotion, well, there is indeed an equivalent epiphany. I don't have to be as fast as anyone else, not even myself; I can just relish mobility itself. That's enough for me.

It's always been there:
the warning whisper
the urge for a different direction
the unspoken call from a connection.

More often, from this less crowded way of living,
an imagined face slips in without distraction,
then the real time communication soon follows.

Prior to a lightning strike, invisible tendrils connect
marking the path the bolt will follow.
The unseen and the seen are always dancing,
co-creating.

Sometimes I wonder
how I embrace or miss opportunities,
how I'm utilizing or avoiding the moment.
On a morning like this,
when the words I'm searching for
are being spoken by a friend far away
and
when I can receive, rejoice, and respond
in an instant ...

I know we are becoming prepared for what is needed,
remind myself to be gentle even with the reluctant self
that wants to remain hidden
and safe from the storm.

October

Daily Exercise

Every day I make a note of at least one thing I do not understand, and another of what I could not hope to accomplish by myself.

Of course, I must limit this exercise so as not to tax the awareness of the extent of my ignorance and helplessness.

Just a slow reality drip is required to keep ego grounded, to water down any tendency towards the wayward boast or offhand judgment of another's plight.

It's the reverse resumé-making of an elder. Rather than rocking and reminiscing in re-fabricated glory, it reminds me to be restrained around the unfathomable, encourages me to sink deeper into the shared genetic pool from which we all arise.

It's not a self-improvement plan—I tire too easily for that—but a prescription I wrote myself for getting through another day without forgetting how those I'll never see or know make my life possible.

70,000 new cases around the country in a 24-hour period. Even the president has tested positive. No one is safe anywhere.

Recently, I returned to playing golf. 9 holes is all I can manage, but I'm walking and carrying a small bag with 5-6 clubs. I had tried to use my push cart and full bag, but it was too difficult to get up the hills with it. Part of the struggle with my recovery is in my head: accepting and adapting to a diminished body.

It would be easy to give up golf now, but where else would I exercise like this while feeling safe from the virus? Instead, I respond to an infomercial and buy an easy-to-hit GX-7 driver with a senior shaft. Technology to the rescue?

I can't help but compare the distance lost with each club I hit. And I think of what my body used to love to do.

More than on a golf course, it was in the mountains I felt truly alive, hiking for most of a day, making mountain goat ascents to dramatic views, followed by rapid, rock-dancing descents.

Maps were made only after a discovery, reluctantly, for sharing a location with a trusted comrade. And trails were seldom used, so finding one's vehicle before darkness was the welcome signal to relax some vigilance, start the fire, break out whatever was left behind in the cooler, and recount the day's adventure.

Those starry nights of myth on cold, hard ground uttered secrets and spells this body can no longer understand, nor endure.

But I can still gaze into embers, feel the warmth and wonder of the once-blazing fire of youth while whittling and worrying words from the comfort of home.

No, it is not the same, but perhaps the plight of an explorer is to become a map maker in the end. A map maker, and perhaps an old man with a small golf bag walking 9 holes in early morning light.

Another presidential debate I could not digest. Candidates talking over each other and ignoring the actual questions asked provided no model for the competent leadership these times require. Who I like or dislike more doesn't matter. A country and a system that produced these two old white men as the best choices to lead it is in trouble.

Then, I'm awake in the night listening safely to the yipping and howling of coyotes perhaps closing in on a kill.

Many years ago, I received a call from Chicago about my father being taken to the hospital with a possible heart attack. Unable to get a flight until the next day, too restless to be in town, I went out into the desert for the night.

I found a good spot in a sandy wash, put down my sleeping bag and began stargazing while thinking about and praying for my father. However, it soon became obvious that I was sharing this piece of real estate with a pack of coyotes.

For some reason, I didn't want to be chased away, insisted to myself to stay the night, as if it somehow mattered. Still, I held a knife in one hand and wrapped my belt around the other, so I could swing the buckle as a weapon.

Every so often, the coyotes would run into the clearing where I was, and I would spring to my feet, ready to fight to the death. Then my mind would return to images of my father in the hospital while also waiting for the coyotes to attack. It was a long, difficult night. I didn't sleep much as sounds of their various chases and periodic howls punctuated my silent vigil. And yet nothing happened, externally.

When the sun finally rose, I knew everything would be okay with my dad. And it indeed turned out to be a false alarm. His heart was okay, and he would live for quite a few years more.

Do I think my intense vigil had anything to do with his diagnosis? Of course not. But in facing my own fear of dying and mustering a willingness for life-and-death battle, I gained the strength and clarity to return to Chicago, not the next day as originally thought, but soon after.

I was able then to work with him in the family business. We got to know each other as men, not just as a father and son. And I committed to therapy, personal growth workshops, 12-step groups, and a supportive spiritual community. The life I know and love today began then.

So, what's my point? I think today we are at a crossroads as a people. There's much work to be done, but we're stuck in the place of finger-pointing, denial, and blame. And there are many who are ready, maybe even eager for combat and violence.

What my story reminds me is being ready for anything is a powerful place to be, and that a path that brings us to confront what we fear is also the way to what we love.

Soul Search
Came up against my own fierce inertia the other day.
To what is not important.
It could have been to anything threatening the fragile illusion that all is well.
Sometimes, I have a hair trigger, yet sluggish bullets that can't even penetrate

my own resistance.

In my make-believe fortress, the needs and tasks of maintaining life and home are relentlessly mounting.

Look, we have all learned to do without much of what once pulled us through such tedious muck: the delectable night out on a gyrating town; the joyful ruckus of friends gathering;

everything that happens with music, dance, art, and theater; and the sweet retreat of a targeted getaway.

If we're lucky, the slow horror of dreams unraveling might still seem distant ...

I want to stop this writing now! Walk away from whatever words will follow next.

But what if the path I'm searching for is just beyond the dark I avoid?
And the light only obscured by the shadows
of what must finally be embraced?

Black Lives Matter protests and arrests continue. Another mass shooting. 83,010 new cases of the virus in the last 24 hours. Mask mandates are being debated again.

Dear Mona, Oh Mona, Mona,

I have done the unthinkable. I have let someone else's fingers, scissors, and comb run through my hair. Can you forgive me?

The circumstances were beyond my control. It happened in Florida. There was this party, and I was drinking, and there was this girl, and I was smoking. We were having a good time. You know how those things go. One thing leads to another, and before I knew it, she was cutting my hair.

I felt cheap and dirty in the morning. And then I thought of you and felt guilty for my unfaithfulness. I can only hope you will take me back.

I'm doing my best to make it grow back, and though I won't be able to face you with a clear conscience, at least I'll have a full head of hair.

Tender or not, there is a "bar" in barber, and I'm thinking it must be time to go for a haircut. Of course, Susan has been doing a fine job cutting my hair, even Phil S. Ponce, my barber, said so when I finally saw him.

Susan has fewer customers than he does, is easier to get an appointment with, and I really do enjoy sitting in our backyard while she fusses over me, but still, it was time to take a chance. I wanted to hear news of the outside world, and Phil is one of my best and most uplifting sources. Humans must recalibrate periodically in the presence of each other or risk being usurped by their own eccentricity.

One of my first memories of having my hair cut was a painful one with Benny the Barber. It was at a barbershop on Touhy Avenue in the Rogers Park neighborhood of Chicago. He cut a section too short and then had to cut the rest of my hair to match. I was traumatized and wore a baseball cap everywhere until it grew back.

When the Sixties came, my hair grew long, and all I needed was a headband to style my hair.

By the time I considered a haircut again, spinning striped barber poles had given way to stylists and salons. It was now possible to have one's head massaged and pampered by men or women. I learned phrases like "feathered" and "layered" when describing what I wanted. And I enjoyed having women, like Mona, cut my hair.

Cindy once invited me to her home for a full hair treatment. She washed and conditioned my hair inside the house, and then we went outside for the cutting. The warmth of the sunlight, her touch, and careful attention were hypnotic, erotic, and dreamy. No words were spoken. We got along well that way.

Walking over to the Racquet Club to see Phil this morning, I remembered when he was the first man to cut my hair since Benny the Butcher. And how an 82-year-old nurse, whose hair Phil had just finished cutting, stood next to me for a while, as if she knew the significance of the moment. She even took a comb to my hair for some reason.

Guys who worked around there would saunter in, grab something from the fridge, and sit in the empty barber chair. I had entered the Twilight Zone. And I liked it. I didn't close my eyes.

I participated in the conversations, but I never looked in the mirror until he was done. I had surrendered into something different, something about men and trust, while letting go of something else, about women, and what I once wanted from them.

And I got a great haircut.

Back in the chair this morning, we started slowly with election politics and picked up energy at local gossip. But even constricted by mask strings, my ears really perked up around the peculiar economic news.

I had already been wondering about all the housing market activity. I figured that people were relocating in response to working from home, wanting some distance from crowded cities, and, now that they had spent significant time at home with partners and family, were reversing the downsizing trend.

Still, how could so many afford it? Stranger yet was this: Auto sales have come roaring back, almost doubling since a low in April. Over 15 million in August. Almost 16 million in September. What is going on?!

Sure, the stock market has acted as if there's no pandemic pulling the economy down, but that's the playground of the rich, right? They make their own rules. However, all these big-ticket item purchases suggest something unreported unfolding. Without frequent access to barbers or bartenders, I was clueless and thus surprised.

The country itself has massive debt. Millions are struggling to pay their bills, feed their families, keep a roof over their heads. But instead of tightening their belts, so many were apparently letting it all hang out!

Life as we once knew it is reorganizing around yet-unnamed principles. Perhaps the explanation is as simple as this: Without travel, dining out, and entertainment expenses, people used to paying high monthly credit card bills are now reallocating resources.

I can only hope that our long-held tradition of giving to those in need is continuing, especially this year. I'll probably schedule a December haircut so I can keep up with any good tidings.

Perhaps some good tithings are in order as well.

I still have the need to scratch a thing
or two off the lists
I no longer keep
but
a day holds secrets
I feebly try to uncover.

There is an urge to discover
what is called for today
and a tug of war
from the refuge of old patterns
but
I find no answers in old stories —
no shelter, nor comfort in ways past.

Even as we long for each other
there is little to say
but
we can't go back
and the path ahead
is not yet formed.

I would hold your hand
assure you of what I can't possibly know
but
even that is spared
as we wait
alone
together.

A vaccine is announced for possibly as early as next month! An epic election is underway. I'm no prophet, but I can sing "Anticipation" along with Carly Simon and anyone else who wants to join in.

I wonder how we all are doing with this "keeping me waiting" thing.

I catch myself imagining scenarios (both jubilant and horrific), wanting "this" to be over, hoping to return to once cherished ways.

One honest look in the mirror, however, or any wrong step, reminds me I am not the same. Each excursion on familiar streets reveals more casualties of closures and dreams. Nothing will be the same again.

Many months ago, when there was still something novel about speculations of how the virus might reshape us, a global reboot was suggested, one where we would emerge with new sensibilities. Instead of measuring growth externally, midst mindless consuming and waste, the forced retreat would allow us all time to reflect and repent. (Ha ha!)

It's ironic that one of humanity's most deadly and ancient diseases was long known as consumption. Renamed tuberculosis, we learned to treat it, so anything is possible, right?

Recently, David Attenborough, who at 94 actively campaigns to save the planet, was asked what we can do to help. His simple response, "Waste not!" I guess that's all any of us need to remember if we are ever to cure the consumption that is still destroying everything.

I have had many jobs in my life, but when asked what I did for a living, I often replied that I was an educator. However, I never attempted to persuade students to believe as I did. I trusted that if inspired to think critically, to understand oneself honestly, and to listen to others openly, natural curiosity and intelligence would lead them in optimal directions.

I didn't come to such a philosophy on my own. I had mentors.

When thinking of mentors, I tend to remember one teacher in particular whose presence, more than his ideas, stimulated timelessness. I'd find myself unconsciously mimicking his gestures and phrases until they became integrated with what became my own teaching style. The key to understanding always seems to be linked to another, doesn't it? Certainly, the way to apprehend and express knowledge is a thing learned from those who came before. We all exist in a continuum of other minds and others' thoughts.

I did not start out to become a teacher. I was corralled in a hallway by a department chair in need of a last-minute replacement for an instructor. As was my way back then, I said yes without much thought, and within 24 hours I was in front of my first class.

That summer, I was invited to participate in the first Southern Arizona Writing Project. It was an exciting time in education as the approach to teaching writing was undergoing a radical shift. Like disciples, we spread the good word to schools across the state. Those who knew what a disruptive presence I was as a student might appreciate how much I enjoyed coaching teachers to lighten up, be writers themselves, and engage more genuinely in the classroom.

Once, while visiting Chicago, I arranged to do a presentation at the high school I had attended. This was going to be grand! Yet upon arrival, I found myself checking the roster for just one name. She was still there. Then, vivid memories arose.

Frosted blonde hair, pale almost pearl skin, peach-colored lipstick on quivering lips. Long, false eyelashes that spoke of a female teacher imagining herself some other kind of woman, but whose flickering eyelashes, hiding darting eyes, revealed instead something fragile, something delicately hinged. I thought her nervous then, but perhaps neurotic might be more accurate.

Her body was long and angular with expressive, ivory hands and feet, always painted. Her looks, her movements, her expressions came back to me. They represented something. Her message. Her plea. Was I just hearing it now all these years later?

She always spoke from so deep inside herself. Her whole body showed the strains of the exertion. She wanted us to see. She wanted us to understand— our world, ourselves, each other.

Each class might be her last. She must eventually crack, like fine china, into pieces that would never come together again. But she didn't. She remained on the edge, torturing herself with the incredible task of bringing light to adolescent barbarians.

I never understood her drive. And I didn't see her that day. Somehow, I couldn't, knowing now that whatever it was she was afflicted with, she had given to me. She was the forgotten reason I had said yes that day in the hall.

Have I mentioned that younger me used to write letters to older me? He was a creative but undisciplined chap and had this notion that he would just scribble notes for some older version of himself as a guide for future projects. Amusing, huh?

Hey, truth is, I have used some of his ideas for posts, but mostly he was too impatient, didn't leave enough direction, presumed I would share enough of his brilliance to understand him, including what he did not spell out.

I don't resent (much) that he assumed I would have nothing better to do (or write about) than to decipher his ramblings for subject matter. He often pictured his older self as a more disciplined yet boring continuation of himself. I can't argue with him, however annoying he has become to me.

Recently, I came across a different kind of communication from a 35-year-old me. Here's the *Reader's Digest* rendition:

Dear Lee,
If I survive to be you, love is the reason.
That is the kernel of what I want to say to you.
I hope you are pursuing what gives you joy in your work, in your community,
in your home, and loving it all intensely.
That's all there really is. Don't get freaked out about money. It will always come
and it will always go. It's just a by-product, a means to an end, without
any sustenance
of its own.
So, be well Lee. Take care of yourself, your health, your body.
Pray. Eat well. Sleep well. Wake up early. Laugh. Love.
Let go regularly.
Be creative, enthusiastic, and productive.
I love you. That's why you are today.
Love, Yourself

You know, that arrogant little snit is kind of growing on me.

94,000 new cases around the country within the last 24 hours. I've become more neurotic and paranoid than before about getting this coronavirus. I can't bear the thought of going back to the hospital, and I still feel so fragile. I keep hand wipes everywhere and am uncomfortable being close to other people.

Spending so much time at home has given me ample opportunity to study at the paws of the house masters—our indoor cats.

Everyone knows that cats stay flexible and agile with minimal stretching and frequent naps. Although most of their unique skills are unfortunately out of reach, there is an applicable behavior of theirs to which I currently aspire and could actually possibly obtain.

Simply, it is this: they both have places to retreat when they want to be left alone. And they both are vocal and persistent when they want closeness and touch. It's as easy and as natural as that. Wow!

They display the rhythms of intimacy and solitude without any hesitation or explanation. And in their cat-clarity, they give us permission to be more tidal in our own ebbs and flows, learning to live together as mostly indoor humans in this brave new world.

Raised by dogs
More recently, adopted by cats
I understand the need for others
as well as the desire to be alone.
My dog self wonders when will we play again with friends,
sniffs and reaches out to make contact,
whines and wags anxiously at the door.
The cat in me has hid the phone,
is ruffled by anything that interferes with the simple rhythms
of eating, stretching, scratching, and sleeping.
Truth be told, I no longer bark, seldom howl,
and there's really nothing I want
to throw, fetch, or catch.
So, perhaps it's okay to age like a purring cat
being stroked on a sunlit lap
during these very long, long days.

It's early enough when even the cats aren't interested in what I'm doing awake. Hot taste of coffee bridges the dreamworld to this one. I pick up a pencil, wait for instructions.

None come. I doodle. Hear "do little" in that word. Okay, I'll try. (My first smile in this still dark day.)

In the quiet, I can sometimes feel the urges of where to connect, who to support. I write letters. I'm never as alone as I suppose. Only my own petulant pouting can keep me separate.

If love is what we need, why aren't we more loving?

With that very thought, a cat shows up in search of a lap! With the first stroke of soft fur, comes a purr. The steady vibrating sound requires tending. Did you know that cats that roar can't purr?

Who is being more soothed in this exchange of touch and sound? I'm reminded of the Breema method of massage, where the distinction between giving and receiving disappears.

So, even as consciousness argues bitterly with itself about what kind of existence we shall try next, I just need to remember this: keep giving to others what I, too, desire.

Days away from the election event horizon, out shopping, experiencing some street stress, I found myself thinking of sanctuary and places of refuge.

In a parking lot, near River and Craycroft Roads, I saw a stout bag lady. It was a cold morning, but she was in short sleeves seemingly unaffected by the weather. Talking cheerfully to herself, she arranged her various bags, balancing the weight perhaps before she trekked off to elsewhere.

Where did she spend the long, bone-chilling night? And how could she now appear to be so light?

In the store, I resolved to approach her on the way back to my truck, but she was gone.

Being close to the Rillito, I wondered about a nearby hideout I once knew. Might she have found her way there? I didn't investigate but remembered instead my last trip to the spot, went back home and dug this up:

Return

There is this place, green lit by sunlight filtered through dusty salt cedar branches where I used to go to be alone with my thoughts.

When I returned after being away a long time, there was the debris of a clubhouse, old wood, torn sheet metal, and a fallen tire with thick rope tied around it.

I expected to feel good in this magical hideaway, but there was a sense that the place had been overrun by something that was no longer light nor playful.

I sat and tried to recapture the warm and safe feelings I once had there, but all I could picture in my mind were savage youth playing dark games.

I felt sad and empty as if the dream of a happy childhood had somehow been punctured and I was left with only the insults suffered and the wishes made by the small child peeking out from somewhere lost inside.

As someone with a home for his groceries, I wrote those words. But having the luxury to reflect upon what went right or wrong in a life does not markedly improve my, or anyone else's, existence, does it?

Yet old wounds and past mistakes keep colliding, obstructing our way forward. Tell me this: On what path does a family member allow one of their own no shelter? And then, what kind of community permits this to continue?

I am indeed perplexed. What must finally be surrendered, or embraced, for us to offer each other a steady hand?

Tsunami

No need for polls or pundits to explain.
Opinions washed away as voice after voice join a rising wave
lifting and cleansing a nation with clarity.

Millions have already cast their votes.
Tens of millions more tomorrow.
A hundred, no, two hundred million more
are lining up to be heard.

Nothing can hold back these waters.
No matter which vessel boarded,
whatever allegiance sworn,
a transcendent event is upon us.

Everything will be revealed.
Whatever becomes known soon belongs to all:
from starting a fire to rolling the first wheel;
from electricity transforming the way we lived
to how CPUs are shaping it now.

Long ago, the printing press allowed knowledge to be retained,
shared widely, thus taking power away from the few.
Today, satellites circling the globe connect us,
and everything known, instantaneously.
My brother sneezes in Sweden.
I bless him from Tucson.

With every question immediately answered,
what is missing?
What is keeping us from stepping
into the full maturity of our species?

It's not the responsibility of those in power to let go.
It is the time of the many to be heard.
It's not the election itself that will matter most,
but the historic numbers reclaiming, reforming,
demanding democracy; ushering in the Age of Equality.

We won't ever all agree. That is not the point.
But we can all be counted,
take what is ours to wield,
and then, we the people can decide together
what our collective future will be.

November

The sun seemed late to rise,
or was it just me?
Why this reluctance to join
a welcome change of season?

Along with the fading heat
go the faces unseen this summer past.

Friends and family touch virtually.
We follow each other's stories.
But all those with whom we would share the unexpected
laughter and insights of summer travel
like the hosts and guests
together at the long morning table
of a bed and breakfast
bonding over coffee, tea, and telling tales.

Or at the beer gardens, on the ferry rides,
and through all that shopping,
always kibitzing, swapping tidbits of ourselves,
both taking in and spreading the spirit of summer,
its celebration of movement and interaction.

Anything can be contagious.
I miss what we are not giving each other,
what we can't know from
these small kitchen tables.

Are you struggling there?
Can you somehow feel
we still care?

2 30,000 dead from COVID-19 in the United States and over 9 million known cases. Texas and California have each passed 1 million cases.

I was getting ready to begin 2nd grade when Barack Obama was born. He was the first president younger than me. Today, I'm on Medicare, feeling even older than I look, and resenting these old white guys running for and becoming president in their seventies. WTF?! They are ruining aging comfortably for the rest of us!

I've watched them both for years jetting around the country, campaigning, debating, making appearances, being interviewed, giving speeches, and just have to ask, "Don't you nap?"

I fall asleep doing things I enjoy, forget where I'm going and why, and try to avoid driving as much as possible, so really, you feel okay running the country?

Remember when we wondered if Ronald Reagan was too old to be president? Ha! He wasn't yet 70 at his first inauguration. Quit pushing that bar! Get a rocking chair already! Geez! Never thought I'd feel like an underachiever in retirement. Thanks a lot.

Imagine a presidential election where both candidates say they have won!

Not knowing:
an anxious surrender into patience,
wanting to understand
how so many watching the same story unfold
can view it so differently.
What does it mean going forward?
Can we solve real problems without agreement?

Will we still obey the same laws?
Does a red light mean stop anymore?
Or, like a cape to a bull, signal an urge to charge
towards extinction?

There are fewer false claims, less fear and hate, arriving in our mailbox. Political signs are disappearing from along the streets. No one calls for my vote anymore. I almost watched a Ford commercial just because it began with, "Something we can all agree on … ."

In the cessation of ugly attacks, my ears ringing as if surviving aerial bombardment, I wander aimlessly through our quiet neighborhood, grateful for the reprieve.

Some are jubilant, or at least relieved; others are angry or despondent. I praise the mostly peaceful process that got us here.

And I'm dazed by what it would mean to my fragile sense of self to have over 70 million both for and against me. This is not sports where winning or losing is all, but governance where the will of the people should be heard and served.

We stand upon common ground that must be shaped by understanding, compromise, and agreement lest it erupt into a battleground where we and so very much can fall.

Solace

Something unusual, almost tropical, in the early morning air.
In the stillness, I imagined an alarm.
But sunrise, colored long and bright,
kneaded away my anxiety:
"Breathe into this moment, Lee."
A mosquito (of all things!) disturbed my oncoming serenity.

I think I shall move only half as fast today,
perhaps to somewhere beyond the clamor in the news;

maybe even set aside concerns
for what may or may not be occurring elsewhere.

Seek out instead the solace of gratitude,
within the miracle we somehow find ourselves in,
with whatever awareness given—
ignored or cultivated.

It's actually getting worse. I'm finding wearing clothes to be a hassle. Don't get me wrong. This is not a nudist's cry for help. There is much best left unseen under these various layers. It's just that dressing as if for an Arctic expedition in the morning, then peeling and recombining with every warming hour seems to take more of my attention and energy these days.

Even a trip to the bathroom requires gymnastic and logistical skills I am obviously losing. And I can no longer pop out of bed comfortably barefoot onto a cold tile floor. I have to remember to strategically leave socks or slippers somewhere close by.

I understand this is nothing to complain about. It's just weather and life. Nights and mornings are cold in the desert, but it usually warms up. No big deal. People come here to get away from the real cold. But it points to something else I'm becoming concerned about: I'm spending way too much time at home and sober.

Stumbling into and out of clothes when drinking was often amusing, even when it disrupted my honorable momentum or other intentions. Perhaps that is what is missing now: more laughing at myself?!

With that thought, I'm already starting to smile. I just might be onto something. 2020 has been the least funny year imaginable. Yet laughter can dissolve so much toxicity.

Is that it? Do I have too many undissolved solids circulating, affecting my tolerance for weather changes, nasty politics, aggressive drivers, stupid virus spreaders … ?

Yeah, I don't feel like laughing much either after beginning that list, but I did catch myself, and stopped adding to it.

It's hard to be funny, but perhaps some silly art project: how about bathroom selfies with a tangled heap of fabric and limb decorating a hard, cold floor?

In an attempt at breaking the monotony of so much repetition, I've started re-naming the days of the week. Here's the first round:

- MoanDay
- Too soonDay
- When?!Day
- SoreDay
- Why?Day
- What's next?Day
- Again?!Day

Doesn't really help though. Perhaps the months next? What about this year? Nah, no one can forget 2020, Groundhog Year.

This morning I had an ultrasound that signaled all clear for getting off blood thinners! The drug I've been on is not only expensive, it added to my feeling of being an old man who needed to be extra careful doing anything.

Not that I'm doing anything dangerous, but I was carrying bandages around just in case a small scratch turned into a big deal. I can relax about that and fully concentrate on what I've been missing:

"Do I miss her ample and fair, beguiling ways? Or her alluring mounds and slopes? Oh, the hours we spent together in both bliss and frustration!

One would challenge me to read and understand how she moved. Another demanded more strength and length. And then there were those who simply took my breath away with their sublime or majestic beauty. I loved them all, performed better with one than another.

So it goes.

Who's keeping score? Well, not to brag about it, but I used to score quite well. Could even go around several times in a day. But now, with interests and body profoundly changed, there's just one for me. And, truth be told, I seldom go all the way. I'm content to just stroll, enjoy the moment, rather than to ride right through it. But even as I slow, I can honestly say: 'I do it all fore love.'"

250,000 dead and over 12 million cases reported around the country as traveling for family Thanksgiving gatherings begin. We will stay home with cats.

With You, Home

Lost in the museum of us
there are no visitors,
dust accumulates.
On display or not
what is boxed or stacked
serves no one.

Would the weight a collector carries
while in pursuit of what's next
be unbearable if the past were truly felt?
(Do people even go to each other's
homes anymore?)
But you are here with me
with all we hold,
honor or obey.

In the realness of you
richer than any fantasy
I sometimes stumble,
have trouble making a plan.
How to know what some
mangy future might demand?

We've spoken many truths
(perhaps withheld a few)
while practicing the alchemy
of turning feelings into this life
we are living, not the one first imagined.

It may still be the once-targeted
exotic existence will be visited
and we will leave this almost holy retreat
that has kept us safe,
has kept us more together
than even the dreams of those lighter
than life fantasies of what love could be.

A black cat on each side of me like bookends. Might I be the last unread book in the house? Often, I do write to discover the unrealized, to make connections between fading experiences, unformed thoughts, and what is emerging around me. There seems to be no end to it.

A friend recently remarked that my social media posts are like reading a book while it's being written and that I myself have become like a literary character on the screen. I suppose we are all our own narrators. It's rare that someone else will do it for us unless we are—or part of something—extraordinary.

No matter. Examined and crafted or not, discarded or shared, the slim volume of a self can never be fully grasped, nor emptied.

There's something oddly comforting and astonishing about that, even if it can also be so exhausting … for the teller of the tales as well as for those in earshot.

The cats, however, only blink, purr, and go back to sleep. Consciousness takes many forms, never ceasing in its evolutionary experiments.

Our holiday meal:
Only the cats get turkey
The rest is for us!

December

Accepting Beauty

I leave words as cairns
marking the places from where
I sing my love songs.

Once, I would have wanted to keep
these exotic fields of fragrant flowers hidden,
fearing others would trample
what I have come to cherish.

Yet the recognition of this serene beauty
arrives only from my own long years of frustration:
attempts to reach what was never mine to have.

Another, prancing or trudging towards
their own promise of paradise,
might not even notice me
on this perfectly contoured boulder
midst nature's startling bouquet of color and comfort,
watching clouds stretch and change
as if it were the most natural thing to do.

We live somewhere between rock and cloud,
are something of each,
and yet these bones must move;
emotions, rest.

So it is that what we pursue might be opposite
of what we need, even as we inch our way
to a balance we cannot hold, only lament
or enjoy, as petals drop, seeds spread,
in service to life and death:
their persistent lover's dance and quarrel
of what just may be an endless creation.

As expected, holiday travel and family gatherings have led to another spike. In a 24-hour period, with just 30 states reporting, there are more than 200,000 new cases. Here in Pima County, cases have nearly doubled to almost 1,000 per day.

And in the last four days, over 10,000 deaths around the country.

I hear of these daily death tolls from the virus like another weather report, not comprehending all the accompanying grief set loose.

To make it more real, I urge myself to watch the "In Memoriam" section of the *PBS NewsHour* to see the faces, hear the stories, attempt to understand what's slipping away from us all in the thousands of deaths, each and every day.

When it's time to look at something, reminders can pop up like billboards or advertisements blaring out, "Pay attention!" I seem to be in such a place. The issue: relationships. Well, what else? Okay, specifically, "Communication in the Time of COVID."

I'm not intentionally ignoring or shunning anyone, but I find Zooming unsatisfying, have long disliked the phone, and socially safe gatherings increasingly feel neither safe nor quite so social.

Some restraint and distancing have taken hold, have become second nature. I know I've become more reluctant to reach out, can regret an offer soon after making one, and now instinctively pull away from any planning.

I've heard stories of others disappearing, not responding, or simply forgoing or forgetting the social niceties that previously lubricated all our complex ongoing interactions. Should I/we be concerned?

We tell ourselves and each other that it will be better once there's a vaccine, but I wonder. Does a caterpillar know what kind of creature it is destined to become? Do the dreams of wings precede the flight?

I know so little, but I study history, look for clues, absorb the news, write what's in me, and perhaps along the way imagine how I and others will emerge from these cocoons of ours.

After writing those words, I check in with a friend and real estate partner, Chris, who most bizarrely was in the hospital the week after I was for a very similar operation. In his case, there were more tumors, more of his stomach was removed, and he needed follow-up treatment.

We've been comparing our recovery progress, celebrating small steps like being able to enjoy some wine again, or getting back on a bicycle. I'm impressed and a little envious at how quickly he has returned to doing what he wants. What's wrong with me? Am I letting fear slow me down even more than this body?

I think about other role models, about elders, about what really is my path forward. I notice a weight in repetition yet an ease in routine. And I often miss my own truth until I can see it outside of myself.

For a long time, I've carried with me an image of an older man who walked nine holes twice a week with his pals at the same city course. He was gray and thin, too fragile to push a cart or even use shoulder straps. Instead, he had a small bag with a few clubs that he hugged to his chest as he walked. Okay, he was adorable, but really?!

I caught up to them several times on early summer mornings when hoping to play a quick nine before heat and work. I would join them for a few holes, chatting, trying to grasp what pleasure they still got from this activity before blasting ahead again into my own mighty reality.

Time flies.

I woke up this morning from a dream of dancing girls that had morphed into challenging golf holes I might never play again. But are they really out of reach?

In golf, one can move up a tee box or two to still be able to reach where a younger self would have landed. Along the way, one can revisit the markers of past shots, measure loss by the need for ever-longer clubs to gain the same distance. Acceptance and ego duke it out.

If ego wins, the game is over. Clubs will gather dust or be handed down to another.

If acceptance becomes the invisible partner, one might leave both cart and scorecard behind, carry half as many clubs, walk into a different yet still perfect green moment.

How far could it be from there to that embrace, from where what is precious is held close and dear without consideration or concern for how it may appear?

It seems that is who I am becoming with my small bag, a handful of clubs, and less concern about score than ever before.

What once seemed like a lifetime supply of yellow pads, partially used notebooks, and accumulated scratch paper have all been burned through this year. As with many materials not being replenished, I've become increasingly creative in utilizing what is available.

Even in our micro-bubble, Susan and I can see how the relationship between preserving an environment and sustaining an economy must be utterly re-imagined.

I'm writing now with a pencil that I carried with me (but only recently sharpened) since emptying my office at Sierra Tucson Adolescent Care in 1993. Managed Care had made the healthy model of adolescent care impossible, and the facility was closing down.

As the teacher, I was the last employee. I moved my office to home where I continued to negotiate with the home schools of patients. My final task was to coordinate their eventual return to school and to have it include any credit they earned during treatment.

My attention, lost for a moment on the tragedy of another Camelot not surviving, returns to what is in front of me now: paper. The paper has a watermark with an image of a crown and this information: Eaton's Parchment Linen -100% Cotton Fibre - Berkshire USA.

I was using this quality paper between 1975 -1985 for typing manuscript submissions on my Remington manual typewriter. The paper left from that era has made every move, survived every purge since.

These last blank sheets will not see 2021 unscathed. What was once only for sharing my finished best to the world is now where I doodle and draft, something akin to wearing a wedding tuxedo while cleaning the bathroom. But there is a satisfying and sensory pleasure in the soft scraping sound of parchment grabbing lead. And I'm learning to accept that now is the time for using everything saved, doing anything long put off.

No longer intimidated by the need to match and clothe only polished words with fine linen, I am free to savor my own process as long as it lasts, and trust that in the end there will be enough, that there has always been enough.

Earthbound
Crafting consciousness by inking words on paper is a slow process
with circles and arrows, crossed out dead ends, and always starting over ...
listening for the music of phrases that match what I could not speak, did not know,
but believe in the birthing to be true.
And then, somehow, it's done (except for the tinkering).
Another piece of the puzzle
in a mind alive and aware
spinning on a planet somewhere.

No one chore asks much anymore—until a wandering attention, partly tired of daily repetition or restless for surprise, bumbles a simple task, and, lo and behold, there's something new to do!

From these age-altered bodies, we laugh more than swear at this because, well, we've tried other responses, together or on our own, have learned each other's sound-sensitive preferences, cultivated even discord to be something more harmonious.

More often than before, the music playing in our home is instrumental. Words can distract. Still, we frequently change radio stations rather than just choosing something from our own collection. It seems necessary to keep open some channel to the outside world.

I've heard from others able to stay home how their days fill even without jobs or plans. I'm familiar with the equation: the expansion-contraction balancing of time and task. But there is also a delayed awe in just what is required of and accomplished by every working parent and householder in an ordinary life.

I have the luxury of humoring myself with a peculiar sense of order, as if socks sorted and folded in a drawer might somehow matter. But, you see, that's it really. That's the gift no one promised but was long sensed possible: the freedom to understand the mystery of self by following it around, untethered, allowing it to express what otherwise would be unknown. It takes time for this. Time with few demands.

So, I can sit home this morning, without an eye on the clock, and be grateful for what has been given, and even for what has been taken away.

Startled by some pecker's tapping on our metal chimney cap, and whatever I was thinking about is gone.

We live uneasily above veins of gold, our untapped inner wealth. Yet there is nothing here to steal, no deed proving what is ours or what has risen from other sources. With some effort perhaps, these riches could be converted into a legal tender, but why?

All I seem to mine are but by-products, reflections, of a life mostly well-lived.

Then the whine of leaf blowers interrupts.

More and more, I cringe and retreat from the cacophony of uneven needs, disparate desires colliding out there. Have I become that much more sensitive from being so isolated?

An unwanted phone ring, the near horror and shock of a doorbell, a neighbor's dog's anxious bark, and I become undone.

Is it from listening so intently for something else—attempting to gauge the slight difference in timbre between what is dross and what is of value—while panning these streams of memory and consciousness that the unexpected sound is so jarring?

I know quiet is a lot to ask for even in the relative slowdown of our pandemic-starved economy, but we've been lured into trusting. Who expected city life to become as quiet as it has? And so, at home we engage in a receptive state of mind we'd once go elsewhere to experience. Perhaps that is why we are caught off-guard now when some screech bursts into our silent bubble.

In life past, I would go, or Susan and I would deliberately go in search of silence. We'd hike to it, or even travel and pay to be somewhere to relax into it for days. We'd bring books and projects and revel in long periods of no interruptions.

I celebrate the accomplishment and the blessing of human enclaves of silence: a neighborhood library; the refuge of a retreat center; the ongoing miracle of a monastery. And I miss escaping to these places.

We're not packing our bags anytime soon, but with each honking horn or wailing siren, Susan and I whisper a wee bit louder to each other, wondering when we will ever be at such a place again.

In this home with Susan, I have a den. In it, of course, is the reclining massage chair that follows me everywhere. Next to it is the dictionary stand that Ellen had made for me when we were living together. There are very few things that have survived all my moves and purges. My friendship with Ellen is like that too.

We were high school sweethearts. My mom had died the year before we met. Ellen's big Greek family adopted me, filled a hole I didn't know how to talk about. I used to say to her that I wished we had met when we were older. I just couldn't sit still.

Of course, I would come back to her. But I graduated high school a year before she did and wanted to do some roaming alone. When it was getting close to her graduation and to making a decision about college and a future together, I disappeared without a word.

Obviously, I didn't know much about how to be in a relationship. I was better at meeting people in the moment. I fancied myself a wanderer rather than just someone who ran from the complications of intimate interactions.

Riding a freight train through the mountains of Northern California, watching the stars, I knew I had made a mistake.

She had enrolled at the University of Arizona, and I showed up one day hoping she'd have me back. She did. Altogether, we were involved with each other for over six years. I could not, however, stop meeting other women.

Ellen was patient, loving, and forgiving, but eventually moved on, created a wonderful life with someone else.

When still a teen, I spent a summer in Israel. Ellen and I wrote each other letters. I was living and working at a kibbutz. In the nearby Beit She'an Valley, a man digging to build a bomb shelter discovered a mosaic floor. I volunteered for the heavy lifting part of the excavation: shoveling and wheelbarrowing under the morning sun, wearing just boots, quick dry shorts, and a hat. Tanned and muscled, I'd go from the site to the showers, wash my clothes along with myself, then sun dry before lunch.

It was liberating to have one task for the day, to be done early, not have to think about the kitchen at all, just enjoy the company of others all doing their share.

Every evening, there was music, singing, and dancing. Are you kidding me?! Why wouldn't everyone want to live like this? It began a search for something similar that took me to many places, hoping to find something like it again.

In 1976, armed with a degree in creative writing, I went searching for community again, for something like what I'd experienced in Israel. The Tucson area had become my base camp because of a community just outside the city limits.

I found my way to it because of responding to an ad in the *Aquarian Almanac*. They were looking for an editor and invited me to attend a meeting being held at this eight-plus-acre oasis.

The first structure on that land was an adobe stage stop built in the 19th century. Then, early in the 20th century, a ranch house. In the 1950s, the Valley School for Girls was established there, went under around 1970, was first converted to a quirky rental property, then bought by a group from the nearby St. Francis in the Foothills congregation.

Their inspiration was the original community of Saint Francis: San Damiano. Americanized, it became known as Damian Ranch, later, Damian Community.

When I stumbled upon it, it was still a rest stop and watering hole along the Rainbow Gathering Trail. I met people there with names like Sky, Blue Thunder, and Spirit. There were tepees in the wash, drums playing, naked bodies swimming and dancing, and, well, I was young and interested in it all.

Funny, how not having boundaries then meant expanding one's awareness and being able to merge sexually with strangers. I had no idea what I was really getting myself into at that property and wouldn't know for many more years to come.

Something of what I had experienced in the Israeli desert was happening there then, and I kept coming back. I didn't find anything like it anywhere else, although I searched the planet for another ten years before returning to Damian to live. I remember saying to myself then, "This is where I will make my stand. I will not run again, from anything."

I didn't write often during the years I was taking care of that rustic and historic property. The haphazard growth and age of the structures required me to develop an anticipatory sense for possible problems. If I may say so, I became quite competent at preventative maintenance, at catching little things prior to them becoming larger expensive ones.

This relentless vigilance cost me though. The uninterrupted solitude needed for introspection and then drafting ideas was just not possible. My attention was on what was going on around me, not inside me. I also had a young son and neighbors whose urgent needs of the moment superseded my own. We all make choices and sacrifices.

I only mention it now because even though the community is no longer my headache, the part of my brain that anticipates what might be going wrong has not relaxed. I see negative potential everywhere. Yes, it's a good trait for defensive driving and, sure, it helps with caring for a home, but it is exhausting.

Today, midst political-economic-pandemic-climatic crises, my attention, once confined to around eight acres, has expanded to larger issues.

Of course, no one is asking for my advice on how to manage the world, but that doesn't stop me from thinking about it. Sure, Susan and I wonder about our own future, worry about some close to us, but we also see more people forced to live in the wash near us.

Here in Pima County alone, 259 encampments have been counted with perhaps up to 2,000 people living without more than a tent. The last head count was 1,380 in 2018, but their numbers have been rising with the pandemic's disruption of the economy.

My overwatch mechanism cries, "Tilt!" This is not right.

I want a magic wand, a few billion dollars, or to live among others who care for life on this planet. How do we get there from here?

One good idea I've been reading about are Pallet Shelter tiny homes. The model is being implemented in over fifty cities around the country. Quick assembly structures of 64 and 100 square feet that include fold-up beds, locking doors, a desk, and room for storage are placed in villages.

Each unit has electricity, heating, and AC along with on-site food, restrooms, showers, and laundry. Some offer social services, including medical and behavioral health support. I can also imagine how these shelter villages are an opportunity for utilizing more solar and alternative energy.

There is needed work to be done around our cities. Why not create more of these micro-house villages and give people a chance to contribute in exchange for a safe place to live?

300,000 deaths now in our country related to this virus, but the vaccines are now being given to those front-line health workers! Hallelujah!

Other than an occasional cricket, the random stink bug, a fly or two, or a rare lizard appearance, our cats don't interact much with many life forms. A small snake surprised us all recently. We're still talking about it. Oh yeah, a scorpion might drop by, but the cats are immune to their charms.

Even all together, it's not much company, yet they neither hang out nor play with each other. They're sisters, for goodness sakes. Well, I guess that doesn't mean much when it comes to societal preferences, right?

I remember reading in one of Susan's books, *Genome* by Matt Ridley, how Arabs and Jews have almost identical Y chromosomes. In other words, they have the same paternal ancestors. They are more closely related to each other genetically than to any other ethnicity. Such is the way of things.

It's one thing to dislike from a distance, but to really hate another, boy oh boy, there's nothing like knowing someone with the audacity to reflect back what we reject or neglect in ourselves.

Susan, who worked with the guy whose lab began the Middle Eastern chromosome study, soothes me by saying the cats will accept each other more as they age.

I guess I understand that, but I wonder how long it will take for the rest of us to get along. And when, for crying out loud, will we start listening to scientists again?! Hey, don't look at me. I married one.

In Mississippi, a 2-year-old was dropped off with a bag of clothes at a Goodwill outlet. In Nigeria, hundreds of children were kidnapped from a school. Between being unwanted or impersonally valued, I'm not sure which story is ultimately more troubling.

But this week's news was not done. NBC reported that a former Israeli Defense Ministry head claimed aliens have an underground base on Mars and have been in contact with the U.S. government.

Meanwhile, in that very government, over a hundred newly elected representatives alleged fraud in their own election without a trace of ironic understanding.

Fingers point in all directions, but I think it's the competition for dwindling resources between increasing populations, midst climatic uncertainty, driving the insanity.

In study after study of mammals in crowded conditions, historical patterns of interaction and reproduction broke down. The collapse became known as a "behavioral sink." In some experiments with rats and mice, infant mortality was as high as 96%. In other words, self-extinction is a built-in regulatory response to what is abnormal and unsustainable.

I recommend reading some of ethologist John Calhoun's findings from close to fifteen years of research. He created conditions that allowed rodent populations to dramatically increase and carefully noted the results. Females were either unable to carry a pregnancy to term, did not survive birthing, or if all lived, the maternal instincts seemed absent or inconsistent. Males became either extremely overactive or withdrawn, deviated from their normal sexual expression, and could even become cannibalistic. The end result, extinction.

My own aversion to crowds began long before fear of contagion, but there's nothing like a deadly virus to remind those still able to discern the important difference between borders and boundaries that neither walls nor slogans can alter what is a simple math problem: less of everything, for more of everyone, in a closed system such as a planet, will require shared solutions. If not, the chaotic grabbing and tribal animosity between conflicting anarchistic fiefdoms will continue to devolve into a make-believe, do-it-yourself reality.

I fear for what havoc our baser nature unleashed can wreak, which is why I made the bet I did with Susan about civilization unraveling. I don't want to be right, but meanwhile state after state, country after country, pushes for more reproduction while making both birth control and abortion more difficult. It's as if we unconsciously are repeating Calhoun's experiments with ourselves.

I'm often grateful for a cup of water by the bed at night. It wasn't always that way. In fact, growing up, nobody in my family did it, and I can't tell you why not. It was never discussed, nor presented as an option. If awake and thirsty in the night, you'd somehow have to make your way downstairs to the kitchen for a drink. Or suffer through the night. Did I mention ours was a Jewish family? Suffering was just the shoulder shrug start to another story.

I really can't say when it was or who it was that nudged me into the habit I now have of bringing water to bedside. Hey, don't laugh or shake your head at me. Look how long everybody lugged baggage around before adding wheels! Come on, we even invented the word "luggage" rather than utilizing the prehistoric technology long available to us. How Jewish is that?!

We're all funny that way when it comes to putting up with what we are already used to doing. It takes an initial concentrated effort to break a habit or change a routine. I'm trying to cultivate an attention towards more life-improving customs, so am open to suggestions. I appreciate that about social media. I've already learned how previously tedious tasks, like peeling garlic, can be simplified. So, thanks to those who share such discoveries.

I suppose once enough of us understand the implications of Quantum Entanglement communication, I will too.

18 million cases of this coronavirus around the country and 319,000 dead from it. A suicide bomber in Nashville on Christmas, and yet another mass shooting, this time at a bowling alley in Illinois.

Three Conversations

God, in you, sits on a rock
looks at a flowering, willowy, river plant
remarks to no one in particular,
"I don't remember how I did that."

Who do you want me to be:
the one you wake up with
or the one you go to sleep with?
"Both," she said.
"Of course," I realized.

Sometimes, we have to hold hands
look into each other's eyes, and ask,
"Are you okay in there?"

And with the year coming to a close, rather than with anything profound in mind, I'm questioning when did the frequent wardrobe changes of winter become aerobic endurance tests demanding balance, flexibility, and advanced spatial awareness skills?

From Jock to Klutz: The Wrong Way Home is the new working title for my memoir. Oh well, it's not a race or a competition, is it? Is it?!

By the way, I don't run. For anything. But I catch myself now and then speeding up. It can happen anywhere, but thankfully not so much driving anymore. It's more about my attention leaving a task before its completion. The results are seldom efficient, nor pretty. Not sure if the culprit is more often impatience or boredom with the same repetitive actions.

Meanwhile, with the new year almost in sight, a vaccine already being administered, we are all restless to move on. I get it. But what my purplish bruises and the various debris in my clumsy wake tell me is that when I am most anxious or eager is precisely the moment for slowing, for breathing deeper, and becoming more aware and receptive.

Old habits may no longer serve us. The life we once relished, or strove for, may be gone. Who knows?

Perhaps we should strive to enter 2021 with a question and an open heart rather than with a command and mind made up …

It seems I should attempt to reflect upon a year worth forgetting. While others will provide more details, I know this: more survived than not. And yet the loss of life, and way of life, is staggering.

So, what's next? Damned if I know!

When possible, though, I will get vaccinated. I almost died this summer, and there was nothing Susan nor I could have done about it without the expert care of others. And after 10 days in the hospital (and still getting incomprehensible bills four months later), I certainly understand much is broken. However, to not trust in the cumulative knowledge of our species is baffling.

My hunch is that our very helplessness is at the core of the problem. Who grows and prepares all of what they eat? Who builds their own homes? What about all of our technology? How many understand how it all works? Our own isolated dependence scares us. We lash out with a misguided fury born of an inability to solve our own problems.

Once upon a time, I had a 1971 VW convertible (Clementine, which was, no joke, the actual name Volkswagen gave the paint). I cared for her mostly myself, even carried spare parts to make repairs anywhere. If I saw another VW by the side of the road, I'd stop and often surprise someone with just what was needed to get them going again. We'd all feel better after such a moment.

I miss the feeling of being able to competently assist another, or of receiving unexpected yet vital aid for no other reason than that it was needed.

These fragile human bodies of ours do best in a network of mutual care and support.

That's what 2020 has certainly underlined and emphasized for me. Is it wrong to wish for a similar awareness (minus the near-death episode) for others in 2021?

Part Two: 2021

January

Cookbook

"In the beginning was the Word,
and the Word was with God,
and the Word was God."

If there were a word that should be spoken
since that first word started it all so long ago,
what would it be?

I know I've searched for the one that would bring more love,
uttered many more in pursuit of laughter,
or attempting to repair so much broken.

I wonder about the last word
that will end it all.
Will it be spoken by man,
bereft of life's desire?
Something like, "Launch!"
or simply, "Fire!"

Or will it come thundering from above?
Sounding, "ENOUGH!"
You know, really tough love.
Nuclear orgasm—of cosmic dimensions—
a Big Bang of sorts.

One that puts the genie back in the bottle,
and then the bottle in something like Pandora's Box,
only locking it this time
then throwing away the key.

As tempting as that may be
to any actual and frustrated Creator,
how could one resist trying again,
hoping to finally see something greater?

The U.S. has now officially surpassed 20 million cases of COVID-19. There are more than 125,000 hospitalized, the 4th consecutive record-high day.

Resolutions have always seemed to me a prelude to some failure and potential self-loathing, but a new year seems to call forth at least the process of intention.

There was a time in my youth when I jettisoned everything to see how high (while mushroom-fueled) I might rise if untethered by the ordinary.

Just months ago, near death and mostly from a hospital bed, I said goodbyes and made amends. In such moments, a genuine glimpse at the intertwined eternal immensity told me all I needed to know. I am already everywhere that ever was, will ever be. We all are.

It seems to me that the struggle of consciousness is in grappling with what we are. How much of the totality to embrace? How awake and aware can a mind in a body bear to be? Awe-full and awful are but fluctuating reactions to All That Is.

Everything can certainly be too much.

So, how much—of anything—is enough?

I do not believe it is possible to have nothing, no matter how impoverished our circumstance. Human beings are star sparks of the divine encased by flesh and bone grown from the earth itself. What a concept! Possibly, the result of infinite Oneness bored with itself, wanting the surprise of otherness, the pleasures and pains of physical sensations.

These bodies of ours are designed for pleasure and pain. In that, all are equally wealthy. Praise be! What masterpieces of co-creation we are!

So, in 2021, what in this miracle will I choose to cultivate? How will I approach this opportunity of still being alive? Do I have any stuff left to strut?

There is something in my awareness I am struggling with: How can I be any healthier than the planet I am living on? Doesn't caring for myself require caring for all of life?

Whoa! I think I better start small, but without forgetting that tending to even one thing can be caring for everything.

Over 1,000 people died from the virus this past week in Los Angeles County alone, but nothing is as shocking as seeing the Capitol building being stormed.

Really?! It has come to this?

I ask Susan if we can call off our $2,000 bottle of wine bet. I don't want to win. I don't want any energetic part of what is happening. I want to be wrong, and I'm afraid that I am not.

We agree the bet is over. Instead, we will buy and share good wine with others as we can. It helps that we have a nice backyard with a view of the mountains, a table with six chairs where we can gather with friends and appreciate what is still working in this shared existence.

In hard times, it does help to laugh. I can sometimes add to the amusement of a moment, but I don't tell jokes. My father told jokes. Some, over and over. I resisted fully listening, often groaning and turning away from the repetition. As a result, I never developed the capacity for remembering a joke. His younger brother, my 94-year-old Uncle Marty, still consistently sends me some of the funniest emails I get. I, in turn, often pass them along.

At 29, I don't expect my son to step into this branch of the family business … but perhaps it's his destiny as well. We'll see. A person could do worse than to be the one who shares smiles and brings laughter. In youth, one can rely on agility, flexibility, and countless chances to get through life's challenges, but there comes a time when laughter might just be the only answer.

I have several friends who can tell a good tale, find and expose the funny bone. A couple of them, like Elliot Glicksman and David Fitzsimmons, even get on stage in front of paying audiences to do so. Imagine that. Oh, I've given talks and speeches, sang and performed, even read my own writings in front of seated people, but never tried comedy. That takes real courage. If I'm acting or reading, I can get lost in what I'm doing without knowing how it's going until the end when the enthusiasm (or lack of it) in the applause informs.

However, when people gather to laugh, and you're up there alone, not delivering what they came for—Oh my!—it must be like being adrift on a leaky dinghy, taking on water, sinking, with no rescue possible, just silent witnesses watching. No, I prefer to chime in with whatever wit from my place within the circle, or to pass on what comes to me and surprises with laughter.

There was a day when the value of remembering jokes, along with the skill in delivering them, helped a group of us transcend a terrible time. It was on a camping trip with the Rogers Park guys celebrating our 40th birthdays. We were up in Utah's Uinta Mountains for a few days before The Rain began. A downpour.

There were six of us standing close together under a tarp we'd tied between trees—cold, wet, and watching our lovely campsite flood. Morale could have gotten pretty low, but one of us, 'Da Gar' stepped up. He surprised us all with a nonstop monologue, physical comedy, and storytelling that kept us laughing and engaged for hours.

The rain wouldn't quit. Eventually, we abandoned everything, dashed to the vehicles, drove down to a town, and checked into some hotel. 'Da Gar' collapsed on a bed, fully clothed, and slept through the rest of the day. We honored his gift to us by letting him be.

We had grown up together yet had no clue he could do what he did. Where did it all come from? None of us have ever forgotten his spirit-saving performance.

It may have been what saved a tradition before it began. That was the first of our adult guys' trips. We did one almost every year after that until the pandemic.

And I'm grateful for the many who have shared their talents, their humor, music, and insights during this past year. Yes, we'd certainly be lost without those on the frontlines taking care of our bodies and those figuring out how to fight this virus, but today especially, after witnessing what happened in Washington D.C., I want to shout out to all those who have been taking care of our spirit.

In these relentlessly hard times, we can see the worst in any of us, but over and over again, people do step up with what is needed most: a vaccine, resistance to overturn an election, or the universal antidote of laughter.

Much of the past year has been unbearably hard and heartbreaking. If not for the creative comic spirit of so many, I don't know how we could have endured it. So, thank you all. Thank you for the guffaws, the grins, and the spins that have allowed us to digest the toxic and the unpalatable. Maybe one day soon we can all laugh together again.

Some thoughts only come after your parents are gone.
Responsibility has been wordlessly passed from them unto you.

When no one is left to carry you,
turn to lift another.
Freedom is not as we dreamed.
It's more tender chore within a choice.
Still, rejoice!

Rejoice, if you have arrived at this place
in the endless continuum of lives
with more than can be held.
Let what from you spills freely
fill the cups of the thirsty.

And give thanks for letting go,
for being in lightening—
as lightening your load lightens another's.
For one, an anchor; the other, a treasure.

Someone is waiting for what you no longer need,
for what no longer serves.
Someone has relinquished something precious,
ready to be apprehended by you.
Only in service is it felt,
never seen.

You know what's not funny? Yet another report citing the dangers of something I regularly consume! *The American Journal of Clinical Nutrition* published the research of Dutch scientists about the dangers of drinking unfiltered coffee. It seems it can increase the risk of heart disease and stroke by up to 10% by raising blood levels of a compound called homocysteine.

Really?! Did I need to know this during a pandemic and not long after stomach surgery? Do you even understand what my French press means to me? How many passions must one surrender?

Wait. How long has this been known? Never mind. I'm glad I had the time I did with my morning ritual. It's ruined now. Once something is known as bad for us, it can never be savored in quite the same way again. Oh, I might still choose such a brew from time to time, but I will always be aware of the darkness in the choice. Damnit!

While reading the news of late, I wonder how many are grappling with similar thoughts about other things, like who they might have believed in, and what they have supported.

In this household of four (two human, two feline), I'm what passes for the only male. So be it. The cats have no intention of helping with today's plumbing project. They will still want what they want when they want it though. In fact, they have become more demanding as our time together has burgeoned. Familiarity breeds complaints. And we all must wrestle with our expectations.

One cat, for example, known around here as Bear, thinks she can and should sing opera. It's a troubling, although amusing (the irritating kind) fancy. Still, who are we to extinguish her flame? Or her preferred time to practice? Yep, when we're going to sleep. However much we say we'd like to help her take this show on the road, we keep her safely indoors. Such is the role of responsible guardians: We limit what's possible in favor of what's sustainable.

I expect to accomplish what needs to be done today, but whenever the water must be shut off to replace old valves, anything can happen. One must prepare for and guard against the worst.

This week in our country feels somewhat similar. I trust enough know what must be done and how to pull it off efficiently and securely. I'm always glad when my role is simply to stay out of the way. I can do that.

And, yes, I do hear the clamoring—not unlike our less than musical cat's—of those who believe they are singing some battle hymn to the republic, but instead are sounding the screeches from too many grapes of wrath consumed.

Our other cat, Bean, came to me this morning as if to say it was her turn to be written about. After 11 years, she still has some kitten energy. If bored enough, she will even follow me around the house. If I dare close a door on her, she will tap on it as if to say, "Uh, excuse me. I'm out here. You're in there. And this is in my way." Paw, paw.

I suppose she recognizes in me her best chance for a certain kind of play, or treat. Her sister is seldom interested in playing with any of us. Neurosis is not just a human thing. Oops! Almost started back on Bear again. Attention often does drift to the problem child.

Bean is the innocent, forever present, alert to her surroundings, even with what's happening outside the window. She might scratch some furniture while climbing on and exploring everything, over and over again, but all in just being a cat. Whereas, when left alone, her sister might willfully destroy what we forgot to secure or barf on a countertop where she had no business being other than to leave her opinion regarding our neglect.

Interesting to note, Bean is the one most scared of visitors and has several hiding places. Bear doesn't much care. Anyone who will touch her is accepted. She is not shy in asking for the love she wants and, as a result, is the quintessential purring cat and often Susan's personal lap warmer.

Bean has learned to indulge in some tender moments as well over the years, but it's not really her nature, nor what she seems to really need from us. Of course, this is all shameless personification and projection, but we are spending a lot of time together. Hey, we do know some people too! We even talk to them, once in a while, but no one plays laser tag with me like the Bean.

We've been warned. Things are intense. What else might happen in these last days of transition? Okay, many of us have gained great expertise at staying home. However, whatever this energy is, it reaches everywhere!

My last few days were warped by attempting a tight-quartered plumbing project with a body less flexible than when I somehow managed to replace everything under the kitchen sink a few years ago.

Oh well. I only partially flooded the house, and in the end, I managed to overcome the builder's shortcuts and restore the delicate order, the fragile balance required to harness resources for our convenience.

But I sure am sore this morning. In my pain, there is empathy. Empathy for all those who must put on tired bodies every morning and do what must be done. There are so many incredible stories of endurance, longevity, and accomplishment.

But must we suffer so? I know, it comes with this fleshy territory. Still, I can imagine another way. I'm not holding my breath. In fact, I do try to utilize my breath as a tool.

My current meditation drill is about acceptance while inhaling, just taking in what is. Then, while exhaling, releasing my own resistance. In doing so, I ask myself, perhaps allow myself, to surrender to the creative force of the eternal moment.

Hey, it gives me something to do midst so much out of my control. And, tell the truth, it's not such a bad place to be.

Born in a segregated nation where mothers stayed home to care for their households, it is indeed a momentous day. A biracial woman is about to be sworn in as vice president.

I know many are frustrated with how long change seems to take, but just think, from the Emancipation Proclamation to the Civil Rights Act was about a hundred years. 45 years later, we had our first black president.

Now, 12 years from that day, a woman of black and Asian descent will be a heartbeat away from the highest office! Notice the trend?

Like it or not, it is as MLK reminded us: "The arc of the moral universe is long, but it bends towards justice." And, I might add, towards equality of race and gender.

The other night I listened to three former presidents as they stood in the Memorial Amphitheater at Arlington National Cemetery, participating in a moment together, sharing their thoughts and prayers. Through them, I caught a glimpse of a place where we already meet, red and blue, like the colors in the flag so many have lived and died for.

Alchemy

Just the sight of snow whitening distant peaks
lightens the valley, transforms the desert,
as if quenching the thirst from drought,
soothing the lasting burn from heat endured,
easing the fear of scorching yet to come.

But then the beauty begins to fade ...
the more magical a thing, the more fleeting it seems.
Snowmelt like tears running down the face of mountains,
in trickles and streams, nourishes all below.
How then can I lament the loss of what I only witness from afar?

For so many years, I'd be up at first light
to hike or climb my way to a rare snowfall.
My footprints would dot the pureness,
mark a return, make a strident statement
of a zest now diminished.

Oh, I've already been out in my truck a few times this week,
catching uplifting views, scanning but not quite planning
anything
yet.

For that, I'd have to trick this old body into believing
something it seems to have forgotten—
about the joy of letting go
of being as a child playing in snow,

someone who doesn't need to know
anything, really, but go, go, go!

I hear an inner parent reminding to bundle up,
and Captain Picard commanding to "Make it so."

On cold nights, I get in bed first to warm up the side Susan will eventually sleep on. We will both read until too tired to continue. She will typically last longer, which has always puzzled me since she almost always falls asleep if we attempt to watch something on television. Perhaps the effort in imagining from the printed word is the more exhilarating.

Roughly five years her senior, I've never understood not being able to stay awake … until this past year. Oh, certainly some combination of reasons can explain it, but who cares? It's just another piece of our new reality to incorporate: the nap! Intentional or not, it will happen.

Like with everyone else, much has changed for us. Of course, there has been the obvious abdication of travel, restaurants, and entertainment, but there have been some unexpected changes as well. Even the soundtrack for our days together has shuffled. Sure, we still choose from our own collection, but mostly we've surrendered to the radio. The surprise (to me) is the gains KUAT (classical) have made on our perennial favorite, KXCI (community).

Perhaps most significant has been how our cooking and eating rhythms have transformed in such planet-friendly, person-healthy ways. My diet more so than Susan's. My reduced capacity is part of it, as well as our agreement to not have meat in the house. We both drink less. And we're usually done eating for the day by 5pm! I wonder how that will hold up post-pandemic.

There is so much unknown, within and without. I see how my own neurotic tendencies have amplified. And I imagine that trend has spread in others as well, along with the virus—in the fear of it or in the denial of it.

We are greatly defined by what we consume, what we choose to share or reject. I, for one, choose to reject conspiracy theories, from anyone; news, concerned with ratings, interspersed with advertisements; and even market opportunities driven by social media rather than fundamentals.

I know I can't fix the crazy around me. I will strive to live as if to one day inhabit a world that makes sustainable sense. And as long as I am able, I will share what I have. Consider it one man's feeble attempt to warm up another's side of the bed.

I had to grow more me than needed to find my own discordant yet rhythmic, nighttime voice. Yes, I'm talking about snoring. I know, some accomplishments are less celebrated than others. Just ask Susan. And because her opinion matters to me, I was also happy to reverse engineer this less than musical apparatus.

Okay, surgery (and the resultant weight loss and sobriety) did most of the grunt removal. But (and here's the important piece) I wanted to change my unconscious, disruptive ways.

For most of my adult life, I never needed an alarm clock. I'd just program myself to wake up at a certain time, and I did. How did that work? Is there some part of a self that keeps wakeful watch, eyeing the clock in the dark? Or is there some unknown internal mechanism functioning?

Like much of what the brain/mind configuration is busy at, I am neither consciously in charge nor aware of how it does what it does. So it goes.

When I was a child, I believed I had discovered the way to go to sleep with the dreams I desired. By balling my fists and twisting them in opposite ways over my eyes, I could change channels. Critically, I was not only able to find a suitable dream in progress but avoid the haunting or terrifying ones that had invaded my directory.

In the pursuit of facing and then vanquishing my inner demons, I unwittingly lost that particular ability. Oh well. It served me when I needed it most.

Today, almost every word I write begins in the hand-off between sleep and rising. What I'm saying to this Secret Self, my inner Night Watchman, is that I'm listening. And I trust in what you tirelessly offer me to better myself.

4 a.m.

Extracting essence from experience like squeezing a sponge,
as if there might be something in these last drops
that will reveal where I went wrong.

Last summer, from an imagined death bed,
I made many amends, said some "just in case" farewells,
and emptied a reservoir of unspoken words.

But my life went on—almost weightless—without the burden
of the unfinished, the unresolved, and the misunderstood
expectations of a lifetime.

I never fully realized how much of what I carried for others anchored me
until in the honeymoon of healing where the problems on my mind
became mostly my own.

Today, reluctant to fill what took such force to drain,
I catch myself on the verge of inviting back the drama,
but instead turn to this writing to avoid the karma
and spare myself the pain of starting over again.

There is something missing, I admit.
I suspect it is a longing for what is not,
but what could be, here and now,
if only we'd commit, and heaven permit.

80,000 of our fellow citizens are now dead from the virus. Although there have been relatives of friends, no one close to us has died. It would seem by now that everyone would have seen or heard of the pain some family has to bear.

I've heard of children losing both parents within days of each other. What can ever be done for them? There's just too much suffering to take in, and so little one can do.

I'm saddened that to wear or not wear a mask has become so charged with defiance politics. For me, each time I put on a mask, I'm saying to myself as well as to others, "I care, and I want to help." Amazing how that one conscious ritual changes my perception from being restricted and inconvenienced to being on the support team for those combating this killer on the front lines of hospitals and laboratories.

Even retired, in a pandemic, with really nowhere to go, I can find myself feeling uncomfortably rushed or, conversely, annoyed with how long some things take. On the road in traffic or being put on hold on the phone, either the fast face of impatience or the restless countenance of anxiety can still get to me. Knowing there's an invisible enemy that could be closing in doesn't help matters, especially waiting in line at the grocery store.

I might have had some tendency towards becoming a germaphobe prior to the current fear, but now I don't want to touch anything or anyone outside of my home.

I'm also more sensitive these days to feeling wrong or being where I don't belong. And to any plan made, a gravity well, affecting the self-propelled trajectory of an aimless day. Yet the vacuum of too much empty space can sap more energy than it restores. Oh, and God help me if the list of what must be done becomes too large and is coupled with the frustration of failed technology. Meltdown Danger!

So it seems I've become not unlike a hot house plant who needs everything to be just so. Not too hot. Not too cold. Not too busy. Not too slow.

Not so long ago, striking a crisp iron shot stiff pleased me most, but I am happiest today simply absorbing beauty in nature or literature, or with pen or pencil in hand quietly pursuing the right word to capture an otherwise elusive thought. The reward of that is often in the discovery, with some small pleasure in the crafting. After that, any response from some electronic distance is welcomed.

And I like to walk and talk with Susan. Lately, we've been venturing out to places around town. Short trips in her car to spots where we've either never been before or had never experienced so empty, such as the university campus. It feels strangely daring.

There is something eerie and accessible about wandering around where it was once so crowded. Our attention, freed from avoiding other bodies, can absorb details previously missed, but always the science fiction sense that something is wrong here.

February

Restless

Yeah, I missed your birthday.
Not forgotten, just nothing to say.
And no, the phone is still not on.
What is there to talk about
we don't already know
or might yet want to hear?

We seldom leave the neighborhood,
take few chances,
just taking care of what we can
from this home
without secrets
only the surprises
from all that ages
and two black cats
roaming free
in our shared cages.

A shooting in Oklahoma leaves five adults and one child dead. No motive is yet known.

A more contagious variant of the coronavirus from the United Kingdom is moving rapidly around the country. Known cases are doubling every nine days.

I still wear the hospital socks from August. They grip our tile floors well and, like the gray beard that also remains from my hospital stay, remind me to keep checking in with my fragile as well as my rambunctious self.

Whenever trimming and shaving around the additional growth, I question if it may be time to take down this aging advertisement, as if looking younger might actually persuade likewise behavior.

Just yesterday, I finished some spot patching and roof coating that began in pursuit of a small leak that appeared during last week's rain. It had been a while since I'd been on the roof and was pleased to find past work had paid off: no full-on re-coating was needed. In this era where procrastination and putting things off have become survival attributes, this was most welcome.

Like others, our wish list for post-pandemic travel keeps growing, but we are also considering what we can do without or experience in other ways as we try to imagine how to participate in a different, more ecological economy.

Our trips to walk around previously unexplored parts of our own city is part of that plan. Instead of ending such an excursion sitting at a restaurant, we call ahead for take-out to bring home, so as to still support our favorite places in our endless staycation.

Years ago, we co-decorated an electric pencil sharpener that recently stopped functioning. Reluctant to just throw it away, I took it apart, discovered a worn gear, then identified and ordered a replacement part, which we now patiently await.

The old formula of time and cost would have dictated simply getting a new one, but now, time-rich, this tinkering path feels both frugal and right. And it kind of fits for a gray-bearded guy.

On an easy day to be outdoors, without any particular weather calling attention to itself, we went on a hike. With no wind to push against, nor heat to sap strength, the distinction between landscape and self was lessened. Just some conscious, mobile beings crunching trail, observing the medley of color and shape in mountain desert under cloudy sky.

Sometimes, walking energizes side-by-side conversation. Other times, it's more single-file meditation. In a quiet place, with bone on rock and spirit skyward, I tried to imagine how many steps I've taken in this life, how much of this or that I've consumed. The thought of all that it takes to keep just one body moving through the years around a planet heavy with too much and too many. When I started to multiply by generations and billions, I just had to surrender in amazement for all that Earth provides.

Instead of returning by trail, we surprised ourselves, made our way into a narrow wash below, and then scrambled over and down rocks, around cacti, and through brush, without knowing if we'd be blocked and forced to turn back.

It was okay. Without trail markers or worn pathways, one's attention can only be on the next step, intermittently scanning far enough ahead to know there is still a way forward.

We used to do this quite often, partly in pursuit of solitude, partly for the spontaneous responsive interaction of balancing motion with obstacles. It's still the best exercise I can imagine for tuning mind and body with its sustaining source. And it reminds me to trust without having to understand; and to enjoy without knowing how the story ends.

Beard stubble, coffee grounds, lead pencil shavings—some of my morning particulate waste. Not collecting, just noticing. No photos needed. One can picture it.

I often have to shudder-stop myself from imagining how others live. I'm squeamish about many things, avoid much in search of some serenity. It's not exactly a hero's journey.

The collective waste from humans more than bothers me; it downright disgusts. Led more by Susan, we use as little as possible, even downsized our garbage bin to the smallest size available, but it still takes us weeks to fill.

We pick up the litter of others. Any object that can't be recycled, we imagine how it might be repurposed, perhaps as part of a barrier in the garden, a container for plants, or an art project anywhere. We have a collection of take-out containers we're still wondering what to do with (I suspect home-baked treats will be delivered in them for the foreseeable future).

But more than refuse, I worry about water. The math of more and more people moving to a region where there seems to be less and less precipitation is a word problem that even a preschooler would understand.

Still, besides governing our own usage or reporting leaks when seen, I don't feel called to organize or petition the clouds. It will be what it will be, and we will respond accordingly. Tough decisions about growth, tourism, landscaping, agriculture, ranching, mining, swimming pools, golf, and even decorative fountains will have to be made. I suspect I won't be consulted, perhaps can even trust that the eventual catastrophic crisis will help clarify what are now legal and historic use hurdles.

There are, of course, scores of issues and problems needing to be resolved, but what has my attention, what I see on every walk along the Rillito, are people without homes.

Around the world, the number of refugees, migrants, and homeless are increasing. Tens of millions of people without homes. The numbers are staggering. The challenges, immense.

I have become an advocate for Tiny Home Villages. If humans insist on reproducing on a planet that cannot grow larger, we are going to have to learn how to take up less space, use fewer resources, and find alternative ways of feeding ourselves.

Susan has been following, studying, and supporting lab-grown protein as an alternative to animal protein. Looking ahead, it's either that or eating insects. Once again, I'm with the scientists.

With less than two-thirds of the original, I literally have less stomach—for anything! Certainly, I eat and drink less. And I know the pandemic magnified some latent neurotic tendencies, which were then further amplified by my surgically accelerated aging process. The result? I can barely tolerate drama or conflict now in just about any form. Music needs to be softer, more thoughtful. Complexity is better than repetition. Instrumental over most lyrics. So it goes.

Can't imagine being in a crowded place again. I'm on the verge of wanting a driverless vehicle, or maybe following the lead of some friends and having only one vehicle for the two of us. Susan still seems to not mind driving.

Have I mentioned I worry? I'm sure I have. That's another unfortunate characteristic of this new territory: I repeat myself.

Anyone else
wonder where your get up and go got up and went?
Avoid mirrors for days, then suddenly get all dressed up for no reason at all?
Anyone else wear the same clothes over and over?
Or reach out to friends one moment, hide the next?

Do you have a list of things you're putting off until the pandemic has passed?
Are you wondering how long some of those things can possibly wait?
Then, in an attempt to lower such anxiety, start a project you immediately regret but now can't turn back?

What about everything you thought you'd do on your way to lockdown realization?
The languages, art, healing, skills, amends, instruments, whatever.
How have you done?
I still don't know how to use this computer I'm on every day!
I skim around its capability like a caveman who has found fire
but is clueless as to how to make it on his own.

But mostly what I wanted to ask you is this: Anyone else wonder why even good news doesn't feel as good as you think it should?
Do you still even watch the news?
I do. Even though it reminds me of all that is going wrong, or about to go wrong, everywhere, in the entire world.
So, I turn away in search of some serenity … for a while,
but keep coming back to this abuser
who turns my curiosity into alarm,
my desire to be informed and responsible into overwhelm.

But what if news coverage focused more on what's best about us?
Began and ended with feel good stories?
What if we were bombarded instead by all that's possible and accomplished through cooperation and perseverance, through kindness and generosity?
How would that change who we are?
Would anyone else, just for the hell freeze over of it, like to see us try

so that perhaps before we all die, we might witness this unlikely but angelic pig come to fly?

These viral days, like sandpaper, have worn away much. And then there are the hammer blows. I learned this morning of the passing of John Putnam, a man I never met, but with whom I spent countless Saturday mornings, from 6 a.m. to 8 a.m.

John, on radio station KXCI, filled our home with the sounds of Hawaiian musicians. His gentle voice, a caring companion, sharing his quiet passion for the islands. Mostly, I listened from the kitchen, allowing the music to shape the choices that would become our first meal of the day. Susan will tell you, I looked forward to Saturday morning all week. As he would say, we were "ohana"—family.

And now he's gone. As I write these words, I hear his voice. KXCI is playing an archived program. They will play another next week. I'll be considering it his memorial tribute, will break out a favorite Hawaiian shirt, then sing and dance Aloha to John.

Today, February 21st, 2021, is my son Ryan's 29th birthday. He was conceived and raised at Damian. His imminent arrival was the reason I went from being a roommate with two other guys there to buying in as an owner and sharing a place with his mom, Lorie.

With the help of her father, Roger, we did an extensive remodeling of the unit still known by its former school designation, Headmaster. He was 60 then, knew how to do just about everything, and was a joy to work with. If there's a better man than Roger out there, I've yet to meet him. But that is when my neighbors realized I was handy.

At the time, I was the educational counselor at Sierra Tucson Adolescent Care where I was cross-trained in various therapeutic programs.

Not having boundaries at that time in my life meant I became the guy who people would call for both personal and plumbing problems, for relationship as well as building repairs. All this while learning to be a father, a partner, and to stay in one place, no matter how hard things got.

Ryan was the reason for my perseverance.

Before he even makes a sound, something calls me out of my sleep, and I find myself alert, listening. I hear the rustle of his legs pushing on his blanket. He's restless. I get ready to respond to a cry I know is coming, like waking up before the alarm clock goes off.

I get up and go to him, place my hand gently on his back to share warmth and comfort. Sometimes, whatever was stirring him passes, and he drifts back to sleep. Sometimes, I lift him and carry him back and forth down the hallways of Headmaster.

Somehow, holding and loving him in the dark, I am finally able to reach my own abandoned infant self and now know, everything will be okay for both of us.

As I became enmeshed in the fabric of the community, boundaries blurred even more, caring became taking care. Like a spider, I became someone who felt and reacted to every vibration, sensing and resolving whatever might disturb or upset the web. But I wasn't really present or available for something essential with Lorie.

She moved out. We had never married. Our commitment has always been to meet in what was best for our son. We still meet there with mostly joy.

Can't say exactly how long ago it was I realized I needed to extract myself from those caretaking patterns. Or what kind of surgery it would take to separate my nervous system from those surroundings. I read once how if one leaned against even the most massive glacier, over time the glacier would give.

Susan helped me lean in a different direction. She moved into the community in 1997 and had her own place next door to mine. Side-by-side intimacy helped me get through what I could not before. Each with our own space allowed sensitivity and respect for our differences as an ongoing foundation. Something like an invitation, rather than an expectation, was part of our daily rhythms, and so the health of the individual as well as the couple were both being nurtured.

We married in 2001, ten years after we first met.

She didn't have the lifetime attachment to the ideal of communal living as I did though and got tired of the pettiness of the residents and of their endless squabbles, which prompted our purchase of the townhouse in 2011.

I wasn't quite ready to leave, so went back and forth between the old and new properties until microscopically slow yet steady, my mind always grinding and buzzing with possible scenarios, something inside me moved. I began to detach from the threads. And like ice calving, the old dreams finally fell away.

25 years after moving into Headmaster, I remodeled it again. This time to sublet. I took on all the projects I had put off while raising Ryan, teaching at Pima Community College, and taking care of much of the community's needs.

Besides the usual painting, I replaced the windows, doors, even the toilets, and in the process found myself thinking of Walking Bob.

When just out of graduate school, eager to write a novel, I went to Bisbee where I met him, stayed in one of his unheated apartments during the winter. I wanted to rent a house he had just finished remodeling. He took great pride in showing it to me. Everything glistened. It was his masterpiece. He liked showing it off, but he just couldn't let anyone actually live there. I didn't understand, thought he was crazy. He was gone on walking tours for months at a time. Why wouldn't he want his property occupied?

After completing these projects, I understood his desire to preserve, for however long possible, something pristine.

Part of my process was sorting through the accumulated stuff that was a byproduct of staying in one place for so long. I estimated that I have recycled or repurposed over 80% of my possessions. It gave me a very satisfying kind of joy to find the right homes for my things and to watch the weight of all the plans, possible projects, nostalgia, and miscellaneous mishegoss disappear.

What's left was the distillation, which I took with me to begin a life living with my wife away from Damian.

It's been over a year since I've been in an office supply store. I went to one today to load up on ink and paper. Sure, I could have gone anytime, but it's been kind of a fun challenge utilizing and using up everything in the house first. You know, all the saved but forgotten, the perhaps one day, stuff.

Somehow, this morning, feeling deprived, but not really from a lack of good ink, I gathered up some favorite but dry pens and resolutely ventured out in search of recharge. Surprisingly, a Cross refill of black archival ink for a fine felt tip rolling ball has revived more than just my pen.

It occurred to me that a few strategic dollars spent close to home had accomplished what some previous and expensive getaways had not: spiritual restoration!

As mentioned, I also treated myself to a fresh pack of lined paper. Big deal, huh? But, for most of my life, I have primarily used scrap paper for my drafting process. It started with the childhood discovery that a Chicago printing business on Touhy Ave discarded all kinds of misprints, partial pads, and flawed reams in the alley shared with our home on Fitch Ave.

I have had an endless stash of paper ever since. It has helped free me to play with writing without feeling as if I might be wasting paper. The paper had already been thrown away!

Today begins a new era. All the odd remnants gathered over a lifetime have finally been consumed. At 66 years and a couple of months old, I sit with clean, fresh paper in front of me and a fully loaded sleek pen poised and at the ready.

Now, if only I had something left to say ...

I get stuck. Not just with writing. It happens between things. I'm in one place, know the next thing to do, but am frozen, unable to move. It's like the feeling of being in a room, wondering why I came here, but without any motion.

Like a power outage, it happens without warning and lasts for an unpredictable amount of time. There's no reset button to push. The electricity comes back on when it does. Until then, I'm paralyzed.

And it's happening more frequently. What if it's some sort of possession?! "Who ya gonna call?"

I'm not tired. My mind is alert in such moments, just incapable of authorizing any action, like some incompetent manager in a numbing bureaucracy.

Could it be something in my diet? Perhaps a laxative-induced sense of urgency would help? Or perhaps a stronger sense of purpose is the answer?

I've been advised by my elders to stay engaged and be productive. But maybe the repetitive nature of these unvaccinated days has worn some sprocket teeth down, making engagement more difficult? Who does that kind of repair?

I see the need for repair everywhere. Maybe that's it. Maybe there's just so much to do, and so many obstacles, it's overwhelming.

I wonder what that one best step to take next, for all of us, would be—if, that is, we ever could all agree.

Good news! Pfizer and Moderna announced that their vaccines are 94% effective against the new strains of the coronavirus. Surely, enough of us will agree to get vaccinated and stop this thing.

Another windy morning when I was planning on walking nine holes. Lately it seems as if the weather is plotting against me. Okay, not really. It was my mom who took weather personally and dramatically, especially when traveling. She believed rain followed us, but punished her specifically for some unspoken mistake. I took some of that on, but mostly have rejected that I am responsible for or similarly cursed by the weather.

And I am not one of those who gloat about living in Arizona when others are freezing elsewhere. After all, who wants to be here in summer? However, I did notice that about three-quarters of the country was covered in snow, with record lows everywhere.

Truth is, this has all been feeling biblical for some time. Remind me, where on the Plague Parade are we now? We're already through the original top ten, right? I won't even ask, "What's next?" I just want to know what we can do to make it right.

You know, some kind of booming voice, speaking in every language simultaneously, through every device, on every screen, out of the mouths of every creature, on everything growing, on the rippling of the waters, in the wind, skywriting with clouds the message we can't seem to understand: "Take care of this planet! You will not get another like it."

Strange how my fantasies have changed during this past year. I remember thinking it strange when they first became about hitting great golf shots on exotic destination courses rather than what else might happen around such places.

More than uncertain weather, it's our changing dreams that define us.

Acceptance

Fifty some years after last dialing it
I still know her phone number.
Whatever came first, always remains so.

When surveying a life's journey
we must return to where we began,
gauge from there what success might be:
distance traveled perhaps,
but more by what remained constant
and then by how much has changed.

I understand the desire to reach back
with wiser hands,
alter this or that,
see where a different course might have led.

Some believe there are infinite realms
for every thought to have its way.
I'm okay with just this one.

It's more than enough to know how what came before
brought me to where I am and to whom I now co-create
a life so worth learning to cherish.

There is no point in dialing that unforgotten number,
but she who once would answer
has found a forest peace with dogs and daughters,
and I can truly smile knowing that as well.

Recently, I heard from a friend in Phoenix that her childhood home had been demolished. There were no invitations or announcements, just the jarring experience of one day discovering a hole where once was her home. Just like that, only the absence of what had contained so much. A home, full of family memories, an external storage expected to last, was now gone.

I felt her shock of reality displacement, how her own cells in the dust, marks of growth on a door jamb, art shadows and argument on the walls, had all vanished. Whatever was left or lost in a move will never be found or wondered about again by another. A connection had been severed. Does it somehow diminish or does it liberate one?

I think back to a visit to Chicago, ringing a doorbell, recognizing at once its chiming pattern, and then how I shared stories with the current inhabitants as they gave me a tour of what had been my childhood home. One such visit was enough, but the familiar houseboat-inspired structure on Fitch Avenue in Rogers Park remains an important touchstone in my life journey.

All these thoughts motivated me to take a drive to a previous dwelling here on the west side of Tucson. I found it when in graduate school and working as a garbageman for the city. It was more than I could afford on my own, but I loved its spaciousness and its closeness to the Tucson Mountains. I had roommates.

For a time, Julie was one. She had lived with me, Ellen, and Jody when we were all undergraduates. She eventually finished her MBA and moved on.

Diane was another. She came after her marriage ended in New Jersey and met her eventual life partner while living there.

Funny how life works: it was Diane calling me in Chicago, looking for a house sitter while she and Brad traveled, that brought me back to Tucson, where I reconnected with Lorie, which led to Ryan emerging into the world.

With memory tapes already rolling, I headed west on Grant Road past Silverbell Road, made the right turn that led to the dirt road, saw the street sign, but the house itself was not there. I walked all around, disoriented, as if in a parallel dimension where I did not belong. It felt as if a piece of my past had been erased, and I was oddly lost without it there.

I kept checking to see if I might have gone wrong somehow, but everything else was where it was supposed to be. I went down in the adjacent wash where I used to walk, found a rock, and sat for a while.

I remembered how Julie and I once hosted a Thanksgiving dinner at the now missing house. Fast Freddy, an eventual chef, but then a garbageman I had partnered with, had given me some tips for the meal, so I did most of the cooking. Julie cleaned up but poured the grease down the drain and clogged it up tight. I wonder what she would say if I told her that was the last time I hosted a Thanksgiving gathering.

Memories kept coming as I sat there. It was riding with Fast Freddy when I saw a woman with long brown hair still wrapped in a towel, fresh from a shower, rushing to bring out her garbage in time. Rather than being concerned about her state of undress, she seemed embarrassed about the condition of the leaning, white wood fencing in front of the property.

The scene made an impression and after work, I stopped by in Clementine, which always carried tools for most situations. I fixed the fence and was just leaving when she pulled up. She recognized me as her garbageman. My plan for an anonymous good deed was busted. Denise and I became friends for life.

I became part of her family. Her parents' house near Sierra Vista, AZ was the place where I'd leave vehicles during my Forest Service years. In exchange, I'd housesit when they were gone, taking care of the dog and chickens.

While sitting and looking around this desert arroyo, it occurred to me that it had to be a flood that swallowed the building and altered the landscape, along with my sense of reality. Yet perhaps the discombobulated state of mind had opened up a different kind of door for me.

This was also the one and only house where Cindy and I had ever lived together. And it seems now the tale I've been trying to tell for years is getting ready to come out.

At home, instead of trying to find out exactly what happened to the house on Grannen Road, I go to my journals. I find an old poem where one line said it all: "If every man has a sense of perfect design, then she in fact embodied mine."

It wasn't until I met my birth mother that I understood who it really was I was seeing in Cindy and where the intensity of my feelings had originated. But I'm getting ahead of the story here.

All because of that house. Not only was it not there, but the land beneath it was gone as well.

If I'm supposed to interpret that, I can't. I completed a Master's degree in English Literature while living at that house but am at a loss to understand how its obliteration fits into this telling. Has its disappearance forced me to grapple with a significant Sticky Karma crossroad in my life?

It was the time when I met Judith. She was a waitress at a restaurant near campus, and her appearance sparked many things, including pushing me towards, then accompanying me on, the search for my biological origins, and all on our way to Africa.

March

Meditation Meds

I look for her.
He waits on me.
They wonder if they are forgotten.
Others burn and run from attention.
There are so many of us
spinning stories separately.

If not expanding,
soon we are contracting into them.

My dreams are all wrong.
I keep thinking there is somewhere to be
if only I could arrive intact, complete,
confusing rest with destination
emptiness with attainment.

I watch too much of the world's sufferings,
see not enough of its beauty.

I met a man once, in words, who explained
how he measured himself
not by the results of his actions,
but rather by how true they were
to what he believed.

174

The first slice of sun rising
up behind the Rincon Mountains
seems to stir a breeze.
Purple penstemon sway.
A glimpse of beauty, a present breath,
another day.

It seems there are a thousand worthy causes
and an infinite number of ways
to only one reward.

The CDC announced that fully vaccinated people can now meet indoors without masks! 30 million have already been vaccinated as mass vaccination sites are set up all around the country.

Yet, with over 500,000 lives lost, we have the highest virus death toll of any nation.

On the second awakening of the day, I won't attempt as much as after the first. Caffeine-propelled productivity is a morning ride taken until hunger snuffs it. I don't fight the post-lunch drowsiness anymore. I nap. My advice? For every day, live twice.

Whatever can be done in a busy morning is enough. During many jobs, I've witnessed the common drop in energy and efficiency after lunchtime. The corporate answer: make phone calls or schedule meetings for afternoons to share the work from earlier hours and plan for tomorrow's.

It helps to close one's eyes after lunch, even for a few moments, to both signal and accept the shift. If you're lucky enough to control your own daily schedule, leave the second half blank. Allow what you need to reveal itself when there is a time to respond. Perhaps a walk or a stretch. Get lost in a book. Reach out to someone, not from any should, but from listening to inner whispers. It's an opportunity to live more in sync with intuition and heart, rather than morning determination and mind.

It's the slow way to end a day, aligned to watch the sun set, prepare an evening meal, meet the night—and all that darkness brings—with the balance and presence needed to bear the gaze of billions of years of starlight streaming and twinkling simultaneously in and out of your consciousness.

Scrolling

... for something, perhaps, but not searching.
Something more aimless,
scrolling without knowing,
like taking a pulse, the temperature of the moment.

Who's okay? Who's not?
Will I, should I, respond?

How often do we visit each other this way?
Leave no trace, just take a peek, grab an impression
we might carry for a bit, think about returning, or not ...

Unlike how we once gathered and organized,
these devices and platforms allow us choice,
perspective previously unimagined.
Seems as if we were distancing long before the pandemic,
doesn't it?
Understood the mathematical trajectory of going viral
before being asked to mask.

Even friendship has taken on some attributes of a math problem:
How can we be connected simultaneously to everyone from every time
in our lives and still have meaningful exchanges?

So, we scroll, like taking a stroll, past much,
watching for where heart and curiosity land us,
learning as much about ourselves as each other
along the way.

Lately, I've noticed myself not enjoying the second cup of coffee, or another glass of wine, as much as the first. Have already stopped going for second helpings, no matter how delicious. And it's not just about food or drink. I'm discovering a desire for less of everything, have even come to distrust wanting more of almost anything. Susan models this and encourages me to learn to savor.

I've begun to savor-surrender: a relaxation into the moment, a bit foreign but welcome. It feels as if something long out of whack is coming into balance. It happens not just with tasting, but when moving/stretching slowly and consciously; when breathing cooled air under snow-dusted mountains; feeling sunlight warm through skin and closed eyes; even in choosing and typing these words.

Ever consider how closely aligned the word "savor" is with "savior"? Can't help but wonder if all it takes is removing the "I" to more fully relish and cherish existence. Why? Can't explain it, but the boundaries between things disappear when fully sensing what is being experienced.

Oh yeah, I know, boundaries are necessary. Not having them can be a drag. I know that too. And they're not always easy to construct, recognize, or reinforce. However, their rigid enthusiasm can also keep out what is essential: the ceaseless creative flow of life.

Today I received my first vaccination at the University of Arizona. I didn't even have to get out of the car—medical fast food technology, just like the speed in which this vaccine was developed.

Susan drove. There was no traffic along the way, but upon arrival there were several long lines of vehicles and dozens of staff and volunteers assisting in this public safety effort.

We were directed to one of the lines for those 65 or older. I couldn't help but compare how the different lines moved, but it's not as if we had anywhere else to be. Still, it was strange to be around so many people and to watch how this quickly assembled apparatus for administering vaccines operated.

Folks with vests and clipboards advanced us from station to station. The shot itself was the fastest part of the whole process. It came with a vaccination sticker and a sucker.

We were then directed to a waiting area, just in case there were any side effects. Holding the sucker, I remembered reluctant trips to doctors being rewarded with a choice of lollipop. And I thought back to being a kid, lined up with my family at Stephen Decatur Elementary School to receive a sugar cube in a tiny paper cup as a polio vaccination. All the neighbors were chatting and enjoying being together. At least, that's my recollection of it.

Polio had plagued humans for thousands of years and ravaged our country in the first half of the 20th Century. (Read Philip Roth's *Nemesis* for what it was like in 1944.) Thankfully, today, it seems a distant memory. Mass vaccination worked then. Will it work now? Back then we seemed to collectively trust more in the competency of our system than we do now.

Getting a drive-through shot at the UA last night was not quite the jovial community moment as in my childhood memory, but it was fast, friendly, and efficient. And in that unexpected taste of sweetness, there was still a link to something like collective hope and some future success.

Former Tucson mayor, Bob Walkup, died. Years ago, I played and wrote about an unexpected round of golf with him. My friend, David (known by many as Fitz), cartoonist and columnist at the *Arizona Daily Star*, asked me to write a condensed version for the editorial page. I did.

In the mysterious way inspiration works, doing so helped me decide to enter my club's annual member-pro event next month. It will be my first attempt at playing 18 holes since my surgery. I tell myself I can always quit whenever and just ride around in a cart, enjoying the company of men again.

Not wanting to be embarrassed by my lack of strength at the golf event next month, I consulted with our club's PGA pro, Chris Dompier. He holds several local course records and is the best teaching pro I've ever known. We met at the range and talked about small adjustments to maximize the distance I could still get without jeopardizing accuracy.

I showed him the snake-like scar from my stomach surgery. He didn't flinch.

In the past few days, there have been shootings in Atlanta massage parlors, a Dallas nightclub, and now a Boulder supermarket. Even without the pandemic, it doesn't seem safe to go anywhere anymore.

Whose death
will be the one that will finally be enough?
Will it be his, or hers, or must it be yours?

But if you are left and they are gone
what will you do with the words unspoken?
Where will you go with heart and life so broken?

What if someone nearby is struggling
with what is simple for you?

What if we walked our days watching for moments,
not in fear, but to extend a hand, lend an ear?

Might we more often reach the one about to burst
and through timely and unexpected relief
spare the world another shot of grief?

Three days after the initial sadness from hearing of yet another mass shooting, I learned that I knew one of the victims, Jody Waters.

Honestly, I had mostly forgotten about her. Hadn't seen her since college. But this now more personal shock was stirring memories.

Jody and Julie were my girlfriend Ellen's best friends, and the four of us shared a house and guest house as undergraduates. I was immersed in their women's world back then. It was an important part of my education.

With her twinkling active eyes, Jody was mischievous and quick. We often clashed, but also laughed, competing perhaps for Ellen's attention.

I remember her zipping around in a forest green VW bug. She'd even drive alone from Tucson back to her home in Barrington, Illinois. I thought it was too dangerous for her to do. She didn't care. She did as she pleased, and it all worked out.

Until, that is, one short ordinary trip to a store at the very wrong time.

We got along best when talking about an upcoming date she had, or in her after-date debriefing. She could be funny. And fun. I'm thinking of our legendary water fights.

This morning, I saw a photograph of her and her two grown daughters, recognized her in them, but was mostly struck by their loss, their shock, their grief.

A few years ago, I had a brief exchange with a neighbor who couldn't believe that anyone could fully understand what it felt like to have their house vandalized like his was. I argued for the existence of human empathy. I still would.

However, what was just yesterday another American tragedy that I heard about and then moved on from, now leaves me trembling and haunted.

This was not my loss. Jody and I hadn't spoken in years. It is our collective loss, and knowing her shocked me into that awareness. It can happen to me, to you, anywhere, anytime.

I don't care which side of gun control anyone is on. None of us is safe nor distant from this kind of random horror. It is spreading like a virus, and we have to figure it out!

In a lost year,
how many have died?
In a lost year,
how many dreams were boarded or closed,
put up for sale?

Who can track all the losses,
foresee what else we might be losing?
Tell me, where does so much pain and grief go?
How does it get contained and processed,
absorbed and transformed?

I too feel the restless eagerness to return
to what was once commonplace,
but even if what was remembered were still somehow there,

with all the players alive and waiting in all the places of gathering,
with all the ways of celebrating, could I join them?

Can you grasp all that has changed,
what is being asked? If so, please explain it to me.

A look around the globe reveals a growing suffering,
along with the tragedy of migrants and refugees.
And in the many wars not being won,
but more in those not even being fought,
a grim face of the future rises
like a specter wailing at a barren moon.

Sometimes, I imagine Stephanie's face about to be struck by a car running a red light.

I met Stephanie when she was living with a lover of mine who was unhappy about me choosing to stay with Ellen rather than be with her.

How far should I go back in these tellings? How much do I want my wife to know?

For my 50th birthday, Susan put together a book for me. She contacted the people in my life she could find and asked them to contribute a page. Somehow, I figured out what she was doing before it was finished. I must admit that I panicked a bit thinking about what the various women in my life might reveal to her. But it worked out, even if one did mention still wanting to have a baby with me.

In the end, I wound up with the best gift I had ever received. Not just the tributes, memories, and love, but how it integrated my past with my present life with Susan.

Stephanie and I were not lovers in the conventional sense, but time with her was like stepping into another dimension. With an aura of incense and accurate visions of what was to be, she was unlike any human being I had ever known. She wrote poems that revealed both herself and myself to me, and I was drawn to be around her, no matter the consequence.

Her presence and what it awoke in me, followed by her death, sent my life suddenly careening on a different trajectory. In retrospect, I would say it began the search for knowing more about consciousness and what else might be possible.

Ironically, in terms of my relationship with Ellen, Stephanie, the woman I could not have, was the one who made me unavailable in a way Ellen could no longer tolerate.

An absence
more profound
than a presence.
A thought, unspoken,
a feeling, unshared, now broken
become something solid
… to carry
or bury.
In death,
what could not be joined
comes back together,
like pieces, minus one,
in the game of Life.
In this reset,
what is missing
changes everything.

On the morning after the second vaccine shot, a flashlight moon lit up our bedroom as if inspecting for changes. I stretched and turned a bit, testing for soreness.

On the way home, we noticed a Saturday night, masquerading as normal, in progress.

Now, the expectant glow of a new day colors the eastern sky; one black cat sits on my lap as I write. She, as well as her sister, have grown quite accustomed to the past year's rhythms of increased attention.

Our state has lifted all COVID restrictions.

We have yet to make any plans.

Wouldn't it be nice if there were valid health reasoning and evidence behind the rush to return to what once was?

Seems we have all been released to live as we please, according to whatever light that appeals, like so many winged things urgently zapping in the night ...

April

Four million doses of the vaccine have been administered in just one day. Normal is being talked about as something that might resume in the near future. Yet hospitalizations and case numbers are increasing.

Relief
a popular word, a welcome feeling.
The vaccinated often speak of it.
As did those who, with held breath, watched
a recent historic guilty verdict.

We sigh and exhale relaxed
when dire consequences pass us by.

In golf, when one gets a drop without penalty
from some kind of obstruction, it is called relief.

When aid and assistance are provided
for those in need it is the charitable work of relief.

In art, something pronounced, even sunken,
can be brought to attention in relief.

Its origins suggest a thing raised,
and I understand now how
my own relief has lifted me.

All adults are now eligible to receive a vaccination. We are just learning about the serious health issues with what's being called long COVID, and yet about one-third of Americans are saying they probably won't get vaccinated. Hello, Vaccine Hesitancy, meet long COVID.

Susan and I have already decided we won't attempt any big trips this summer, but perhaps, once she has had both shots as well, we'll visit some friends and favorite places in Northern Arizona.

However, we are running out of projects to do around the house. If you are one of us, one who has been attracted to and gathered up sea-polished shells and other shiny things from previous travels, how cluttered is your nest? What's it like to dust?

I suspect even the most monkish have accumulated some curios and baubles, maybe even a few gewgaws and doodads. And almost everybody has at least a whatnot and thingamajig drawer, right? Can you ever find anything in there?

Here's a thought in response to seeing more families out and about, attempting to keep their kids engaged: gather up some of your gimcracks and knickknacks and start placing them in strategic spots for kids to find. Imagine, a National Treasure Hunt! They could be put up in trees, under bushes, next to flowers, near signs, on fenceposts, or near benches. Let's decorate!

Hey, if you're opposed to the littering, or just not ready to fully let go, what about some outdoor home display? That's actually what inspired this writing. A neighbor has been painting designs on a tree stump and then started placing all kinds of rocks and stones around it. Totally changed the way we experience that area. It's like visiting some monument.

And just think of all those beach vacations that have been canceled. We can let other people's kids fill up their houses with our bric-a-brac, souvenirs, and ornaments. Won't their parents be thrilled? Or we can impress our neighbors with our extraordinary collectible prowess by erecting cairns and shrines as beacons of everywhere we've been and all we ever hoped to be.

The world is changing, but it's still possible to leave smiles while walking in our own wonderlands.

Reunion

What is the weight of this thing released?
How long before the gravity of these long months
lets go its crushing grip, allows welcome lightness,
an ease again in doing what was once simple and natural
like breathing the same air as friends and family
with only a residual twinge of fear stifling the laugh
needing to burst but cannot erupt?

Something has changed; something is crippled,
but behind the altered eyes of those I care about
I recognize the hunger and the hesitancy inherent
in this moment we know not how to approach, but do,
anxiously trying to fit into old clothes and with smiles
that barely contain an enthusiasm far beyond
what such a gathering once would muster.

In those welcoming hugs, the solid joy
for what has been dearly missed,
like a life jacket tightly cinched
on those still bobbing in an ocean
of all that has been lost.

On a morning bike ride, I stopped to sit in a desert park area. I hadn't noticed a guy on the other side of some creosote bushes until he started talking to me. Surprised, I engaged for a few minutes. He had the demeanor of an old street warrior and actually reminded me of someone I knew. The exchange was friendly, but he said something that stayed with me. It was about how it was getting harder and harder to live in the cracks.

At the time, I asked him if his age was the reason.

He shook his head no and said, "There's just too many of us, and people are less friendly and less giving. Everyone's a potential threat or rival rather than someone to share even a few moments with."

I mumbled something about the pandemic changing everything but never asked him exactly what those "cracks" were. However, I too remember times when getting by with less worked because of the generosity and hospitality of others. Meaningful exchanges with strangers were more commonplace, often therapeutic. Wrong turns could be pathways to serendipity. Any conversation might reveal a missing piece of the larger, shared puzzle.

Something besides phones and the internet connected us, urged us where, when, and how to go. Friends, traveling separately, would find their way to each other in foreign cities, at crowded concerts, before cellphones, and not even marvel at how it was accomplished.

What did we know then that we have now forgotten? Of course, it didn't always proceed as planned, but sometimes the space left by one absence allowed the chance presence of another. Acceptance and Trust were frequent companions. I miss them, and their precocious offspring, Fortuity.

I still try to court them by leaving my truck behind, walking random ways without hurry or destination, but they are seldom found.

Maybe it's the smile-covering masks and distancing? Perhaps my age-slowed perception makes it harder to recognize them? Or could it be that something else today inhabits the cracks where something kinder once blossomed?

Coming home from this chance meeting, I considered the golf event I would be heading to later in the day, and how golf courses had become the place for me where strangers could still slip into my day.

I thought back to the decision to return to golf competition that came after writing about how Mayor Walkup and I had met and played together one early morning on a city golf course.

An interesting side story is what I heard from Fitz after he attended Mayor Walkup's memorial. On display, there were photos and memorabilia from his life, and at the center of them all, framed, was the article I had written about him.

Fitz phoned as soon as he could, left me a message about how writing indeed matters. He had heard me wondering about it in the past. He had in fact twisted my arm a bit to write that one for the *Arizona Daily Star*.

Earth Day:

Dear Mom,
I know I don't always take the time to fully appreciate all of the wonderful gifts you have given, including this precious life, which you have long-sustained so well.
The marvels of your beauty and your bounty are astonishing. And it so pains me to see you, or any of your offspring, suffering.
Though I can never forget how my very life depends upon yours, I really don't do enough to preserve your myriad and startling existence.
On behalf of your many children, forgive us, please.
We vow to do better for you, our mother, Earth.
Lee

Speaking of Earth Day, near the bottom of the food chain, at the bottom of the world, something of great concern is happening with a crustacean barely 2 inches long. They are krill, and their numbers are declining significantly.

I learned the why of it recently from a NOVA episode. Seasonal sea ice has been forming later, melting earlier. As a result, less of the summer algae and plankton (food source for the krill) is captured on the bottom of the ice where the krill feed.

Krill are the basis of the marine food web, which means less food for whales, squid, seals, sharks, fish, penguins, and other seabirds. In other words, ultimately, everything will be affected. So it indeed goes.

Meanwhile, we'll keep arguing about how the climate is or is not changing, whether we are responsible or not, and perhaps what should or even could be done about it.

It is both humbling and edifying to contemplate the interconnectedness of things, how much the smallest organisms matter, and how a planetary balance achieved over millennia can be toppled by the only creatures who imagine themselves separate from the whole that sustains them.

Amend Corner

From the perspective of my pandemic rocking chair,
I have measured many memories,

noted the ones most vibrant,
searched for some I know not how I lost,
stumbled from some that would explode as if groan grenades.

Those are the ones that instruct,
have led me to believe we need live long enough
to forgive and be forgiven
the burning blunders of youth.

This past year has indeed provided time enough,
even if some of the characters
trapped playing scenes in endless loops
can't be found outside my mind.

So I whisper, "Forgive me" and "I forgive you"
as if talking in my sleep,
a sound somewhere between
a prayer and a weep.

But even among those no longer living,
it is still myself most in need of my forgiving.

May

Dreams Deflating

I try not to listen
my own inner voice, choking,
warning of something dire,
a suffocating darkness ...

We live in bubbles,
even invest in them.
If there's oxygen and sustenance enough in yours
the temptation is to relax a bit, isn't it?

Who can live in endless urgency
or with constant consequence anyway?

And whatever commandments one follows,
there were none uttered regarding vaccinations,
were there?

Oh, perhaps a life of prayer and meditation,
fasting, charity, and cleanliness once sufficed,
but not for this, not for now.

Tell me, who didn't line up for immunity
from smallpox, or polio?
What's different today?

The best people I know have been punctured,
are leaking air, neglect to breathe
as if the future mattered.

Meanwhile, We the People cannot even agree
on what is good or what is bad,
let alone what is necessary for survival.

Ohio has put 5 million dollars into a vaccine lottery to encourage more people to get a shot. Deceased victims of the virus are still being stored in refrigerated trucks as morgues are overwhelmed.

Booster shots are now being recommended in the fight against the variants.

I received a phone call yesterday from the owner of a thriving local business. I wondered why he was the one to return my call for an appointment, but I knew him when he was young and energetically beginning.

He's fifty now, with family, and there was no way to cut the conversation short. His sad and heavy dread of what is unfolding needed words and company.

Those who know me and my reluctant old flip phone might be as surprised as I was that I found no excuse, just listened, shared, and cared. We agreed on wanting a future that looked as it once did from a more pleasant past, but could not agree on the simple act of a shot in the arm, even if not just for oneself but for that future and for all those who will remain in peril in it.

Not agreeing on what seemed to be obvious reminded me of meetings in the community. There were times when negotiating difficult agreements—like how to share costs more fairly—we would meet for hours every week.

On and on, heated discussions would continue. When necessary, I can be logical, patient, persuasive, and on occasion, eloquent, but even when I had actual experience or insight into an issue, it made little difference in these circles.

My fantasies of salvation in community fell apart in those meetings. What I found to be true was that people developed and became attached to their points of view in direct opposition to those they did not like, were offended by, or by those who did not include them in something they wanted in on. In other words, it digressed into a sibling culture where unhealed family issues were projected onto and then complicated what should have been practical management decisions.

And, not entirely but often, those who were drawn to a more communal way of living had more of a desire to be taken care of than to take care of common ground.

It was within this setting that my unhealthy caretaker emerged. It was simply easier for me to just get something done rather than to spend so much unproductive time with others figuring out exactly who should do what. Nobody seemed to mind. Eventually, it became a role I was compensated for, mostly in exchange for the cost of living there.

In the midst of one thing, I catch my mind beginning another. Bored or restless? Impatient or anxious? I have no clue, only wish it would stay with me all the way through.

Like between channels on a radio or tv, nothing is exactly as it should be. And in the disconnect of this shifting focus come more blunders and bruises: things break, everyone loses.

Of course, I've tried many antidotes, like allowing more time for everything, or moving with mindful breath, as if balancing on a wave ...

But no matter my intention or objection, there is a force my mind cannot long resist, an undertow pulling in an unwanted direction.

One day, perhaps, I should just let go, see what this urgent agency might know: some fast secrets under an aging sea churning, yearning to be found below.

Speaking of communal living and keeping costs down, have you noticed how house sales and prices have been rocketing? How does that happen during a pandemic, with businesses closing down and so many out of work? None of it really makes sense to me anymore.

Two shootings in New Orleans, but the one that has me writing about shootings again is the story of a 12-year-old girl shooting and wounding three at a school in Idaho. "Start them young; raise them right!"

Back in Colorado, a disgruntled boyfriend shoots and kills six at a birthday party.

And the Colonial pipeline has been hacked, shutting down nearly half of the East Coast's fuel supply. Cyber ransom wars have begun. "Work from home while disrupting the lives of others."

I've tried going back to the life remembered, but we spit each other out as if something alien. Even with such indigestion, I hang around, uncertain, considering what may be next.

It's getting harder to make or not make a plan, as one path compels, another repels.

Look, I don't understand much of what is trending, nor my own slow pacing in ever-diminishing circles, and yet I know there is much to care for and about.

Don't you sense the approaching appetites of nearly 8 billion, a crushing weight encroaching upon and scraping away a planet's preserves?

Do you follow those with a vision for how so many may get a fair share?

Or are you aligned with those who promise to protect a bit of it for you?

If I were to want both, who would I vote for, what should I support?

Pretend for a moment that vaccines were food. Who has them enough to stockpile and who goes without, even as the bodies pile up faster than they can be burned or buried?

The future no longer waits where it once belonged. It roams today, ravaging through ghost forests and acid seas.

Oh, there is no doubt we are the ones who birthed this beast. Starry-eyed, we once glowingly called it Growth.

It helped us tame everything wild, create immense wealth, but sadly now it only devours.

We slowed it for a while when the world locked down, but had to let it loose again when our only nourishment, no matter the taste, comes from its oily waste.

As the world returns to old conflicts and other previous bad behaviors, I catch myself both judging and despairing. "When will we ever learn?" I almost sing. (Singing would be good, wouldn't it?)

Then I question myself about my own impulsive negative responses, even as I blame others for theirs. And I think of my reluctance to make significant changes, my historic slowness when learning something new.

For Pete's sake (whoever he is), it took stomach surgery, a long lockdown, and a vegetarian wife to finally influence my diet towards a more body-and-planet-friendly one. Hard to recommend that model to others.

I recently read excerpts from old love letters. I kept the first drafts for some now obscure recycling and/or sentimental reasons. The collection a tribute to how ineffective, no matter the polish, my words have been. Though often misguided, I was, however, persistent. Oh, I attempted other forms of writing as well, but mostly with even less success.

Bales of paper later, and in a moment of clarity reflecting on having been a teacher of writing—with the thousands of papers graded, the hundreds of hours in conferences trying to tease out the fullness of students' thoughts— it occurred to me: I was the student, taking the same classes, over and over again. I had an aptitude and an interest, yet it took me all that time and effort to only partially inhabit and utilize this language of ours with any skill ... sigh.

Thinking of it that way, I guess I can be more patient and tolerant of the processes of others.

We will figure it all out, eventually, piece by piece, generation by generation, and at whatever pace we do. No one's urgings will significantly speed things up. So, rather than hoping to convince anyone of anything, I will keep crafting these written offerings, like love letters, to friends and strangers, far and near.

I feel compelled now to say something positive about living in a community. First, there was no better place to raise kids, with, as they say, a village watching and keeping them safe without the constant vigilance of any one parent.

There was a community mailbox where the mail delivered to the property was sorted by us. It was also the place where people would bring what they no longer needed, so an ongoing surprise exchange went on all year long. Plus, it was where we would leave each other messages on an erasable whiteboard. It was the hub and the heart of the community.

Believe it or not, potlucks are on that list. Because the site of Damian included what once had a kitchen and dining area for an entire school, we had a wonderful large place to gather, share meals, and have celebrations.

I remember a night after a few of us had been working to install a hot tub and folks were anxious to try it out. The water wasn't hot enough, so everyone went to their homes to boil water in the largest pots they had. We met back in the pool area, poured the boiling water into the almost hot tub, and then all got in. In so many ways that represented for me what was best about joining with others to rejoice in what can be accomplished together.

Just learned that there is little danger of catching this coronavirus from surface contact. It is mainly spread through inhalation. I wonder if I can feel okay touching things, perhaps stop using antiseptic wipes everywhere.

38% of us are fully vaccinated and mask mandates are being lifted all around the country.

First light. Doors and windows open, an invitation for the cool night air to come on in. Birds have begun to stir.

Bean, alert and watching, chatters at them, a sound of anxious, frustrated instinct. She has never chased let alone caught a bird, but something urges her to want to try.

Her sister, Bear, however, could care less. Her superpower is knowing when we are planning to leave the house and then quickly reminding us to first fill her bowl. We are well-trained and obey. (Okay, usually me.)

I find myself wondering which of them would do better without us?

The Bean is the cute one, almost kitten-like even after all these years, but is afraid of people, so (if she could find her way outdoors) would need to become, late in life, successful at the hunt she has thus far only imagined. Her odds, I'm afraid, would not be very good.

The Bear will take loving from anyone and is not shy about asking for what she wants. I wouldn't think it would take her long to find and train another batch of humans.

Although not as adorable as her sister, she can be a bit quirky (obnoxious). Where her sister squeaks, she shrieks. I often feel yelled at (judged) by her. Truth is, it took the two of us a long while to learn to live together peacefully.

However (and here is her main selling point), her purring pleasure from receiving affection is beyond enthusiastic. Anyone who ever coveted the ultimate lap cat would need look no further.

Conversely, Bean (sometimes, Squeaky), took years before trusting a lap. She and I both have intimacy issues. (Remember me? I'm the one who is just learning to live with my wife.) Perhaps that is why we have found more ways to play together, or to enjoy just sitting side by side.

Time with the Bear takes a certain kind of patient and attentive commitment. Susan's temperament and routines are better suited for Bear's purr-athons, so, typically, they will be found in close contact with each other.

More often than not, Bean and I are content to watch the outside world from separate perches, not needing much from each other, but, I like to think, with some mutual appreciation.

And if we're lucky, we'll never have to know a life alone out there, no matter our ancient inclinations.

A recent mapping of dark matter is challenging current notions of the universe. Some scientists are alarmed at the overturning of the Newton-Einstein apple cart; some are excited at the possibilities of discovering something grand. Most, however, want there to be underlying immutable laws of existence.

But what if there are not?

What if the connective tissue of creation is consciousness that can change its mind?

We puny humans want to know things with certainty, like is the universe endlessly expanding with galaxies accelerating rapidly away from each other, or are the enormous gravity wells of black holes gobbling up stellar material in an inevitable contraction?

Does any of this matter? Do humans have some, however small, part to play in this cosmic drama?

I ask myself, which way am I going? Towards or away from others? Which pull is stronger? Perhaps in the process of making up our minds we are mirroring something both immensely and microscopically similar to us.

Oneness, whether we like it or not, is like that, is capable of encompassing it all.

This particular meditation, especially about moving towards or away from others in a pandemic seems quite appropriate. Even before that, leaving the community felt like a directional shift for me, but I've certainly not been accelerating, anywhere.

In fact, the contraction into home space is what is most apparent. Am I becoming a black hole?

But can I be expanding inwardly? Is that a universal equivalent of something yet unnamed? Isn't there speculation that black holes could be passageways to alternate universes?

So, even as I collapse into myself, might I be growing into somewhere else?

Accompanying Susan, I was able to attend an early celebration of the Event Horizon Telescope's success. It took place, fittingly, at the Flandrau Science Center and Planetarium. The world team that utilized the far ends of our planet to capture a clear image of a black hole was there, either in person or on the screen, sharing the challenges and excitement of their accomplishment.

Once again, I was in awe of the collective genius and determination of scientists. Around them, I had the sense they were the part of the universe learning to watch and know itself.

With the weather warming, I take a moment to appreciate what I did not have to do this season: get the assortment of evaporative coolers at Damian ready for summer. It was always the most dreaded of tasks. There are 23 of them, different makes and models, each requiring some specific kind of attention and maintenance depending upon age and material (metal or fiberglass units).

I tried many ways over the years to tackle this massive project. There was a time when the community had a monthly Work Day, and I would attempt to direct teams to take on some of the grunt aspects of cleaning, sanding, and scraping to prepare for exterior spray painting and the asphalt-based coating of the interior pans. The quality of work was uneven, but it helped.

My son and the sons of other residents helped me from time to time, but none were eager to return to the roofs every season for fussing with these beasts, installing aspen pads or the giant treated cardboard ones for the more modern units.

The water hook-up alone would take me days of connecting and repairing copper lines, replacing valves and fittings that leaked or stopped working altogether. Up and down, up and down the ladders I'd leave strategically around the property.

Every year my goal was to finish earlier in the year and not get stuck putting in long hot days once everyone was clamoring for relief from the heat. I also learned to pace myself with how much I did in any one day. The job was going to take a certain amount of time no matter what, but if I started in March, for example, I could be done in April without sunstroke or heat exhaustion. If one survives youthful exuberance and impatience, there is always a better way of doing things.

Yeah, I know, it wasn't exactly mapping stars, but that's not what's troubling me looking back. I want to feel more relief than I am today for not having to do it anymore. Why is that not happening? Is that the hidden disappointment in retirement? Not doing something does not give lasting pleasure. Cessation of a burden only provides temporary reprieve. So, do I need to keep finding something else I don't like doing and then quit, over and over again?

There were some things, given enough practice and patience, I thought I would have become much better at than I did, but one by one I've let them all go as my body dictated a different plan.

For a long time though, golf and sex were two activities that defied the pattern, for even as the body demanded less frequency, overall course management kept improving. Sure, distance matters, but the short game, oh the short game …

No, I haven't given up entirely, but if you'd ask me today what skills of mine might still be advancing, I'd have to say only the indoor sports of writing and cooking (sans barbecue).

Yes, there are similarities between these two as well. Mainly, they're about choosing quality ingredients/words, then mixing, preparing, and presenting them in tasteful combinations. I find nourishment in both as each process allows creativity, craft, and intuition to play together. I find pleasure in, even learn from, that.

Gestalt & Pepper

After a lifetime of reading in and eating out
(consumption as distraction perhaps),
I now compose and cook daily
(Composition as giving back?).

All that time filling up something
part-reservoir, part-laboratory.

And now words, tastes, ingredients, ideas
flow, come together in a surprising mix,
revealing a life's gestalt,
a sprinkle of pepper and poetry.

Only one other sits at this table,
samples the day's combinations.
Sometimes smiling, she might empty a plate,
though never asks for more.

Then, these small audience postings ...
no reservation needed, but no menu either.

At their own tables, a handful of regulars, a few tourists,
maybe a wandering storm chaser, a looky-loo or two.

Some react, some even reply;
others I'll never know stopped by.

Not complaining, or asking for anything,
just reflecting on a reality unexpected,

this life I am still trying to embrace
with what for me might pass as grace.

Eventually, I'll learn the details of her death. For now, there's just her picture and the few words that shocked, informing us she was gone.

Not a make-plans-with friend, but someone whose similar interests and Tucson trajectories brought us together here and there through the years. Over meals and drinks at the bars at Feast and Pastiche especially, we learned how she and Frank lived as Susan and I long did: next door to each other, rather than in the same dwelling.

So, there was a connection between kindred and literate couples on an unusual path. And we enjoyed chatting it up over excellent meals at these fine locally owned establishments. Perhaps we toasted and celebrated each other's good sense in attempting to fashion lives that truly nourished and matched their occupants. Certainly, welcome company.

We are on the verge of returning to some of those places. We might even sit at the bar again, with, of course, some space between others. If so, I imagine one empty stool will seem different than all the others ... I'll feel you there, Jeanne.

Just a few nights after learning about Jeanne, several of the old bar gang did gather again at Feast. For me and Susan it was our return to indoor dining. Bill and Debra were there. Ann showed up. Jack and Mary Lou as well. Lisa was behind the bar, just like in our heyday. Lew and Cliff, co-founders of what Lew called his Algonquin Circle, were not healthy enough to join us.

We used to meet every Tuesday night. The entire bar was reserved for us. We'd share bottles of wine, movie titles, and bring books for each other. The conversation was always lively.

Over a year of tape had been edited from our collective reel, and no one knew exactly where to pick up the conversation on this first evening back at the bar. It stopped and started with alternating levity and sincerity. We were all Rip Van Winkles wondering what had changed while we were gone.

Had anyone heard about Jerry? No one knew. We all had known that Fern had passed away, and she was toasted along with Jeanne.

I saw worry lines around eyes that seemed to plead for something jolly; eyes that offered a hesitant understanding for anything softly spoken. I felt my own rust and neuroses, but also a grateful caring. It extended to the familiar faces of staff and other former regulars.

And there were blunders and apologies from staff getting reacquainted with the rush of others' demands. A couple who never had the need before now had their dog with them. I watched the proprietor, Doug Levy's brow furrow with each bark. I didn't ask about any change in policy. He had just reopened his dining room and was sharing his concern about finding people to work, a question rippling through restaurants. There was, however, no shortage of customers.

We learned about trips planned, graduations, weight gained or lost, kids back home, ominous diagnoses, happy recoveries, and about all the strange, invisible ways our lives remained intertwined and connected, whether we left our houses or not.

Summer was almost upon us. Historically, a tough time for local restaurants. In previous years, Susan and I would support ones we would hate to see close. Often, in near-empty dining rooms was when we'd get to know the owners and employees.

It's hard to say today what this summer will bring and how we will respond. Maybe it's time for me to wait on tables. Susan had done it. I never did.

My louder self emerges and calls out, "Hey Doug, want to teach an old dog some new tricks?"

He shakes his head and says that would be the last thing either one of us would want.

More shootings in Chicago and then another at a rail yard in San Jose, but it is the one in Miami that has me breaking my vow to stop writing about gun violence. Three men wearing ski masks, armed with assault rifles and handguns, randomly spray bullets at a concert crowd, wounding twenty-three and killing three. Has this become a thing to do with your pals? How does that conversation even begin? "What do you want to do tonight?"

It's as if we are now living in an extreme violence video game.

No matter how early, how dark it is when I get up, she is always waiting, eager to greet, ready to eat. To keep her from crying and waking Susan, her first meal is my priority number one.

For the past few mornings, there's been no urgency, no appetite. We've been concerned. Yesterday, an x-ray revealed a tumor.

Of the two 12-year-old cats, Miss Squeaky Bean has been the forever young one: enthusiastic, playful, curious about everything. How sad, strange, and jarring for that to have suddenly changed.

During the past month or so, I didn't recognize her more frequent insistence for attention as some instinctual last hurrah. Still, I welcomed her desire to sit by me more often, certainly engaged with her more, but, not knowing what I do today, perhaps gave her less than I would now if only she'd join me again in the various games and contact rituals we've fashioned …

I'm thinking of getting her a harness, taking her out into the world she has known so little of, hoping to find some pleasant routines we can share towards the end of our time together.

June

Chased birds with our eyes
Sitting out with dying cat
Wagged each other's tails

So many things I've looked for, touched, tasted, even consumed without ever being satisfied for long. Hungers can be like that.

Today, I shop more than search, cook more than order, care more than desire.

Isn't "home" always where we ultimately long to be? If not, perhaps it hasn't been found yet?

Even nomads travel with the familiar, the ones who allow home to be something mobile.

We must belong to something: a landscape, an ecosystem, a community of creatures.

Under the influence of marriage to a gentle soul, I grew up to be someone who includes cats as family. And now a member of our family is leaving, taking such a sweet piece of home with her.

No, there's nowhere else I need to be, just here by her side, purring love and gratitude together.

You know that battle everyone loses, that invincible foe who will not bargain, will make no deal. Even those who do grim deeds in his stead are not spared his icy grip. No talisman, prayer, nor medicinal charm can long keep him at bay. Run, hide, fight, or surrender—it does not matter one iota—no one survives.

And so I watch our cat go about her last days: eating and drinking just enough to fuel her own movement; finding comfortable spots to rest; welcoming the touch and closeness of her people.

Every now and then she will disappear to a place we've yet to discover. Not for long, but enough to remind me she is on her own journey, and to respect it.

There's something of acceptance and appreciation in this time with her. It's not just what I imagine is her peace with the process, but what reflecting on her life illuminates for me.

She spent most of her life inside the same structure and yet never seemed to bore of it. She remained curious even of the familiar, enthusiastic about the same activities, and easily found pleasure playing alone or with one of us. She still has no problem asking for what she wants, or changing her mind about it.

Yeah, one could do worse than to have someone like that around, displaying what both living and dying can look like.

Sitting together during her last hours, thinking she was asleep, I carefully started to stand up when her tail wrapped around my arm and held me there.

In all our years playing together, she had never done anything like that before. I got the message and relaxed back into the glide chair. Her purring resumed.

I had just whispered to her my love and appreciation for sharing life together. Perhaps this was her reply.

Yeah, I know, we all tell ourselves stories, but what else can we do? At least this one sweetens my sadness.

Her expectant eyes
And those heart-opening squeaks
With me forever

We both had secret tumors. Mine burst and was removed. Hers stayed hidden too long.

I have a bum knee that swelled up just days after we learned we were soon to lose her. She then started limping as well, her only sign of discomfort.

Have I been living with my feline totem guide?

Somehow, the way it worked out, I was having my knee drained and getting cortisone while she was first sedated, then euthanized. Both of us being punctured twice, simultaneously, across town from each other, but receiving two very different forms of relief.

Although I've had my share of loss, I have seldom been present at the moment of death. My friend Ira has assisted with the Jewish ritual washing and preparation of the dead for burial. He has always been more hands on in life than I—but hands on in death too?!

One cold touch of an empty body is enough for me to know the essential component is missing—a discarded garment reminding us that its occupant is gone.

I like the notion of the animating spirit merging back into the source. Where else can it go? Everything recycles.

And we are left with the shell, to do with as we believe is right.

In our case, Susan (bless her eco-friendly heart), found someone who not only came to our home, but then took our little friend for aquamation (if you don't know, look it up), so that which is of the earth will be returned to the earth.

I also like to think that something of my four-legged doppelgänger will hang around, at least as long as my own neurons are firing.

Out among the morning movers: all those pedaling, boarding, rolling, ambulating by various means and at whatever pace; all squeezing their motion between first light and the rising desert fireball. It's crowded now along the Rillito corridor pathway, but soon it will be empty, deserted for the day's duration.

When I was younger, I'd ride my bicycle midday, shirtless, reveling in the solitary heat. Then I'd cap it off with an outside shower and a pool plunge.

Summer was a different kind of okay then than it is now. I miss that body of mine. Oh well, things change.

Back indoors, the last of the six cats Susan and I will have together is eyeing me suspiciously. Yeah, that's our deal—no more pets! At least not until we both agree we are not interested in traveling anymore.

So, until then, this four-legged neurotic critter is it. We certainly saved the worst for last, but I'll be kind and say no more.

"Okay Bear, yes, you can be lovable. No one's going anywhere. Go back to sleep."

Where was I? Right, contemplating what we might be done with while considering what's next:

- Is it time to have just one vehicle?
- What about a place without stairs?
- How much stuff do we really need?
- What else can we do for others, for the environment?
- Do we even need to own another place to live?
- What about drought and this blasting heat?
- Shouldn't we leave while we can?
- Is there a climate on this planet where we'd both be mostly comfortable?

I guess it all comes down to this: How much living and loving can we squeeze through the window still open to us?

It is Flag Day. As I write this, it is estimated that some 33 million shots are being administered daily around the globe. That's somewhere between the populations of Texas and California every day, yet still less than 21% of the world's human inhabitants have received at least one dose of a COVID-19 vaccine. (I grapple with imagining billions of people.)

I was not by a long shot one of the first here to get mine, but was fully vaccinated by the end of March. These world numbers remind me of how good we still have it in these sometimes-United States. In comparison, less than 1% of people living in low-income countries have even received one dose.

If there is a flag I'd like to wave today, it would be a world flag, perhaps one of George Boeree's designs.

I finally used the last basket filter from my long-defunct coffee maker and can now allow myself the right style for cone dripping!

Susan and I both use everything we have in every possible way before discarding or replacing. Frugal 'R' Us.

I want to say I stopped shaving rather than replacing my old electric shaver, but that's only partially accurate. Last summer's trip to the hospital was the actual impetus for my display of hairy gray.

Almost made it a year bearded, but Susan treated me to a state-of-the-art Braun precision foil shaver and I'm young again! (Note on mirror: Objects can appear older the closer you look.)

And there wasn't a conscious connection, but I recently spent time with a woman who had lost her partner of over forty years, then came home and shredded a to-do list of uncompleted tasks.

Just yesterday, after years of tinkering with, babying, and putting up with failing blinds, we had a guy come by with samples of new ones. We did not pick the bargain ones. And to even get to this moment, I had to resist all thoughts of doing it myself. That has always been my first choice—not just for the economics, but for the self-esteem of competency and the satisfaction of accomplishment.

It felt like an extravagant luxury to turn this project over to a professional. Perhaps it's an acknowledgment of what's changing in me, of what I do or do not want to wrestle with anymore. I've never liked working on the strings and chains of blinds, and it's not something I need to overcome. But there's more to it.

We have mother-daughter neighbors. The daughter is older than I am. She manages to get her large trash bin just outside her garage door. It took me a while to realize she was counting on someone else to move it to the street.

We've never spoken about it, but I have become one who moves it there and back. She doesn't know, doesn't ask, but depends on this invisible cooperation. I have become oddly attached to this silent arrangement.

For many years, I was on call to solve the problems of others. Much of my own interests were set aside in all the crises, so to be anonymous but still be able to assist another feels right to me.

Somehow, writing those words moved me to the files where I kept a folder, "Letters and Proclamations." It is the collection of what I had sent around the community over the years, either attempting to inspire a change in the behavior of others or to apologize for my own.

Reading the various chants and cries, the pattern was clear, and increasingly more desperate as my frustration grew. This one was titled "Reflections" and delivered as a holiday blessing in December 1998:

When I was younger, I romanticized about everything, but especially relationships and community living. Today, I still have some pride about living in community, but it's more like how one wears a Purple Heart.

Perhaps I will never fully be at peace with ongoing practices that can't seem to sort plastic from tin, that leaves water running full blast unattended, that uses energy selfishly and unconsciously, that borrows tools or newspapers that are never returned, that makes or leaves messes for others to clean, that is quick to take offense and to offend, but slow to heal and mend.

Which is all to say, I will never be at peace with myself, because everything that exists in the collective exists in me, and when my diligence and attention lapse, I become what I despise in others.

So, what is it that brings about this Jekyll-Hyde transformation? I can name it in myself. It's when I become more important than us.

But when I look through the lens of what is good for the community, which includes those I love and one I am sworn to nurture, I am forced to look further than my lazy or impulsive need of the moment. That's when I have a chance to come from a place of genuine we-ness instead of Lee-ness.

Individually, we are all capable of ingenuity, beauty, and compassion: our lives and homes abound with ample evidence and demonstrations of our talents. I have always celebrated such accomplishments, but my greatest joys here come when we have truly collaborated on a project.

I know what work I can do alone, and it's not as much or as inspired as what gets done when I join with even one other.

This year my holiday prayer is we come to accept our negative and positive inclinations, and we come to see our neighbor as someone who already is who he or she is, not as someone in need of our persuasion, insight, fixing, or healing.

I don't know what Paradise might wait beyond acceptance, but for me today, acceptance would be enough.

My hippie counterpart self, Twisted Eel, in his lost memoir, *Dreams of the Snake Pit*, put it this way: "Sometimes, I think the world is divided between those who need to drink coffee and those who need not to drink coffee."

July

Stalker

We're tired of you,
never wanted you,
told you so,
changed our lives
to avoid and be rid of you,
but still you lurk.

We hear you've changed
in your search for ways
to slip through our defenses,
but we just want to move on
without you around.

You take advantage
of our clueless relatives
to bypass the restraining orders,
the vaccines designed
to keep you away.
Can a virus smirk?

Here's a "Duh!" for you: States with low vaccination rates have 3x the COVID rate than the states with high vaccination rates. Vermont is the place to be with 66% vaccinated and the lowest number of cases.

Meanwhile, here in sunny and bright Arizona, the governor issued a decree that schools can no longer force unvaccinated students to be quarantined. Are we fighting the wrong battles at the worst time? Seems like it to me.

I give up. It just keeps getting weirder out there. I just read about a stand-off between police and a militia in Wakefield, Massachusetts. No one was hurt, but 11 heavily armed men between the ages of 17 and 40 were arrested.

They were part of a group who do not believe themselves bound to U.S. law or obligated to pay taxes. It is estimated there are hundreds of thousands of them. Who knew? I just don't get out very much anymore and am feeling less inclined to do so all the time.

Meanwhile, there were 51 shootings over the weekend in New York. The governor has declared gun violence a disaster emergency, which will allow 138.7 million dollars into gun violence intervention and prevention programs. I wonder what those will look like. There are a few things I'm pretty sure of, like a person whose needs are met is less likely to shoot up a crowd or strap on a suicide bomber's vest than one who is not well-fed and content with life.

I'll be curious to hear if such underlying issues are addressed with these programs.

Meanwhile, Chicago (always second but trying harder) had only 41 shootings over the weekend.

Is this how we now celebrate the 4th of July? We are free to kill each other.

When I traveled overseas to less-visited locations and told anyone I was from Chicago, often the first response was to pretend to spray bullets from an imaginary machine gun and say, "Al Capone."

I'd nod and say, "Yes, that was once Chicago but long ago."

What can any of us say today about our country?

Waking up to a lovely morning enticed me to attempt walking nine holes again. Wrapped my recently drained knee, grabbed my lightweight Sunday bag with six clubs, and off I went.

The sky was sending mixed messages: spots of sunshine, but darkening clouds. Steamy, yet still in the seventies; it felt okay to be outside.

Early solo golf on an empty back nine is a moving meditation for me. I try a variety of swings while watching the desert wake up, striving more to shape a shot rather than to clobber one.

I was pleased to not feel hindered by any swelling or inflammation and was mostly satisfied by the height and the accuracy of the ball flights. Maybe I can still play this game, I thought.

Then, on the 14th hole (par 4, 400 yards), perfect timing in my swing released an unexpected booming drive, and I needed only an 8-iron for my approach to the green.

I imagined a low draw that would bounce in front and roll up. And it did just that, but also went in the hole. An eagle! What a waste. No game, no score, no witness. Oh well, I enjoyed it anyway.

I wanted to continue, but those dark clouds were now everywhere, and a light rain began. I told myself that as long as there was no lightning, I'd keep on.

It was sweet and refreshing to walk in the light sprinkle. Seemed the right thing to be doing with The Open Championship beginning this very morning in the UK.

By the time I teed off on the 18th hole, I was pretty sure I was going to be soaked, but no point quitting then. I had to walk in anyway, so might as well do it swinging.

My third shot missed the par-5 green, and I was tempted to just leave the ball and head for my truck. The sky was black, and the rain was picking up, but I had to finish, and did.

I reached the truck, did a quick clean up, and then came the first crack of lightning. Closed up the back, got in the cab, and then, instantly, the downpour! Yeah, timing—in golf and in life—is everything.

Luckily, we have a garage so that I could get into the house without battling the storm. The wind powered rain sideways, slamming waves of water into our windows, finding and forcing its way around glass and frame into our home.

Susan and I battled back, side by side, with mop and towels—not exactly laughing, but not cussing either—just responding efficiently together to the task at hand (and by foot as needed).

Afterwards, with washing machine filled and running, we sat for a light meal, a bottle of wine, taking in the raw beauty of a cloud-drenched sky coloring above a grateful desert. There would be time for window repair and maintenance later, but right then we just savored the view, the peace, and the quiet joy of sharing it together.

The next morning, I inspected the exterior and discovered that the several thousands of dollars we'd spent to have our house painted was the problem. The untrained crew had caulked over the weep holes in the windows. Are you kidding me?! This is why I do things myself!

And now I'm up again on ladders cutting out the caulk, sanding, and re-painting.

(to be)
… even with matter
and maintenance

My body is complaining about what I just asked it to do. Hey, it's not my fault, I tell it. I'm just adapting and responding to what is necessary, and to the incompetence of others.

When still teaching, my best class experiences came when I first prepared in great detail, then promptly abandoned the plan. (This is not the same as "winging it".)

It was about being receptive, allowing the actual combination of humans in the room to shape genuine and relevant pathways to the material. Such trust grew from confidence in the work of preparation. That's what made leading through listening possible.

A similar challenge has emerged today between wanting to maintain cherished routines while desiring the illumination from letting them go.

How to hold a thing while transcending the need of it?

Can this be true of being in a body as well?

It might explain why it begins to shrink even as it needs more care.

When young, growth came in spurts.
Perhaps we give it back in similar fashion—
surrendering size and desire—
simultaneously letting go of body
while finally learning to be in it.

All of the above is my obscure side of the argument about why we should sell this place and move where the responsibility of care belongs to another. I might be more ready than Susan. She's younger, more fit, healthier, and comes from good genes.

For goodness' sake, her mom, Joan, almost 87, is still working as the baker in her son's restaurant!

Every summer before the pandemic, we'd visit Susan's family and the Bemus Point Inn on Lake Chautauqua. It's no secret; it's the best breakfast in Western New York.

I love Susan's family.

We missed going there last summer and we won't be there this summer either. Damn this pandemic!

Although neither of us want to get on a plane with these new variants—Alpha, Beta, and Delta that I know of—and conflicting information about the usefulness of masks against them, we have convinced ourselves that infrequent indoor dining is okay. No, it's not scientific, but deprivation can alter or suspend one's better judgment.

The other night, feeling spontaneous in a way we haven't since prior to the pandemic, we went out, without a reservation, to a fancy foothills spot. And like in the good old days, we sat at the bar for dinner.

As if by magic, before our food arrived, in walked Mister P.

Our most welcome surprise in seeing him requires some explanation.

It was many years ago that Susan and I first saw him at a nearby table, savoring wine with a solitary flair, and became intrigued. Then, we began to notice him at other fine-dining favorites. We seemed to have similar tastes and rhythms.

We heard servers greet him by name and so referred to him in our speculations as Mister P. He caught us watching him once, which started the ritual of smiling and nodding to acknowledge the awareness of each other's presence in various establishments.

One night, I was watching some sporting event at a restaurant bar without Susan when he came in and sat beside me. It was purely coincidental, but now there was no way to not introduce ourselves to each other. Thus, the exchange of names and history commenced. His worldliness was earned through tireless travel, and he had stories from everywhere. He was delightful company.

I even forgave him for being a devoted Georgia Bulldog fan. He was, after all, fond of the Arizona Wildcats. And we liked the same kind of red wines.

Susan and I recognized something of interest about him long before a word was ever spoken. People must sense the essence of another by various means: some observed, some unknown. I like that. It speaks to me of belonging to a larger family, of the possibility for people to transcend their smaller tribe and to make connections across arbitrary borders.

This night at Vivace he joined us at the bar. Big smiles! Glasses were clinked. We had all survived and had returned to something we had long enjoyed.

Then, another couple he knew joined us. Introductions led to stories. Turned out that one of them, Tom, grew up in my old neighborhood of Rogers Park. We had walked similar paths for a very long time before winding up in this revelatory moment together.

Life was once like this. It was good to feel the familiar embrace again. Not that it signaled a return to what was lost, but rather because it offered a glimpse of the agency that can still help us make sense of things as it weaves our lives back together.

On our way home, there was a lighter and more joyous quality in our interaction. I guess other people really do make a difference.

At home, for whatever reason, I turned on the television. I hadn't been paying much attention to the Olympics, but I was captivated by Simone Biles announcing she needs to withdraw for mental health reasons.

I can't help but think she is channeling something for so many by stepping forward and speaking her truth. No one has ever been as good as she is at what she does. Will her words have more meaning as a result?

Simone

Bounding, twisting, amazing ...
Until the games became weights,
and attention, gravity.

When look at me
became
look at what went wrong,
what then is winning?

What has the accumulation of metal or medal
ever healed?

Only in letting go,
only in saying no
can I give you
your failure back,
can my success be
to find my own way
to yes.

August

What is not burning
is flooding.

Robert Frost had it at least half right
when he wondered if the world would end
in fire or in ice.

His prophetic finger pointed squarely
at the human emotions of desire and hate
as the probable culprits.
Hard to argue that,
but may I add ignorance to the list,
Father Frost?
It is neither hot nor cold,
just stubborn and slow.

With everything known
available at a glance,
we distract ourselves
with games and jokes,
with hype and hoax.

Meanwhile, only everything
needed to survive
is threatened daily.

Oh, we react quickly to revive
what has fallen,
but return to paralyzing debate,
while we dumbly await
the next crushing blow,
a firestorm's inferno,
the rushing flow of waters …
so much it seems
endangers or slaughters.

During the last week, there have been an average of 107,000 new cases of the coronavirus daily—the highest level in six months. 93% are from the Delta variant.

So, what news is bothering you?
Never mind, don't tell me.
Yeah, I'm tired too …
We've all had enough, huh?

A young man was at our home yesterday installing blinds. He was conscientious, careful, thorough, pleasant—and unvaccinated.

Without arguing, I asked him why. Inquiry is almost always the best place to begin. Knowing he had to return to finish the job (and get paid), I gave him some homework: learn the history of successful vaccination programs from the past. (Teachers never really retire, do they?)

Oh, I don't expect to change his or anyone's mind. I'm just trying to understand where it all went so wrong. I remember when still at Pima College and thinking something was broken in the educational pipeline. It seemed every year students were less prepared, which exerted a steady downward pressure on any challenging curriculum.

Teaching argument, however, was one of my motivations to continue as long as I did in that less-than-lucrative field. I chose to emphasize the classical foundation, which was about first finding common ground. In other words, understanding different points of view and not mistaking your own intensity of feeling as a measure of being right. I actually gave more credit for evidence of deeply considering rather than just refuting the opposition.

My motto was "Changing your mind is learning, not losing." I was also notorious for not spelling out assignments upfront or providing a detailed syllabus. Sometimes, one should sneak up on things quietly.

We started the semester sharing personal stories. This genuinely introduced the students to each other and also allowed future themes for more expository writing to be extracted consciously from narrative. As a result, an awareness of the connection between thought and experience developed. Some students would come to the realization that they had never examined how they had come to certain positions. In fact, some even realized that they had inherited them!

By the time we got to argument, we understood a little of how experience had shaped belief. Before finishing the actual writing of this major paper, each student would outline his or her topic in a class circle and then take notes from the resultant debate and discussion. After taking all of that in, I encouraged, when possible, to find integrative solutions for their conclusions.

I'd like to think that along the way from there some lights went on, some conflicts were avoided, compromises were made, problems were solved, but I'll never know for sure. Just like I won't know if this young man will really consider how better off we are without smallpox or polio, or how unfounded opinion has clouded centuries of progress.

Yeah, I'm tired. But you know what? Let's keep talking. Let's keep trying.

A Moment's Majesty

I long to move freely in a world that was,
walk again with a younger you,
remembering this perilous future we were able to flee.

Oh, to dine again on the outskirts of, and within, beautiful notions
we would now know were not to last, were never meant to,
and so would savor them all the more.

I met a man once who made a travel film
of places that were no more ...
as if some shell would close behind him,
swallowing the polished reality he had just tasted.

Left my refuge twice yesterday
for the company of intoxicating men.
First, to imagine what still might be.
Then, to mark the way for embracing despair.

This morning's sunrise
announced on the faces of passing clouds
arrived as if it had never been here before,
as if this day would be unlike any other,
as if anything and everything
has always, is always, and will always
be possible.

It's not only new cases of the Delta variant that are rising, but drug overdoses as well. We all know stressors are increasing and wonder how this nightmare will ultimately play out.

Sometimes, stories or movies help. I recently watched *The Seventh Cross*, a 1944 black and white starring Spencer Tracy and Swedish actress Signe Hasso. It's set in Nazi Germany. Seven prisoners escaped from a concentration camp. The commandant erected seven crosses to hang them on as captured. The first one taken and killed became the invisible narrator of this compelling tale.

Spencer's character, George, was the last surviving one and was aided by local members of the German underground and other good people. In fact, Toni (Signe Hasso) only met George because she worked in his last refuge. She knew she could turn him in and receive a considerable reward, but did not. Eventually, a spark between them turned into something more, which allowed Spencer's final speech to her, hours before he would board a vessel to freedom.

Toni asked him where he would go and what he would do. He said he had a debt to pay. She thought he meant he wanted to exact revenge on those who imprisoned him and caused the death of his friends. Here was his response:

"No, it's to the people who healed me. There are some whose names I'll never know. I have a debt. Not only for their help, but for what they taught me." (As he spoke, we heard the invisible narrator list the names.)

"Today, I know something I never knew before in my life. I know that no matter how cruelly the world strikes at the souls of men, there is a god given decency in them that will come out, if it gets half a chance, and that's the hope for the human race, and that's the faith we must cling to ... the only thing that will make our lives worth living."

Amen.

The world has emerged from many dark times. And, in preparing to write this, I read something else that gave me hope: suicide rates decreased after 9/11. Seems there is a history of increased togetherness and support when we share a crisis. When will we get there?

Endless Love

Prone to dinginess, then repulsed by it.
Some ancient issue with darkness and dungeons perhaps.

But if we've lived before, I think it best not to know of it.
Just allow the relentless progression of evolution to figure it out.

Attention on now is all that is required.
Let the scholars compile, study the appendix,
while you inhabit your own novel.

Btw, how's your other appendix doing?
Seems we can live without one of those as well,
but once they were more essential.

Much of life is hard to digest
and our ways change faster than DNA.

In a multiverse such as ours
everything possible,

has happened/is happening/will happen
somewhere sometime.

And what I wanted to whisper in your ear
so many lifetimes ago
echoes in the dreams of our descendants
who laugh and play in a reality
we might have imagined together.

Why do I want to know how a story
that cannot end turns out?

Would it change my next step
if I knew how to get there from here
with a once upon a time you
and a me long forgotten?

The 1-2 punch of the pandemic and my stomach surgery seems to have forever altered how I move, eat, and fill my days. So, how does one adequately acknowledge such an occurrence?

Well, I marked my surgery anniversary last week by having another one. Oh, nothing serious: an outpatient procedure on my more troubled leg, just to have the thrill of surgeon's steel slicing through skin again ...

Ah! The smell of one's own blood in the morning!

Those who know me might be scratching their heads. "Lee?! Embracing medical attention?! WTF?!"

Yeah, I've been one of those who has avoided doctors, shunned hospitals, and closed his eyes during film scenes involving scalpels. But, hey, we've all changed in the past year, huh?

Like most of us, I've spent lots of quality time with my own demons: the one who urges another drink; the one afraid of aging and becoming helpless; the one who wonders how to have people in his life without losing his life to them; and most of all, the compulsive controlling one.

We have found something that we all are in agreement about: to preserve this vessel we share.

Of course, there's still the anxious mind to mend. If only I could identify the inner imp that keeps turning on the news and convince that masochistic little shit to cease and desist!

Stepping Lively

An unexpected spring in my step
like a sudden change of season
exposed what had been dormant,
unknown in me.

What had been forgotten,
left seeds ...

Today, in this lightness of motion,
a first growth sprouted through the icy grip
that held me fast this long year past.

In a world shut down, staggering back with loss,
then forth with caution, or recklessness,
the distinction between what I could no longer do
and what just should not be done
blurred.

It's not that I miss what was once my stomach,
rather the freedom from not knowing how fragile I am,
how flawed we are, how fleeting everything.

I do miss his island music, her soothing voice,
the curious looks and squeaks of one small being,
and all the easy laughter gatherings
with people at places that are no more.

In that brief glimpse this morning
of a bygone trust and agility,

I remembered what it was once like to move
in a world I had yet to learn to fear.

Five years ago, Susan and I were sitting at a combined concert of Southern Arizona choruses. I might have whispered to her that would be something we could do together. We were already thinking about what life would be like when we both were retired.

A few months later, we were at a welcoming for Desert Voices. There was a solo voice check for proper placement in a section. I asked if there were a shower stall I could use. There wasn't, but I was deemed a bass anyway.

Susan is the musical one. When I first met her, she was preparing for a piano recital. Since then, she's been in a clarinet choir, picked up the guitar again, and started on a ukulele. I did sing in a choir as a kid, and I can change radio stations with the best of them.

Still, it was a blast. Susan would rehearse with me at home with the piano to help me learn my parts. The bass line was definitely not the melody, and I do not read music. We participated in several concerts for two and half years before the pandemic shut things down.

Desert Voices is a LGBTQIA+ chorus filled with some of the most beautiful and fun human beings I have ever been around. Now, the chorus is getting ready to start up again, with special singing masks of all things. With all that I've gone through health-wise, I'm bowing out. Susan will continue.

Rehearsals have always been on Wednesday nights, and we often would not get home until 10 p.m. That has become exceedingly late for me. Besides, Wednesday nights are Men & Martinis up at the club, a pleasure I've foregone for the sake of rehearsing.

I am sad to not be able to do both.

A strange thing happened at one of the last rehearsals I attended. My section was done, and I stepped outside the building for some reason. I was surprised by a voice from nowhere calling my name. Then, a woman stepped out of the shadows and introduced herself, telling me I was her teacher at Pima College.

I remembered her story, told to me long ago by her sister: She was afflicted with an incurable disease that was shutting down her liver and kidneys; she was near death; and then, I learned that night from her, she spent five years in a wheelchair.

Now at the age of 41, helping asylum seekers, she was full of joy and gratitude for life.

Susan, along with other sopranos and altos, was still inside rehearsing. I had thought to be in there listening while waiting for them to finish.

Not sure exactly why I went out at that precise moment, but in talking to her I felt that special energy that weaves us all together at work.

She reminded me of a gift I gave her. I am still unwrapping the gift of her presence, of the persistence of life, and what to do with second chances. She was given one. I've more recently been given my own.

Love's Inventory

Is it more what I've seen or have heard
that has moved me to better grasp the love word?
Sometimes a smell can attract as well as repel.
But if I had to choose
between a taste and an embrace,
all I need know is whose.

September

Cilantro & Laughter

There's more of each
in a life with her.

More music and flowers,
plants and cats,
and healthy habits
I would not have without her.

A simple neighborhood walk with her
can become something revelatory
in her excitement for growing things.

She's the one who will catch an insect
in the house to take outside.

Like her diet, nothing must die
for her to live.

There is little waste
in this life we've fashioned,
yet there are containers
of every sort, for saving what
we do not always know.

But there might be a use for anything,
and nothing is done until the last drop
is gone.

It's how I feel about this life with her
in these containers of ours
that hold all the pleasure,
all the love I've ever wanted
as we strive to find our way together
until the last drops of a life well loved
are finally gone …

I used to keep track of how long certain tasks at Damian would take—billable hours—every expenditure of energy somehow compensated. If not cash or fitness, pleasure was an acceptable return on my investment.

Back when things made sense to me.

Nowadays, I volunteer, take care of our home as I can, get no paychecks, imagine the worst, pray for the best, strive for this tiny space in a chaotic world to have some balance and order.

I still watch the news, but in increasingly numb horror and dread, as if knowing what's coming might help, as if it were still a good citizen's responsibility.

Something is indeed unraveling, but no one need hear that from me.

We each sit at our own console, navigating a way in this crowded cyber arcade, unmanageable and malfunctioning, disconnected from the rising fury of a planet wronged. Until—flooded, smoked, parched, starved, burned, or blown—we emerge into daylight, dazed, wondering what went wrong.

I long for a wisdom from up ahead, but no one has been where we are now. So, where does the voice urging me to seek, restore, cultivate, and protect beauty come from?

Seems to me it might be a path without argument or competition. We won't have to agree on what it is, just each listen and watch for what it stirs inside. Then, go there, wherever that may be, and care for whatever it is that speaks beauty to you.

And, with that in mind, it's September, Susan's birthday month, and our 20th wedding anniversary. As a gift to us both, I'm done with the virus, shootings, and the bad behavior of others. I'm all about the love in my life for the rest of the month!

After those words, I heard the news that the son of my friends has died. I don't ask the details, but everything stopped in the shock and the pain.

Where love makes a world,
grief breaks it.
Only in remembering the love
can parents survive being the ones
still alive.

When the future has been ripped away,
nothing can make sense.
There's nowhere to go,
nothing to do
or be said.

I suppose one just wakes up to the day that is,
takes care of self and the other.
And, if possible, feel the love from so many of us
surrounding you both.

Before Billy Joel sang it, Wordsworth penned, "The good die first," and Lord Byron, who lifted it from Herodotus, "Whom the god loves die young." In other words, the notion that the youngest, the best, the purest, and the most innocent leave us early has been around "for the longest time." (I can't help myself, Billy!)

In the original tale, Hera rewarded the sons who hitched themselves to a cart to take their mother to a festival for the goddess. The mother, a priestess, asked Hera for them to have the greatest gift. The sons then went to sleep in the temple and never woke up. And so, in theory, death, and wherever that brought them, was how they were honored.

We all have a list of those who left us too soon. A child. A sibling. A parent. A lover or a friend. An idol outside of our home. It's probably just chance, but having a mind means at least attempting to make sense out of what might have no reason.

There may be an afterlife. There may be other lifetimes. There may be stories unfolding through time and across dimensions too distant for us to comprehend. And, as some say, this incarnation may only be a school where souls develop and evolve. Some graduate early. Some may come to finish a task, nudge another, return a favor. As another chubby hero of mine was known to say, "I see nothing."

However, as always, I return to cats to try and understand. The one who left us; the one who remained. Born in the same moment and yet with such different characteristics and life spans. The one whose very presence opened my heart is gone. She was the essence of cat innocence and perhaps needed be nothing more. Her surviving sister is not as easy to love, not as content at even being a cat. What might she be learning? What might she be teaching us by staying and complaining her way through yet another day?

I have no idea, but as I learn to accept, anticipate, and meet her somewhere in this labyrinth, I can feel my heart opening again to what is here as well as to what is gone.

The good may indeed die young, but those of us who remain may yet have the chance to learn to live and love better.

Yawning Yo-Yo

Stretching in and kvetching out of shape,
I drink and sleep to forget,
wake and write to remember
the loss of a dear face
or a welcome place,
a way of life,
her husband, his wife.

*So much to grieve
so little to believe.*

*Yet something has been extracted
I have no word for,
no memory of—
nothing to sweeten the tears
from its parting.*

*The signs are still up,
but the road to the life imagined
is gone.
Some still search for it,
invest as if it will return.*

*Some wait in whatever refuge
for what, like youth or innocence,
can never come back.
What grief is that?*

*Not the hair-tearing wail of a child gone.
Not that loud,
more hollow and numb,
the absence of what wasn't
without the pain of losing what was.*

*So I stretch into the void,
relish the benefit of a cat-like yawn,
then shrink from everything destroyed,
all the while praying for a different dawn.*

And then we learn that the giant heart of Lew "Bojangles" Harper stopped beating this week.

Okay, no one ever called him Bojangles, and I never saw him dance, but he had silver hair, eyes of age, and he talked of life. And when he let go a laugh, it certainly felt as if he were dancing.

What we did do together was meet at the bar at Feast every Tuesday night for many years. We shared books, stories, and fine red wine because, well, we both once did "drinks a bit."

He was more than a regular at Feast; he was a patron, loved and greeted warmly by just about everyone who worked or frequently dined there. He seemed to care about everyone and was as generous a human being as I've ever known. We had to enforce alternating paying for bottles of wine; otherwise, he would grab all the tabs.

Just last month, we received a card celebrating 60 years with his life partner, Clifford. Lew's sight had been going, but he managed to write a personal note of love to us along with the printed message of their amazing journey as a gay couple from 1961 on.

Imagine that!

I can't. Not really. But their bond was something to behold. As was Lew's devotion to Clifford after his stroke. I can't imagine a life for Cliff without Lew by his side.

If there is an afterlife, they will surely meet up, click their heels, jump so high, and dance in the joy of finding each other again.

So long, my friend. Love you.

I have not always been a man who could say I loved another, especially aloud to a man. The path to love and loving has been roundabout and challenging.

I've always been mystified by how so many seem to find their way to it. And I've been curious about large and loving families reveling in each other's company. Were they really having as much fun together as it appeared? How did they get to such places?

And how did someone like me make it to 20 years of faithful marriage and loving partnership?

I suppose that has been the story I've been getting at in fits and starts throughout these past 21 months. What I know is this: It began with longing rather than belonging. As a result, I felt the most when pursuing or escaping what I did not know how to have or to hold.

If I could have, I would have had a happy loving family in one building with Lorie and Ryan. Even though I was 37 when Ryan was born, I had not learned how to have any of that.

I don't remember the name of that Colorado canyon. I remember it was hot, seemingly inaccessible, and the rocks shown brightly with reflected light. I was there because of her. I had hopes of reconciliation.

We couldn't agree on where to walk. Not a good start. Then, a beautiful black and red snake darted across our path. We followed. We walked quietly, haltingly, as if waiting for something to happen: perhaps another kind of snake-sign that would tell us where to go in our lives.

I felt clumsy. We lost the path we were on when we left it looking for a creek. The brush was thick and thorny and tore at our skin and clothes. We struggled far apart from each other. I felt a panic growing. Nothing was going the way I wished.

Then she turned to me and said, "Open your mouth."

I looked directly into her clearwater blue eyes for the first time that day and opened my mouth.

She softly placed a dark red raspberry on my tongue. I received it in grateful communion. I rolled it around in my mouth feeling its bumpy texture as if it were the last and only raspberry. I didn't want the moment to end.

Still connected by our eyes, I desperately wanted to bite the raspberry. I did. It exploded in my mouth like the love I wanted to feel.

In the first millisecond, it tasted sour and acrid like desert air, then the moisture and sweetness filled my mouth. My knees gave way. I so wanted us to blend like the opposite tastes of that raspberry in my mouth. I wanted to cry. Imagine wanting to cry over a berry.

I finally swallowed it and felt the sweetness begin to fade from my mouth.

Nothing between us took its place.

Every raspberry after that (and there were many) placed in each other's mouth was savored less, followed more quickly by another, as much to not let the taste fade as to not face the specter of that first one: It's ecstasy both in the giving and the receiving; and what would never be again.

After Ryan was born, the community had a Welcome to Life blessing circle for him. We sang to him as he went around the circle, held by one person after another. Sharing my son, my new love and joy, with others was the warmest, most inclusive, moment of belonging I had ever experienced.

My father and his wife made yearly visits. My Uncle Marty and Aunt Lois came to see him. Even from my mother's side of the family, my Uncle Bill and Aunt Shirley broke the long silence and came to Tucson to meet my new family. It was as if Ryan were both the attractant and the cure for my family everywhere.

I was done running or searching, was ready to make a stand. I dug in for the long battles of managing the community, but took no one's side. I had a vision of cooperation and insisted it was possible.

While still teaching as an associate at Pima Community College, I left my position at Saint Francis in the Foothills to assist in the opening and fashioning of the Sierra Tucson Adolescent Care program. It was a salaried job that matched my status as a parent who was in it for the duration.

It was a busy and exhilarating time, but I didn't address the distance growing between me and Lorie. And then, it was too late.

Susan and I had already known each other for years from working with the youth and being in a support group together. She heard my side of the story then as I heard about her issues with work, relationships, and expressing herself. We were friends. I had visited her in the hospital after she had open heart surgery. That should have been a clue to me that I cared more about her than I had admitted to myself. I avoided hospitals as much as possible.

But there was no rush to each other, just a gradual awareness of how something felt different in each other's presence.

I had no intention of complicating the parenting arrangement Lorie and I had arrived at, and so if I were to date anyone it would be when Ryan was with Lorie. I didn't want to confuse Ryan with different women in my life. Now that I was both single and stationary, it was easier for my past to drop by and visit.

In ways that I cannot explain, and with the help of someone who I once wanted to be with but couldn't then, a different kind of passion grew in me. Maybe it came from failing with Lorie after having decided to be parents together.

Living at Damian was a fellow teacher, another man named Jim. He used to lead trips down into the Grand Canyon, and I had gone on one with him. We became good friends. He was the one who mentioned my name to a department chair looking for faculty to cover classes at the downtown campus of Pima Community College.

During this time of upheaval in my life, he offered me the experience of a creative wellness retreat on the island of Skyros. It was an unbelievable gift that, with some difficulty and much gratitude, I accepted.

It was June 1997. I participated in the program in Atsitsa for a while, but something larger was bursting out of me that couldn't be contained by a schedule. I moved to the other side of the island, rented a place on the beach, and let it happen.

Some restraint is required for this part of the telling. I was 42, and at the risk of appearing immodest, I was never more alive, attractive, present, or powerful as I was on Skyros. I stayed up most nights dancing and drinking. During the days I met people easily wherever I went. And more women were interested in being with me than at any time in my life.

I had two epiphanies on Skyros. The first was on a hike with Jim. We went to a high spot on the island, sat at an old temple looking down on the island and the Mediterranean Sea, and talked.

Something about the exertion to get there, the location and the conversation, and I started to see patterns in my behavior. Then, for the first time, I let myself grieve the loss of what Lorie and I had set out to do. And I realized something about maleness and femaleness I had never been able to fully formulate before.

For Love Restored

Time and desert storms, inch by inch, form a scab of earth over abandoned mines, the rusted remains of machinery. All the gold is gone. The waters that once flowed freely—recoiled from cyanide and leaching—have gone underground, like an angry woman vowing not to trust in love again.

Still, rockhounds, prospectors, and hunters sniff and stomp around searching for something of value to take captive, kill, or conquer. Without malice, but mindless, we are drawn to you to fill some emptiness. And the woman that remains unrecognized groans from somewhere inside.

I walk in your desert mountains, with tears, to remember and wake to your ancient and omnipresent beauty. I see the cracked and dried-up places where your waters used to run. I pray for forgiveness and the touch of your healing waters, the refuge of your sacred springs.

Once, you shared your secrets with me, opening like the petals of a flower, but my body left your body, my attention drifted and traveled far away. Now I know I can no longer look for you, except in my own heart and mind. But I sit in the ruins of your temple, grow flowers at your altar, become you, even as you become me, making something old and dying alive and new again.

The second epiphany came on the balcony of my beachside place. There was an older Dutch couple staying in the same building. Each morning, they would bring a small table and two chairs down onto the beach. They'd drink their coffee, read the newspapers, and then go for a barefoot walk, hand in hand, alongside the water and gentle waves.

I watched them every morning I was there. The contentment they had with each other was palpable. Their routine transformed what might have been just a holiday vacation into something that moved me deeply. I wanted it. I wanted to grow old with someone and have what I imagined they had.

Having faced and grieved the past, and even with ample opportunity for loving being presented to me on the island, I knew I was ready for something different and to offer what I could not before.

From Skyros, I called Susan from a payphone and said if she would be with me, I would be hers and no one else's for the remainder of my days.

By December, six years after we first met, Susan moved in next door to me at Damian. Four years later, we married.

Now, this September 15th, 2021, will be our 20th anniversary. How to celebrate that? By returning to the scene of the crime, no doubt. Wait, what I mean by that is that we chose Jerome, Arizona to get married because it was where we had our first fight.

Neither of us can remember what it was about. I guess that was not what mattered. What was important was how respectfully we resolved it, and that appealed to us to have at the foundation of our marriage. Besides, we both thought the patio up at the Jerome Grand Hotel a pretty cool spot for sharing our vows.

Back to the pandemic. We haven't traveled since it began. Is the pet-sitting service we've used in the past still in business? Do we really need to go all the way back to Jerome?

When we find out that our favorite Arizona band, Major Lingo, is having a reunion concert there the weekend before our anniversary, it seems like we must go. I can't imagine being indoors at a concert, but Susan was now eager. I planned the trip.

We didn't have a large wedding. Susan had been married before. I hadn't, but I had a son. Neither of us were young. Our plan was to have a simple ceremony in Jerome, and then have parties in Chicago and New York with our families and friends.

When Denise learned we were going to marry, she, as Clerk of the Court in Cochise County, wanted to be the one who issued and signed our marriage certificate. So, we drove to Sierra Vista to meet her a few days before the date.

On the way, unbelievable news was coming from the radio. Was this another War of the Worlds hoax? It couldn't be real. Everything changed. Our moods darkened. We squabbled. Nothing seemed right anymore.

In Sierra Vista, televisions were on, and we saw the planes crashing into the towers. Numb, we went through the motions. Susan's birthdate was 100 years off. It didn't matter. Okay, it mattered. It got changed, signed, and we all hugged. There was nothing to say. We left in shock.

Just like that, our post-wedding plans were postponed. The wedding itself, however, went on in a light rain. I had driven from Tucson with Jim and Ryan. Susan and our dear friend, Geneve, drove separately. Another family from Damian, with two girls close in age with Ryan, met us there.

A local couple, Andy and Jennifer, officiated together. It was their anniversary that same day. Sally, a former student of mine and in Major Lingo, had connected us to them.

Under the shroud of 9/11, we all joined hands, praying for peace. Each adult had written or prepared something for the moment, but in the sharing of what had been planned, a different emphasis, beyond a wedding, emerged.

When I was traveling as a citizen diplomat in the Soviet Union, I learned about couples including a trip to a memorial cemetery to pledge their marriage to peace. We were making a similar dedication.

And I remembered a popular parting slogan, roughly translated from Russian as: "Wishing you peace in your skies." If only ...

Back to the pandemic: Major Lingo canceled the concert. Honestly, I was fine with that, but we were still going to Jerome. Instead of the concert though, two members of the band, Sally and John, joined us for dinner at the site of our wedding and spontaneously serenaded us at the table.

Jay and Alexis weren't back in time from a trip for the anniversary dinner but met us the following day at a winery. Jay shared an idea for a book, *Watching*, he was working on, and we laughed a bit about all the great concepts we've come up with over the years and how few people have yet to read any of them.

The following morning, Susan and I headed back to Tucson by crossing the Verde Valley towards Pine. The restaurant there I had been thinking about was closed. I really was slipping in the fine art of stomach-inspired traveling. I blamed the pandemic.

Instead, we had lunch by Roosevelt Lake. Perhaps because we were just reliving our own wedding, we talked about the last one we had attended. It was the marriage of Geneve's son Qayyum to Suiko. This took place in Tucson months before the coronavirus was a thing.

Qayyum, as his name suggests, is a reincarnated poet from somewhere ancient and mysterious who manages to find a graceful way of living among us. He was one of the young men who, when it coincided with his wanderings, helped me on the roofs at Damian.

In a momentary lapse in judgment, he asked me to do a reading at the wedding. I brought a tank of tequila, drank a portion of it, and shared all I had learned about love in my life with Susan.

Instructions for a Life Journey Together

- *Pack light! There's enough baggage already.*
- *But carry a journal. It's useful to stay in touch with your individual selves.*
- *Learn to move well together, and separately. Celebrate both!*
- *Travel your own version of First Class, while remembering this sage advice passed on from generation to generation: "No whining on the yacht!" Speaking of wine, red wine, of course, is superior, but white shouldn't be snubbed altogether. Apply this philosophy liberally.*
- *Joyfully, allow him the equivalent of one old recliner.*
- *Gracefully, allow her to change these, and any other rules, as needed. (Except the recliner one.) (You will eventually do that on your own.) (Or so you will think.)*
- *However, there really are no Get Out of Jail Free cards, so tread carefully with what must remain fragile and sacred.*
- *Listen as much, or more, to what is unsaid as to what is said.*
- *You already have everything your hearts have ever wanted.*
- *Wrap it up in all of its disguises and give it away—in gifts and in service.*
- *Laugh long, as that love keeps coming back to you—multiplied!*

In other words, stay heart wealthy, my friends, and keep traveling light, in light, together.

October

Twice already this morning
rain pushed me back indoors.
Still dressed to go out,
not believing this weather can last,
I'm reluctant to adapt.

At home, would I write letters,
contact fading faces,
stir up what has finally settled?

Must there be drama?

Some regrets cannot be repaired.
And so remorse, a code for self,
taps out a more careful way.

When younger, neglect was a teacher
of consequence.
Age does not long allow such luxury.
Attention and care,
the graceful art of pampering without tampering,
are what's required.

A sudden shift in clouds reveals sunlight,
and I have no last words to share,
only the sound of readiness to escape
the confines of what I must let go of
and of what I must maintain.

Of course, I waited until Susan was out of town. There are still some parts of me it's best she doesn't know too much about.

As soon as the garage door closed, I was at it. Heart beating quickly, the long-awaited moment had finally come.

It was more stressful than I remembered. I'm probably getting too old for shit like this. What's a guy my age doing getting himself into such precarious positions anyhow?!

My performance anxiety went through the roof as I turned off the water to the house and then tried to remove the old valve from the improperly installed PEX pipe coming from within the wall behind the toilet.

The last time I took on such a project, I flooded the house, so my reluctance was understandable.

Susan wanted me to call a plumber and go with her and our friends to Bisbee to see a Los Lobos concert. As if I were that kind of guy!

Truth is, I don't really know what kind of guy I am anymore. However, I did manage to contort my arthritic body between toilet and wall and cracked free the crucial old nut without damaging anything … that I know of … yet.

And I replaced all the innards of the toilet, filled the unseen interior with vinegar for a flush-improving cleanse, put on a new valve and supply line, and then turned (cautiously and reverently) the water to the house back on.

No leaks!!

How do you spell RELIEF?

So, now what?

It's Friday afternoon, and Susan's gone until Sunday. What other kind of trouble can I court? I wonder what's happening around town. You know, it's been quite a while since I've been up on our roof …

Truth is, this really does represent a change for us. We don't have to do the things together that we used to do. The Bisbee trip has been an annual getaway with several Tucson friends for a long time. Last year was the first pause in the tradition. It seemed too soon to resume to me, especially on a concert crowded weekend.

Two of the Feast bar people, Jack and Mary Lou, our elders, inspired us to embrace different rhythms. Mary Lou often takes off on adventures while

Jack is content to stay home. I've got a new guiding question: "What Would Jack Do?"

Once, I sought the exhilaration of crowds. Anonymous and buoyant, I'd bounce, mingle, and cut my way past bodies, stopping only when a welcome face met mine in the moment.

Today, I hunt for the gaps left when others retreat. There's something in empty spaces that soothes and fills what freely moving through crowds did long ago. I think it primarily the difference between searching and relinquishing: the looking for, or the giving of blessing.

My wealth is in words, so that's what I share. They emerge from the silence and through the filter of what I've seen and felt.

Last night, I found my way to the door of my old nemesis from a thousand dreams. He lived in ordinary dullness, and I wondered at how someone so unremarkable had haunted and tormented me so.

There really was nothing to say, but we held each other ... then softly began to sing a song my conscious mind can't now recall. The face of a small boy popped up from wherever he had been hiding. In smiling disbelief, he came closer to see if this were really happening.

There is something I've been trying to say for as long as I can remember. A key phrase may appear here or there, but is always lost before captured.

This morning after the dream, I found myself thinking about wabi-sabi, the Japanese philosophy often expressed in art: nothing lasts, nothing is finished, and nothing is perfect.

Maybe more than ever I can understand approaching even the simplest of tasks with such a notion, as when the last line of this writing, like light fading into night, is followed by the dawn of what is yet to be known.

107-day lockdown has ended in Sydney. I'm hearing about borders opening around the world. Proof of vaccination is an issue, but if one wants to leave or enter a country, it's becoming necessary to have it.

The United States has the most deaths from the virus, but Brazil (having just surpassed 600,000 deaths) is right behind us.

Everywhere, the ground is pulsating with chinch bugs and ants. We are not the only ones enjoying this blooming desert!

Hundreds of thousands of varieties of insects, each an ever-changing, creative response to also-evolving plants and predators. What is our role in this ancient and epic arms race? Stay out of the way?

I sat on a rock this morning and was soon covered by busy, crawling things.

I tried to be okay with it but did not last long. Once again, I'm aware I have a place to retreat, while others do not; my ongoing seesaw between gratitude and guilt.

Then I was startled by a coiled rattler on my path. But no rattling. Too cool yet for reptile motion.

So, instead of any historic reaction, and maybe to balance my intolerance of the bugs, I sat down beside it. I took in its hypnotic gray diamond patterns, its triangular viper head, and believed it to be a young Western.

Oh, I thought of moving it to a safer place, but resisted the impulse. Where's safe anyway? And for whom? No, one of my modern governing themes is to meddle less, appreciate more.

So, sitting there with this dormant and deadly beauty, feeling the sun beginning to warm, knowing this moment could not last, I basked in the lazy realization of having survived another desert summer.

Sometimes, Susan and I speak of finding a place we might be without such extreme heat. But, you know, from the proper distance, and at the right times, one can find a bit of heaven even right next to hell.

Is it the season?

Does it matter, really, what reason
friends lose touch,
a day is wasted,
all that will remain broken?

Like a word of truth not spoken,
a trip for joy not taken,
all the projects promising salvation ...

not forgotten, just gradually forsaken,
then gone rotten.

I don't like it when it's too hot or cold.
Neither do I like fast nor slow,
nor any kind of loud, or crowd.
I think both the Left and Right are wrong,
can still hear the teacher say
the Middle Way is where to belong.

Oh, I might lean this way or that,
attempt to digest the news,
avoid the fat,
but where's the common ground,
the place we all may meet?

Is it time to wake or time to sleep?

Restless nights follow days without guidance.
Yet one touch from her settles and soothes a groan
as if to remind me there is no solution alone.

So, what if we started right where we are?
Do just one thing with another, near or far.
Or help a neighbor. Join with those who labor.
Pull weeds. Pick up litter.
Offer what we can. Let go the bitter.
Put on a welcoming smile
and with eager hands, capable or not,
let's fashion together a life worthwhile.

There is yet another new variant picking up speed in its journey from person to person and country to country. Neither Susan nor I have gotten any of them yet, but it seems inevitable.

Speaking of the nearly invisible, we recently watched a NOVA episode on neutrinos. Crazy little things. Elusive too. At least from our point of view.

You know what else fascinates me? Particle accelerators! Amazing how expensive and massive of an apparatus is required to detect and understand the smallest of things. For example, the Large Hadron Collider took ten years and billions of dollars to build. It's an almost 17-mile-long underground circular tunnel. (Oh, and there is already a plan for a 23-billion-dollar, 62-mile-long version!)

Our search for the invisible is quite intense. However, current estimates suggest that everything observable in our universe is only 5% of what actually exists. Read that again please. I'll wait.

Okay? So, what's going on with everything we can't see? Yeah, that's the point of such elaborate research and experiments. For now, we call all that is not visible, dark. Dark energy, 68% of what is. Another 27%, dark matter. But it is we who are in the dark.

It's certainly not within my abilities to understand nor explain much of what our brightest are considering, but that doesn't stop me from thinking about it. I turn to a conscious/unconscious model (call it whatever name for God you fancy) in my attempt to comprehend. What is consciously formed is the 5%. The unformed potential, the unconscious, is the vast remainder.

Turns out there's a previously unknown flavor of neutrino that pops in and out from the dark into the light. Kind of like a spark from a dream informing and connecting our smallness to the immensity of what is, and what is possible.

And then off in the other direction, the final frontier: he finally boldly went where no old man had gone before—for about ten minutes. William Shatner, at the age of 90, got a ride on the Blue Origin New Shepard rocket. Whatever the environmental impact of such a joyride turns out to be, I'm sure it was well worth it.

Hey, there are all kinds of things I'd like to experience, and I have elaborate methods for convincing myself that what I want is okay. Until, that is, I start to multiply my activity by the billions of others who also want their chance.

Obviously, most humans don't have such opportunities, which is how the culture of conspicuous consumption and waste has been able to continue.

But like all pyramid schemes, it will collapse. We've already been seeing the flashing signs, are expecting the sirens any moment.

I really only have the laboratory of my own mind to attempt to comprehend our behavior. And I often catch myself alternating between indulgence and deprivation—forgetting to even drink water most of a day only to then dine out in leisure and luxury. One day I will fastidiously save, reuse, recycle everything; then turn around and throw something away simply because it annoyed me.

Privilege is like that. It can be selfish and intolerant. I feel that way whenever I'm forced to wait in line.

Simultaneously, no amount of savings can diminish a poverty consciousness that still pops up in me, in whose grip everything must be thriftily utilized. I prefer being privileged. Who wouldn't? Yet if I were honest with myself, I'd have to admit that a touch of impoverishment awareness makes me a better fellow earthling.

So, what if the final frontier were between our ears? And rather than swinging from extremes, a sustainable middle way were found?

Then perhaps our real privilege would be to narrow the gap among those sharing this planet. I can imagine another starship captain nodding in agreement and commanding, "Make it so!"

I have a friend, an L.L.C. partner who turned 80 earlier this year. That surprised me, but perhaps not as much as it did him. Still, I can't be that terribly far behind him. And I do find myself peeking ahead to see what those with more accumulated life are doing.

Ryan's grandfather, Roger, turned 90 this year. My Uncle Marty will be turning 95 later this year. He works out in a gym six days a week. Not that long ago, he had a gym buddy who was 104, who called him "Kiddo." Imagine being the younger wingman at 94 to a centenarian who still wanted a night out on the town.

There's a member at the club, "Doc," who at 91 is working on his golf swing, and is a profound conversationalist.

And then there's Dick. I'll let him introduce himself: "I'm the last Dick standing around here."

He's 90 years old and still practicing law. I was incredulous and asked him how many hours he was working. He said 4-5 hours a day, but it would be longer if he had more to do.

He's been working on one case in particular since 1985! It's about how Mexican tile should be classified and charged for by Customs. He's on the side that it shouldn't be labeled "ceramic." Something about the crystallization process. I tell him I come from a family of ceramic tile contractors who stayed away from installing soft tiles. My conversational worth went up in value, and he moved closer, became more animated.

We play in a weekly 9-hole afternoon scramble called Men & Martinis at Skyline C.C. which finishes up on the patio. After our latest round, I find myself lost in conversation with him, forgetting about the others around the table. I'm surprised to look up and see we are the last two remaining.

I tell him his engagement in life shames me a bit, makes all my excuses meaningless. He tries to get me off the hook by saying he has good genes. I don't allow it. I tell him his commitment, his choice, his energy must originate in his mind, and I celebrate that.

When it is finally time to leave (I admit more by my instigation than his), he offers me a ride to my truck in his golf cart. Instinctively, I say I'm okay, and goodnight, but too late I find myself wondering what it would be like to be a passenger hurtling through the darkness in Dick's custom golf cart. Maybe I'll have another chance one night.

Earlier in the afternoon I saw the putting green installed behind his house along the fairway on the 8th hole. It seems that even at 90 one can still attempt to get better at this game, and at life.

My thanks and appreciation to all the elders who are still inspiring me and others by their example.

A Dream Recalled

There's a window through which I've watched many decades go by.
Eyes tiring but remaining alert.
The landscape slowly changes.
Different species prevailing; one's success, another's demise.
Whatever grows, one day, decays.
What once was tamed by younger hands is now lawless and wild again.

I have little desire left to impose my will on anything, really.
The Do Not Disturb signs are more personal reminder than warning.
WE ALL KNOW
something is happening, and that it is accelerating.
It shows up in how we drive: some speed up, wanting to get ahead;
others slow down, hoping to avoid collision.
Who is right? What Rite of Way? My way? Your way? Yaweh?
We piss each other off, scare ourselves, and others—
there are many forms of trembling.

A harmony once found in the rhythm of routine is breaking down.
The American Dream has been recalled.
The Founders can't fix it.
They left no instructions to troubleshoot today's problems.
One party says, "Support us. We will be strong and survive, no matter what!"
The other asks, "Who gets to come with and who gets left?"
Those who want another choice shout in outrage,
"Where can anyone go when everything is gone?"

I think I'd like to plant a tree. Yes, I'd like to plant a tree!
As a man in his sixties, perhaps it should be an Elderberry.
I've heard they do well in a variety of soils, are easy to grow,
and thrive in the company of other kinds of Elderberry.
They can be just a bush or a shrub and have been known to be
an "instant hedge." I like that!
Not just for privacy, but as an elder barrier of sorts.
Rather than retiring to some gated community, or worse,
… imagine joining hands with other elders and saying,
in whatever language, "No Mas!"

But back to the actual tree:
Fragrant, edible flowers and dark purple berries
that have been used to treat all manner of ailment.
Elderberry is good medicine!

Our ancestors knew this, even believed the tree itself would ward off evil.
In our culture of youth we ask much of the young.
Even Harry Potter had to wield a wand of elder.
Picture a world with roles reversed.
Where rather than being the nursed, senior healers, mentors, and guides
remain a gentle force of balance, a wise source of strength.
Adams, Novas, Johns, Scotias, Yorks ... Come plant them with me!
Spread the Black and Lemon Lace. Be a Black Beauty.
Even the birds will love you for it.

Concoct juices, jellies, and jams from these elderberries.
Learn to bake their pies for special gifts.
Brew its tea and talk to neighbors.
Make heavenly elderberry wines and intoxicate the world
with the laughter of twinkling, aging eyes.
Don't just plant an Elderberry—be one!

Often, if I write about something enough, I start to understand why I keep coming back to the same topics, like the death toll from the coronavirus, mass shootings and gun violence and, of all things, driving. Here's the underlying connecting pattern: my fear of the random and increasingly bad behavior of others.

According to the Governors Highway Safety Association, the number of pedestrians being hit by cars has increased by 46% over the past ten years, as opposed to only a 5% increase from all other accidents involving automobiles. I just don't feel safe almost anywhere anymore.

Meanwhile, gun sales have been skyrocketing, and millions do not want to get vaccinated or wear masks and are willing to fight about it.

Okay, now that I've admitted my fear to myself, I can shut up about it. Nothing I can do to change the behavior of others, so my attention needs to return to my own issue. Although, I do wonder how much an armored vehicle would cost us.

Omen/Amen

When there is no blockage,
something, always refilling;
something, always emptying.

An unseen drip into the one;
a leak almost felt in the other.

This writing,
like trying to watch essence moving
from one reservoir to another;
with words, an attempt to translate
what goes on beyond language.

I spent a long morning last week
at a friend's desert sanctuary,
talked about my reluctance to rejoin
whatever remains for us.

It's often in the naming of a thing
its grip begins to relax.
Even a demon can relish the very recognition
diminishing it.

"I'm not your enemy" it wheezes as it fades
back into fears as yet unformed.

Like the deliberate scars from a surgery,
some wounds tell the same story over and over.
I mention to Susan how often it seems
whenever I pay attention to a clock of late, it's 4:44.

Just now, I looked up how long I've survived
since making amends and saying goodbyes:

444 days, yesterday.

It seems that's exactly how long it took for me
to remember how good it is to still be alive
even in a body lighter but not stronger than
the one I also ofttimes failed to love.

Wait, one more thing: restaurants. I know it seems trivial compared to the loss of life, but I am sad about so many cherished places shutting down. *Fortune* magazine reported earlier in the year that 110,000 establishments closed either temporarily or permanently. What matters to me are the ones here in Tucson. I recently saw a list of 25 that are closed for good.

I used to kid that I was probably conceived in a restaurant. So many of the best times with others were spent in them. And, for me, comfort food was not found at home with a sick mother; it came from favorite restaurants. If I talk about the creamy garlic salad dressing at Miller's Steakhouse on Western Avenue in Chicago, there are a handful of people who will immediately understand something about me. They will respond with a reference to the ribs. We will sigh and smile in barbecued harmony.

When I first came to Tucson, such places were hard to find. There were a few high-end ones like The Tack Room, Scordato's, and Palomino's, but it wasn't until LaRocca's opened that I found something like my childhood comfort food. They even had a salad dressing I would buy and give as a gift. They are long closed, but a well-placed whisper to Ralph can still manifest some of the blended elixir.

With respect, nostalgia, gratitude, and sadness, here is my list of the local establishments I will miss the most: Senae Thai Bistro, Downtown Kitchen, Athens on 4th, Caffe Milano, Elvira's, Cafe Poca Cosa, The B Line, Rincon Market, El Indio, Fronimo's, and for other-than-culinary reasons, Chicago Bar and The Meet Rack. Rest in Grease.

November

Rejection Reflection

I keep you where you never age.
Even in dreams, things don't always go as I would like.
Last night though, I hit a tee shot where the ball became an angelic butterfly,
landed near the hole.
A voice from above said, "That's good."
So I didn't even have a chance of missing the putt.

Once, I wanted to taste and know everything.
Not as exhausting as you might imagine, fueled by compulsion,
the restless strategy of seeds:
chasing, clinging, carrying on like that.

Now, young faces no longer, except where I hold,
in trickle or stream, an old dream.

On the radio, a youthful Elton John sings "Levon"
and I remember someone who called me that …
fifty years ago.
I would ask her why today if I could,
but then, a wry smile,
a welcoming glint in her eyes
were enough.

Why say yes or no to anything?
And whose voice—in or out of your head—do you listen to?!

If it's true that we give what we most want
I've long been desperately in need of rescue.
Oh, perhaps not so much anymore,
retreated as I am in familiar routines,
secreted in search for the attitude antidote
to infuse and inform
the days and dreams
still left me.

Well, I'll be hog-tied, tie-dyed, and French fried ... I have a new flipping phone! And, yeah, I passed on the offer to get one smarter.

Still, after 15 years with just my Sanyo Katana, bringing any newer model home was like what I imagine dating would be today: tedious, frustrating, and leaving me wishing there were better instructions, somewhere.

Hey, I did follow the bold "Important" checklist, which had me first go to a site to begin the activation process. Then came the message with a phone number to call with any problems. However, as soon as that process began, my old phone would no longer work. So there I was with two non-functioning phones, a help line to call, and that extra warm feeling of goodwill towards technology and progress.

Sure, it was me who installed the SIM card in the wrong slot, but it did fit so nicely where I put it. So much for logic and intuition. The design of the phone itself seemed an industry effort to convince us throwbacks and Luddites we'd be better off with a smartphone. Every command a secret combination of pads and gestures, hard to decipher, impossible to remember.

Did I mention that the 300 contacts in my old phone couldn't be transferred to the new one?

I think the exact words of the one representative I was finally able to connect with were, "Good luck with that!"

Well, I haven't talked much on a phone in a long time anyway. I don't suppose anyone will even notice that their name won't pop up on a screen on a device already no longer in use.

Diet Bingo

One supplement, a prayer for the heart;
another, a lottery ticket against cancer.
One never knows …

When I was still in my twenties and confronted
by a mysterious illness, a healer convinced me
to go on a fast: eat nothing but watermelon
for too many weeks.

Now, what I once loved
makes me gag.

Beyond what goes in a mouth,
consider the stories we consume
for they shape what comes from us,
the lives we know to want.

I'm uncomfortable with unnecessary drama
on or off the screen.
Mindless action leaves me anxious.
Forget horror altogether.

I change channels quickly,
often land on some sport for both
authenticity and surprise.
There is no script, just people striving,
alone or together.

I'm not proud of this way of spilling time,
nor can I resist rooting, but my loyalties
are shallow and fleeting.
A backstory can sway me one way.
Then, a heroic heart is revealed
and I've switched sides again.

Life is seldom easy,
and there is a hunger unmet.
We are less tolerant of each other,
of how things are going,
yet we want to cheer
for something.

On these fields of play
we witness together the same spirit
that birthed and shaped our world,
can even hope and marvel
at all that might be achieved
when the need to save it
is finally believed.

Have you heard that researchers are concerned at how the virus is spreading among deer populations and how it might be evolving in animals before spreading back to us?

I hear Tom Petty everywhere. Something about this time of year, a call to head out into the great wide open "under them skies of blue."

For Thanksgiving, with most of our family elsewhere, and a reluctance to join the holiday travel flow, Susan and I often go off into the desert somewhere, pretend to get lost, then, when we've had enough of that, be grateful to find the truck and our way home for whatever is in the house to eat.

It doesn't take much to satisfy us.

For many years, upon our return from the desert ritual, we'd stop at Govinda's for a vegetarian buffet and sit on the patio with live sitar music playing while turkeys wandered around inspecting and approving of our fare.

Eventually, it became too popular and crowded for what we like to be thankful for …

Then, along with first noticing becoming older, we started making reservations at the Tasteful Kitchen for a B.Y.O.B sit-down vegan version of Thanksgiving. This required us to skip the getting lost part of our tradition. Aging can be like that. Once losing things gets real, it's hard to remember what is and what is not a game. Good wine helps.

So now we stockpile the house (a little) the week before. Susan might even do some baking.

Anything to avoid the rush, but also in gratitude for each other, the quiet peace of our life together, while thankful for everyone in our lives, each doing what calls clearest to them, even those rebels without a clue.

If these were my last words

Afloat or submerged
somewhere along the endless stream
of doing and not doing,
onward and downward
we go
merrily, merrily, life is but a dream ...

And a goldang repetitive dream at that!
And not really so fricking merry!

But the holiday season is upon us
and we do so try, don't we?

I'm at the point where I weigh the impact of every choice.
What resources shall I help deplete today and for what?
Yes, it can be paralyzing.

My time is also on the preservation list.
I miss more gatherings than I attend,
plant trees instead of showing up with gifts,
wonder why those I've reached out to don't respond
even as I don't return calls.

I have a project or two I hope to complete while in this body,
but haven't figured out what's mine to do
and what is for others.

I have a life partner who inspires me,
helps me make better choices.
On my own, I'd eat straight from the fridge,
but with her I'm inspired to mix ingredients
in ever new combinations and presentations.

Might that be the key?
Find a reason to keep creating.
Discover the motivation
to elevate your aspiration
from what you need to survive
to what allows your soul to thrive.

I can be grateful and give thanks
for having that as I row, row, row my boat …

There are causal chains I can follow in my mind that explain some things to me like how sitting at a daytime bar in Tucson, lamenting my experience taking my Master's examination, led to talking to a man who then offered me a job as a radio announcer in Show Low, Arizona. I said yes, moved into a trailer of his in Pinetop, and became, for a while, "The Voice of the White Mountains."

He, however, was a control freak beyond anything I have yet to experience (give me time) and even pencils and chairs had to be left in exact positions. Once, before my shift had started, I was there early clearing news stories from the AP feed when he came in screaming. The tape carousel had been improperly fed, and the wrong bit was playing. I didn't know. I hadn't even signed on yet, but I was the only one there to yell at. I stuck out my hand; he took it, and I said it was nice working for you, and left right there and then.

With nowhere to go, I went to Albuquerque where Ira was living at the time. When he left for Africa, I went to Alaska, but I knew I would have to follow him there eventually.

That is not exactly all I meant to say, but something about walking away from what is not right, and then sniffing around for what is, was the difference for finding/fashioning the life I now love. But even more than that, the hardest moments were when I knew I needed to leave a sweet deal for something yet unknown.

It might not sound like much now, but being a city employee had many guarantees and opportunities. If I'd stayed there as a garbageman, I would not have found my way to that fire lookout and a spot with the Forest Service that allowed me year-round lodging in beautiful canyons and mountains.

I was at a Saint Francis in the Foothills Celebration one Sunday when the topic of Citizen Diplomacy was mentioned. A trip was being planned for that summer. Out loud, I moaned, "Oh shit!" The light had come on. I knew I would have to leave the Forest Service to go. You could have asked me then or you could ask me now, but I still can't say how or why that certainty is revealed or communicated. All I know is that when something inside says "YES!" there really is no other choice. At least not one I would be able to live with for long.

And so I am grateful for whatever it is in me that listened to yes.

A few days before Thanksgiving, a man drove his car through a holiday parade in Wisconsin, killing 6 and injuring 118.

Hey, I resisted writing about the 11 mass shootings over the Halloween weekend, but I just don't understand the urge to hurt so many. How much pain and anger must one have before exploding like this?

The Sunday afternoon after Thanksgiving, I'm sitting writing these words: "I've been waiting for something, like a promise, that never arrives. Not counting steps but noticing more of them, especially the clumsy ones."

Then a message interrupts. Only thirty minutes previous, Chris had died. Everything stopped. Whatever I had been thinking, erased.

He and I had exchanged emails earlier in the week, after his release from the hospital, so I knew his prognosis was not good but had no clue the end was so near.

I had offered whatever support he desired, but stopped short of saying what was in my heart: "Do you want to talk about dying?"

In 2020, he and I were both in the hospital within weeks of each other to have tumors removed from our stomachs.

We've been partners in a real estate deal for many years. What were the odds of us both having similar surgeries at almost the same time?

We weren't close friends, but had also once been in a small parent support group, so we had the habit of being honest with each other.

After our procedures we would compare notes about our diminished stomach capacity and the slow process of recovery. He seemed less patient about it and was back on his bike long before I was on mine.

His recovery seemed epic, and his life resumed with almost extra vitality. Or so it seemed. Maybe it was instead urgency, a sense of some clock ticking faster, certainly louder than it has been for me. I don't know. I'm a bit numb and dumb now, just moving this pen along as a way to stay with this and not just move on.

I get it though. The one unfailing promise is death. I tell myself in this sad and tender moment there is no need to wait on it. Just get on with whatever life remains.

Chris had a "get it done or get out of the way" approach to projects we worked on together. Was that his way with dying as well? I didn't ask. My regret, my lesson. No matter how awkward or clumsy, Lee, speak what is in your heart.

It is what a good companion on this pain-and-wonder-filled journey would do.

Thank you, Chris, for all of your spirit-infused efforts at being a good man doing more than your share. I can't even imagine what your absence will mean for Marleen and family. I do know there is incredible love and stunned support reaching out from near and far, holding them in your stead.

December

Always Catching Up

I drive a stick shift,
use a flip phone,
seldom take photographs
… of anything.
Don't know what's in or out
but believe eating alternatives, like meatless burgers,
makes more sense than ever.
Any step in a sustainable direction, right?

Sure, simple tasks take me longer and,
yes, I like to nap,
but now call it meditating
as in crossing off yet another positive
from my time-to-finally-do list.
Feeling good is a matter of small
daily choices, isn't it?

Oh, I know the body's trajectory
is ultimately downward,
but I've come to think of it differentLee.
For me, it's become the journey
into the Great Interior.

Want to know what I find funny
about this aging adventure?

(Oops, I can't really wait for your reply.)
But before I continue:
a Steve Goodman song is playing on KXCI.
He was dead at 36.
What was that all about?!

These brief bursts of brilliance …
only to then rejoin (perhaps)
the pervasive consciousness
that permeates, and actually is,
Everything.

I think that is it:
out we go, stumbling;
maybe in some found rhythm
we come back.
Then even more inward we go
until outward we arrive;
each on our own unfathomable
schedule to a destination
incomprehensible.

Let's wrap up this year with a new variant: Omicron. We're on 'O' already? Did I miss something? Or has Hollywood gotten involved and pitching for another Transformers sequel? *The Rise of Omicron!*

Word is, we will need another shot to keep it at bay. I think they're going to call the booster shot Optimus.

Speaking of autobots, I often feel surrounded by automotive extensions of dysfunctional human emotional systems.

To keep it together while driving, I have compiled some reminders for myself:

• When in doubt, and wherever possible, always pee first. So much is easier without that added pressure, especially with staying patient behind the wheel.

• Next, remember the universe itself started small and congested, full of extremes, took its own sweet time fashioning this minuscule gem we find ourselves on.

• And, in absolutely any moment, it can all end, for anybody, and for everybody.

There, now doesn't that put things in perspective? I feel better already. So what if an insignificant life form on a tiny planet in a ho-hum section of one of countless galaxies is late for something or doesn't finish his to-do list?

Here's something else: According to those who closely observe the cosmos, not only is everything moving away from whatever the center once was—it's all still accelerating!

What?! Why?! Riddle me that, Batman! I mean, where is everything going? And what's the hurry? It's as if we are being attracted towards or repelled away from something still unknown to us. Yet no matter what our beliefs, we are all part of the exodus.

I don't expect us to get anywhere in particular during our own infinitesimally brief life span, but I am a bit curious and also slightly concerned. I won't pretend to understand, but wild guessing is a hobby of mine, so here goes:

The earliest images of detected light suggest that what started it all was energy (name it according to personal preference). Matter came later. So, whatever that energy was doing, it eventually created matter. Blah, blah, blah, billions of years later, here we are: conscious combinations of matter and energy in self-propelling sensory containers utterly connected to and dependent upon a single planet and star.

Whatever the source of the evolutionary urge, consciousness is at least a by-product, if not the point. I like to think of us as Creation admiring and experiencing itself from different points of view. Constantly tinkering, adapting, changing—for whatever impulse or reason.

However, the immense force unleashed to move from darkness to light perhaps needs some restraint. Otherwise, this acceleration will continue until oblivion.

Don't you feel it too? As is above, so below. What is pushing galaxies is also accelerating consciousness. It shows up not just in our technology but in our consumption of information, speed of communication, and in our unruly emotional reactions. We are hurtling ever faster, burning up resources, and are unable to stop or even slow.

However this story turns out, I suppose will be okay, but consider this: If we are indeed a conscious piece of the universal puzzle, shouldn't we (rather than just go along for the ride) choose to participate in the development of our awareness? Isn't that what those who meditate have been doing for centuries?

Once upon a time, a few enlightened ones influenced many millions, but now that our numbers are in the billions and the stakes have become planetary, it just might be time for more of us to consciously slow down ... in ... each ... and ... every ... moment.

Let me try to get at this from a different direction. When I was a young man, I thought to cheat winter, moving west as I did, but instead I've grown softer, less tolerant of the cold, and temperatures not even freezing can keep me in bed.

Winter wins. There really is no escape from whatever our weakness.

Darwin explained that it's not the strongest nor the fastest but the most adaptable that survive. So it goes.

How are you adapting? No doubt, a lot has changed in our lifetimes. Perhaps more so in the past few years than before.

My personal barometer of the collective interior is how we are driving. My impression is that we've become more aggressive, less courteous, but a larger study was needed prior to making any generalizations. Well, I've just read one.

In 2020, there were 38,680 roadway deaths, even though we were driving fewer miles. 2021 is on a pace far beyond those numbers. Some of the reasons: speeding, not using seat belts, and being under the influence. What was more telling was the significant increase in single vehicle fatalities. Well, who or what to blame then? We're not just reacting badly to each other, but also acting recklessly on our own. That is worth further examination.

Dr. Frank Farley of Temple University calls it an "arousal breakout." Sounds like something that happens in a crowded strip club, but he suggests it is a rebellion from the isolation, loneliness, and depression brought on by these trying times. In other words, expect more recklessness!

Here's an odd observation: I've even noticed it watching football. Coaches bypassing field goal attempts for less certain 4th-down conversions; going for 2-point conversions and wins rather than a PAT and a tie; and, more often than not, failing.

I'll stay away from politics but will say I do miss genuine conservatism. I might not have always agreed with my elders, but I sure felt safer knowing those with decision power over others would lean towards less risk, side with the percentages.

Oh, reckless arousal is nothing new, and masks like condoms should probably be used more than they are, but it will all eventually be sorted out in the gene pool. Won't it?

Meanwhile, I learned my lesson when trying to run from winter. There is no escape. Not from anything really. Certainly not from flocking or herding behaviors, no matter how risky or stupid they appear to me. My job is to somehow adapt, be patient, take care of what I can, and break out the long underwear as needed.

Alone inside my head, I wonder sometimes, where on earth did THAT thought come from?!

And am I responsible? Well, who else is there to blame in there? Parasites? Malevolent spirits?

Some suggest diet may be a culprit, but let's not go there.

I haven't always had an effective one, but a strong interior governor is needed to pluck or shut out the crazy voices while leaving the wiser ones intact.

There was a time, for example, when I found myself jumping out of airplanes, trusting gear I had no personal verification would function correctly. And not just once. That would have been understandable and forgivable.

Each and every time, my anxiety would build to nearly unbearable levels until the moment when the chute would open and I could peacefully soar, float, and glide across the sky. I guess that silent endless view seemed to make it all worthwhile.

That is until the day when after stepping out on a locked tire, holding on to a wing strut, wondering again how to just let go … letting go … and then the panic of seeing a tangled chute above me. Yeah, imagine that.

In training, we were taught to jettison the malfunctioning main chute and utilize the smaller, little used, reserve one. I could not. What a time for my trust issues to come to surface, huh?

It seemed to me I had let go enough that morning and I would rather just hold on to what was already in my desperate hands rather than turn it all over to the unknown strapped on me.

Instead, while looking up, I alternately tugged on the two lines I had control of until the chute grabbed more air and opened more fully.

I landed a bit hot, kept tumbling upon impact, hoping movement would spare any one part of my body too much stress. I was able to walk away, bruised but uninjured.

However, I credit that day for the ascendancy of a previously neglected aspect of my character, the governor that has mostly watched over my decision-making ever since.

Oh sure, the crazy voices are still in there urging me to take chances, like defying gravity or other laws of physics, but they haven't won any internal elections, just a few card games among the inner politicians amusing themselves, biding their time, in what is for now a mostly stable intimate society.

How to Fashion a Life

First, with exuberance and glee.
Then, after decades of misstep and mistake,
with more caution and hot tea …
or
with whatever it is that slows
your racing mind enough to see
you are not alone
and home is indeed
a splendid place to be.
There will be times, of course, when
everything will still go wrong
and there's nowhere you belong.
Just survive

somehow,
stay alive.
This journey will never cease to surprise,
so hang around, do good as you can,
craft routines that nurture,
and cultivate patience
as one who worships silence
for all that it reveals
even in darkness, in every breath,
like sunlight illuminating
vermillion shades of love
behind closed eyes.

Today is my Uncle Marty's 95th birthday. There is a party for him in Florida. With the new variant raging, we reluctantly decide not to go. He is the elder in our family, always available for wise advice.

I remember a walk he and I took in the neighborhood around what was once known as the Purple Hyatt in Lincolnwood, Illinois. We both were staying there when my dad got married again. My uncle explained some of his insights from being a successful business consultant. When assisting in restructuring, he didn't pay as much attention to credentials, titles, or resumes as to how well a person listened, made eye contact, and communicated. I have applied his prescription whenever hiring or contracting anyone for a task since. It has served me well.

However, his deepest inspiration remains his devotion to his childhood sweetheart, Lois, who passed just after their 70th wedding anniversary. Their daughters, grandchildren, and great-grandchildren carry the gift of their love forward.

And he is still the conduit for what things were like long ago, and just about the only person I talk to for any length of time on the phone. I share with him what I would with my father if he were still alive.

My father's birthday —
Calendar return orbit
spotlights love and loss.

It is now the season of more frequent walks. Susan and I prefer to avoid the pre-holiday madness and stay out of our vehicles as much as possible.

A cacophony of screeching hawks interrupted this morning's walk. In trees, on power lines, flashes of brown, copper, and white taking off, circling and landing, all concentrated on a single desert landscape in front of a house on Allen Street. What the heck?!

Our attention was fully captured in this cessation of ordinary behavior and time. Harris hawks often hunt in pairs, are the most social of raptors, but we counted at least seven in this urgent gathering. What was going on?

Then, a large, healthy gray bobcat emerged below them and departed. Had it hijacked a kill or threatened a nest? Apparently, the calls of the hawks brought all the relations together to convince the freckled bobcat there were better places to be.

A human occupant from the dwelling had also popped out to watch the spectacle. We semi-consciously moved towards each other while caught in this rapture of raptors. But then something looked familiar. Oh no! I know her ... knew her.

It was Judith.

I was shocked near speechless. What was she doing here?! And how was it possible for her to wind up so close to where we live? The last I heard she was in Portland.

When I introduced Susan as my wife, the conversation seemed to dry up. A few more things were said about the moment we were in with these hawks, and then she was on her way to an appointment, and we were headed home.

I felt a sense of narratives rapidly converging and collapsing in this time language can no longer shape or contain. Was something calling us to come together, bridge the gap? I couldn't do it. At least not with her and not this morning.

I say I listen, but I've been locking myself away. I say I've been waiting for direction, for revelation of how a solitary soul might take flight in service of the whole, yet with something like a sense of panic, I am the slinking bobcat, not the soaring hawk.

Ordinary reality for me had just been punctured. Of course, it would be Judith that would instigate what was necessary, get me to look at what I'd been avoiding.

When she was younger, Judith's openness and intuitive curiosity, like some spiritual magnet, led her (and me for a while) down unusual paths.

Because of her, I met a man who channeled an entity called Z. At first, I was skeptical, designed all kinds of questions and methods to test the validity of what was presented as coming from another plane.

I not only became convinced, I helped him open a metaphysical institute here in Tucson. I thought what was being brought forth was of great value for all. But then I watched another man, mentored to become a channel, open himself to multiple entities, and within a short period of time contract a host of illnesses and die. It was as if he were burned alive from inside. I recoiled.

At the time, I was in an investment group that was theoretically taking advantage of channeled insider information to play the market. The predictions were correct; the timing was not. We, and I personally, lost everything. It was clear to me I needed to get away from all of it. And I made a pledge to myself then: I did not need to know what was not mine to know. I would grow into what I needed to know at whatever pace and not attempt any more shortcuts. It was the beginning of building boundaries after being a youth hell-bent on transcending them.

With Judith, much was porous. There were nights when I'd wake up with her in my dream only to find she was having the same dream and then we were both awake and aware in each other's dreams.

I suppose some might find that the ultimate romantic merging, but it was not. It was too much. Yes, perhaps to touch on moments like that during love-making is desirable, but it needs to have boundaries. We did not have them. We were like a two-headed Icarus on track to self-destruct.

In retrospect, we were too immature and undeveloped to harness such intimacy. Our time in Africa exposed that. From the moment I chose to not fling myself into the smoldering crater of Nyiragongo, I began the descent towards somewhere I could live and heal, without her.

During my hospital stay, I revisited the volcano where I considered ending my story but had no amends to make to Judith. I had already given her everything short of my life itself. Yet there is an acknowledgment she still deserves. She is the one who encouraged and then accompanied me on the search for the truth of my birth.

Perhaps her unexpected presence was the catalyst I needed to finally recount that story.

The land where I was born was green and soft, mothering, and I felt I could not breathe there. So I went west where the earth did not cuddle one like a baby, but one could see forever and grow strong with the challenge of open spaces, jagged mountains, and harsh deserts.

Perhaps because I rejected the mother who rejected me, I had to leave the civilized east whose cold winters were like a mother's love withdrawn and find instead the stern paternal hand of the unforgiving desert.

After so many years in desert discipline, it was time to return home, not as a child to measure his worth, but as an adult ready to embrace both mother and father as he finds them, and as they reside within his own heart.

A younger man wrote those words. I often girded my loins for an excursion to Chicago while simultaneously romanticizing and projecting my inner story onto an anthropomorphic landscape. I was, after all, both the victim and the hero in my own mythology.

There are a hundred possible ways to start this story. I have folders filled with papers, notes, records, letters, and scribblings suggesting many of them. Perhaps it was wise to wait almost 40 years after meeting my birth mother to tell this tale. Time has allowed me to condense much of what would be of no interest to anyone else.

Seems fitting to be sitting down to write this on my adopted mother's birthday and with my own birthday tomorrow.

There were many steps to unlocking what custom and the state of Illinois had sealed. The first was to approach my father, assure him my love and gratitude for his love and for the life he provided me.

Then, I told him about my hard-to-diagnose health issues related to the genetic marker HLA-B27. I could not answer the questions about family medical history the doctors needed for more clues as to what was going on in my body.

He took me to the building on Granville Avenue where early in 1955 he was instructed by his lawyer to go to meet the baby that was to be his son. It was not far from where we lived. In fact, it was close to where I went to high school.

My dad remembered one other detail: The woman who gave me to him made him promise I would get a college education.

Armed with an address, I was able to check who owned the building back then, make contact, and find out who was living there at the time. Phone calls and letters eventually revealed a name, Alida Olson, but there was no modern trace of her in the era's phone books. So, now what?

Here comes the first mystical twist in the story. Remember when I answered an ad for an editor at the *Aquarian Almanac*? Well, I didn't take the job with them. Instead, I gave the Aquarian Angels some advice that resonated with their own sense of what needed to happen. In exchange, they gave me two gifts: my first birth chart; and a session with the psychic, Ursula. Both experiences were profound and somewhat unsettling as they challenged my sense of how things functioned on this planet.

One thing that Ursula said without any prior knowledge of me was that someone was looking for me. She then proceeded to describe an older woman whose hair was once dark but was now lightening. I was almost able to picture someone, but there was nothing to do about it, and life went on.

In Chicago, frustrated about the dead end in my rather short search, I slept uneasily. I'm sure my mind was sorting through all the tidbits of information I received from the various conversations I'd had, but I really don't understand how exactly I awoke with a hunch, hurried to the library, grabbed the Boulder, Colorado phone book and found the name, Alida Olson in it.

I had some notion of how I would present myself on the phone, but as soon as she heard my voice, she became insistent on knowing who I really was, as if she had been waiting for me, for this call, for almost 30 years. She was my birthmother's aunt. I had made my first blood connection.

Sorry to interrupt this telling, but here in our Tucson neighborhood, Christmas just began with fireworks at midnight. You know, celebrating when our troops liberated Santa Claus from polar predators, or saved the North Pole from communism, or, well, I really don't know how or why fireworks have become part of Christmas too.

Normally, I'd be more annoyed, but I'm pretending it was meant to arouse me back to work on this. These words have been coming out slowly, as if needing to be squeezed from wherever I've stored them.

Alida had lost touch with her niece, but from her I finally learned my birth mother's name: Irene Gardemalm. Born in Sweden, she was a teenager when she came to live with her Aunt Alida in Chicago. Alida remembered Irene running around with a married man who was "crazy about her" but not much else.

Now that I knew her name, my search had better aim. I went through the *Daily Law Bulletin* records of court proceedings and found the case for the adoption of "Baby Boy Gardemalm." I learned she married a man named Jack in 1959 at the age of 23, which meant she was 18 when I was born. They divorced in 1965. I looked at phone books, used criss-cross directories, and checked census and property records under both names. I even had a contact with the phone company who checked if either she or Jack ever paid a phone bill. Jack had, but it was disconnected. It was as if they had both disappeared.

And, for however the brain processes highly charged undertakings, I started singing "Goodnight, Irene" at random moments.

With the search for Irene at a standstill, I went to Boulder to meet Alida. Judith came with and photographed the reunion.

When her door opened, Alida's first words were, "My little bundle!" And when I saw her, I remembered what Ursula had said all those years ago. This was the woman who had never let me go.

It was a bit too much emotional energy for me. Luckily, Judith could deflect some of Alida's attention away from me. I learned from her that I might have a brother in Sweden, but nothing solid. She thought my father's name was Ed Wendt. And she relayed how Irene was young and unable to be a mom, and that she, Alida, was the one who'd handed me over to another family. She said it was one of the most traumatic experiences in her life. And that she always prayed for me. Could that have been what helped me find her?

We wrote each other letters after that. I saw her one more time before she died, but never met her family as she desired.

The search was over for a while.

Un-fated

Too early? Too late? Could it be timing? Or is it just fate?
Is that why I offer what I do not have, hoping you will receive
what no one can possess?
Still, we try to present it to another, believing,
upon the agreement of reception, it will materialize.
Perhaps you yourself have imagined such an exchange
with someone else who would then also turn away, baffled.
It's neither faith, nor love, that fuels this zany
perpetual e-motion.
True, it can be animated with desire, felt as a longing
(perhaps for something not of this world)
projected upon one living near.
I have come to see it as a random glimpse,
a recognition of something happening elsewhere,
not meant for here, the now we know.
But somehow it can show itself, momentarily,
in the eyes or gestures of someone unsuspecting,
maybe mischievously, or even innocently.
You know, just another quirk of consciousness and existence
that spark these unheralded quests and questions of ours.

I hadn't given up but wasn't sure what was left to do. Perhaps Alida would contact the common family in Sweden and pass around the word of my existence and my search for Irene. Still, if Irene did not want to be found or contacted, who would break rank?

I did have the thought of investigating the rumor of a brother, even caught myself scanning crowded places as if I might recognize a face more connected to mine than any other.

Months went by, and with back issues troubling me, my health became more of a focus. I was bouncing from conventional to alternative to utterly bizarre approaches to resolve the crippling pain. At one point, I was drinking a tea made from creosote that tasted like gasoline. However, that was nothing compared to my 30-day watermelon fast. Nothing. But. Watermelon. I never enjoyed watermelon again.

In December of 1982, Judith and I were in Chicago visiting my family and friends, seeing if we could pick up the trail again. There didn't seem to be anything new to go on. The only thing we found was that, for whatever reason, Jack had registered to vote one year, and so we had an address for him. Wasn't much, considering they had divorced 17 years ago, but maybe he knew something of her current whereabouts.

On our last day in Chicago, we went there, rang the bell, but got no answer. We had plans that night for a Second City show, so that was it.

And that takes us to the second mystical twist in my tale.

As we were getting ready for our night out, I broke out in hives, for the first and what turned out to be the only time in my life. I was itchy and uncomfortable and could not imagine sitting through a show in that condition.

It got worse as we started driving south towards the theater. I told Judith I couldn't do this. We needed to turn around.

Unplanned, and I can't say today by my or by Judith's urging, we stopped one more time at Jack's and rang the bell again, only this time a head popped out from a window above and asked what the hell we wanted.

Thinking fast, I said we were friends of Alida Olson who was trying to locate her niece, Irene. Upon hearing this, and seeing Judith's Swedish-looking face, he smiled and said, "Come on up."

When we got upstairs into the apartment, he introduced us to a woman: "This is Irene."

Again, luckily Judith was with me. Jack's attention was on her. We kept up the act of being friends with Alida. I was vibrating with the unexpected shock of meeting this way. Irene sat back in the shadows, mostly watching. I thought she sensed things were not as they appeared to be.

The energy was so thick, electric, and pulsating in that room, how could she not have felt it? How could I possibly have participated in the seemingly light chatty talk about Alida and about me and Judith on my first encounter with the woman who birthed me?

My hives disappeared. It was as if my body knew what was destined to happen, as if it had somehow conspired to make it happen.

When I first began the search, I imagined the best scenario as somehow meeting her without her knowing who I was. It seemed to me that would take the pressure off, allow us to meet as just people. I had no idea how that could ever be arranged. Yet that is exactly what occurred.

The first sight of her also brought on the realization of how she looked like an older version of Cindy. Wow, the power of imprinting! That explained so much. I had found the teenage face of my mother in Cindy's!

So much more was happening behind the friendly words being shared. Might I look something like my birth father? I had a peculiar sensation that I was somehow acting like him, some deep body knowledge speaking from within me to her again.

And then a phone rang. Judith and I looked at each other. There was no record of either of them having a phone. He answered gruffly and was quickly off it.

When we talked about it later, Judith and I both had a sense of something dark, perhaps criminal going on. In our conversation with them, we learned they had a smoke shop in downtown Chicago. Tobacco and crime have danced together before. Who knew? We certainly weren't going to investigate that!

People have asked me how I could have not broken down and confessed my identity. Perhaps if it had felt different I would have. As it was, they were nearly invisible, as if in hiding for some reason. We obviously didn't bring up their divorce or find out how and why they were together again.

She seemed quite private and reserved. He seemed to dominate her. Jack's enthusiasm was surely about interacting with a young, attractive female. It made the evening almost pleasant, and I didn't mind having that be my first interaction with the source of my existence.

Most of all, it didn't seem fair to spring something like that on her. So, we left as we came, strangers who happened to know a concerned relative. Of course, if Irene contacted Alida, she would discover the rest of the story.

I stepped away from this narrative for a bit. Must admit how difficult it is to piece together exactly how events unfolded 39 years ago. My memory has not always matched the records I've been digging up and reviewing.

This morning I was reading how in Japan there are night-movers who help people disappear without a trace. They have a name for those who have successfully vanished—"jouhatsu."

Of course, that brought me back right to where I left off with my speculations about Jack and Irene. I found it curious to be thinking about them and modern versions of people vanishing.

I've been wondering where one goes, what one does, after evaporating like that. Could there be a place somewhere the rest of us have yet to discover? If so, what is life like there? Were those who found their way to such a hideaway able to leave the problematic parts of themselves behind? Or did they find what most of us eventually do: We were always our own problem?

Nowadays, and really only in comparison to previous versions of myself, I have partially disappeared. However, I do still catch myself wanting to be liked or at least not thought ill of, and now for the first time in a very long time I'm wondering if I might be anything like Irene.

I know several people who have mostly stopped interacting in person with others. It's not just fear of getting sick anymore. We are already sick with something that can't be cured by going back to how we've lived before.

Why did they divorce and then Irene come back to live with Jack? And so, even what is happening today is reconnecting me to unanswered questions from the past. Why were they both almost impossible to find, even by relatives?

Judith and I went back to where we had been staying in San Francisco, moved to Tucson and officially got our own place together. From there I wrote Irene a letter telling her the true identity of the man who showed up at her apartment in December. I kept a copy of it, dated 1/24/83. Two typed pages of single-spaced rambling about me, what led me to look for her, and how I went about it. I apologized for the deception in December and ended it with the hope for future communication.

I didn't hear back. I sent her something short and sweet for Mother's Day. Yeah, I really did.

This was the response I received:

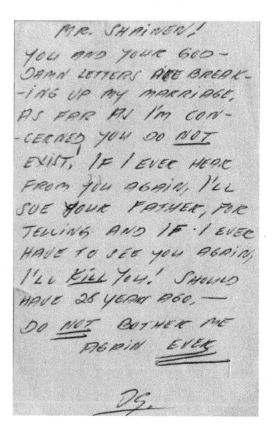

A death threat, on a postcard. All these years later, and I still handle the artifact like toxic waste, still feel the shock of articulated hatred and rejection. Yet I have never disposed of it. It was the key to everything previously unsaid wreaking havoc in my attempts at a life.

Eventually, I shared this response with Alida. She was already not well and was hard to understand, but my translation of what she haltingly shared with me was that Irene had tried to drown me as an infant. No matter what Irene's actual attempt in that moment was, Alida intervened, and I survived.

Alida also shared Irene's fear of Jack. Irene had called her after my first letter, said Jack had read it and beat her. So there is that part of the story to consider as well.

I have seldom been comfortable in other people's homes, in cold water, in caves. I tried re-birthing but froze up, became paralyzed in seizures of tetany. I've come to understand the womb was not a safe place for me, and I have projected that fear elsewhere.

I've talked before about the years I worked with my father at Acorn Tile when I mostly drove the truck to set up and pick up jobs, but also did the jobs myself too small to send a crew. And when not busy, I spent every minute I could in the warehouses sorting and organizing the hundred years of tile, supplies, and equipment from the business my grandfather had started, as if doing so might help make sense of something inside me.

The warehouses contained the history of ceramic tile in America, and I came to be able to identify just about every piece from the color and the backing.

Plumbers knew to come to me for almost-impossible-to-find pieces of tile to save a client a costly new shower or tub wall after a repair. Rich Melman of Lettuce Entertain You Enterprises would wander around in the warehouses looking for inspiration for his next restaurant.

At the time, I lived in Evanston in a sparsely furnished attic apartment. I'd park my vehicle on Friday after work and not start it again until Monday morning. I walked everywhere.

I lived as a monk who consciously re-birthed himself. It was a womb of my own. I grieved there. I wrote, made art, and invited childish expressions to come forth without judgment. I had a therapist, got involved in personal growth trainings and 12-step groups. It was in that attic a place in me, once filled with pain, finally emptied and became receptive, ready for something else.

And I did do something else. I went to Irene's Smoke Shop and confronted her.

It's now late morning on New Year's Eve, 2021. I had hoped to finish the rest of that story before the year's end, but the sun is shining, and I need to move. Susan and I spontaneously agree to a walk along the unpaved side of the Rillito.

The wind picked up and what began as a pleasant stroll became a head down trudge. After a while we surrendered and let the wind push us homeward, testing other directions and options as we went.

It was as if there were only one choice for us. Our path, our timing, led us by the open garage of a neighbor who was spread out on the concrete floor, unmoving, blood around her head. Oh no!

We got her talking, then carefully up to a sitting position to assess the extent of her injury and whether an ambulance was needed immediately. Susan went to get the help of some other neighbors. She found a young couple who had recently moved in. Turned out he was a paramedic, and she, a dental assistant. Neither were squeamish about blood and injury. How lucky was that?

With his help, we got her inside to her favorite chair. They tended to her head wound. Her two cats were involved with everything going on. A television, already on, let us know Betty White had died. Somehow that added to the surreal nature of being in an elderly lady's house for the first time trying to figure out who to call and what to do.

Susan and I looked through papers, found an address book, had her point out someone to call. There was a cousin who lived in Tucson. Susan left her a message. The four of us decided Urgent Care, stitches, and a full examination was necessary.

As we started to mobilize, the cousin called back, said she would be right there. Yes, there was relief to turn this over to her, but there was also gratitude for participating in this rather strange way to end the year and get to know our neighbors.

It was a reminder for me to listen to and trust urges and instincts, to know that I don't have to do anything other than my own part and, once again, to remember how much we need each other, how much better everything is when we come together.

I may just have to stay up late tonight to finish my tale.

Once the Hero's Journey is invoked, there must be obstacles. I took the train from Evanston to downtown Chicago on what must have been the coldest and windiest day of the year. That wasn't the plan, of course, but walking westward on Madison Street towards Irene's shop was against the bitter cold wind. It had to be, right? Each step had to be full of conviction and determination.

Are you really going to do this, Lee? She threatened to kill you. Her man seemed like someone capable of arranging it.

The cold weather allowed me the disguise of a scarf and stocking hat. I was able to enter the large office building that housed the shop in its lobby unnoticed. I was just one of many people moving through it. I waited until Jack stepped out to approach her. She panicked, threatened to call the police, but I was solid, unwavering.

"You need to answer some questions, and then I will leave, and you will never hear from me again."

I asked about my father and their relationship. She said he died in the Korean War. Of course, that made no sense. The war was over the year before I was born. Actually, I didn't believe anything she said. She was nervous and wanted me gone as quickly as possible, so said whatever came in her head. It didn't really matter. I just needed to stand in front of her open-eyed and unafraid.

When there was nothing left to say or ask, I left. I wanted to say, "Goodnight, Irene," but it was midday. However, I smiled inside at the thought. Outside, the wind had stopped. The sun had a warmth unimaginable earlier. I even unbuttoned my overcoat and practically zippity doo dah skipped my way on the same street I had struggled to navigate earlier.

I felt as free, alive, and present as I ever had.

I stayed in that Evanston attic for three years, and while working for Acorn Tile, I had several opportunities to be downtown. As promised, I never said another word to her, but I'd stop in the shop from time to time, buy a newspaper or something, like any other customer who came and went.

On the last stop, she attempted some small talk, appeared to reach out, perhaps recognizing me even though I now had a mustache and different hairstyle. I was just another guy though who nodded his head and departed. I never saw her again. The shop was gone soon after.

Ten years later, walking from my Headmaster unit at Damian Ranch to the Community Room for a meeting, I picked up my mail on the way. There was a letter postmarked from Sweden with the name Gardemalm on the return address. It was from Irene's brother, Jimmy, introducing me through a letter to my brother Glen.

Irene had died. Jimmy and his brother had flown to Chicago to settle her estate. And here's the final mystical twist in my telling. After they closed everything up and exited the apartment, Jimmy had the urge to go back in and take a final look around. When he did, he found a plastic bag full of papers hanging in a closet they had not seen before. He put them in his suitcase and brought them with him back to Sweden.

Eventually, he looked through the bag and found a letter I had written to Irene. She had saved it. And it was the first anyone in her family had ever heard about me. They knew Glen because he was born in Sweden. I was the secret.

Glen, his wife Susanne, and his sons Kenny and John came to Tucson. We were both in our forties when we met. As he said at the time, "It's not often one gets an older brother late in life."

We got along easily. Once, after a romp in the Rincon Mountains, the seven of us, alternating head and feet, all managed to squeeze into the back of my cushioned-for-camping Mazda pickup truck to watch the sunset. I have no similar memory of such intimacy with the family I knew all my life. And we had only been around each other for a few days. Ryan, Kenny, and John were like puppies from the same litter. It was a joy to experience.

My blood did not speak
until I met my brother,
gave silence a name.

Over the years, we went to Sweden; they came back to Tucson; we met in New York; we met in Chicago; Kenny came and stayed with us; Ryan went and stayed with them; and during this pandemic if I mentioned a family Zoom, it was with them.

Irene had written letters to Glen, promised she would come back, but never did. As soon as he was legally able, he signed the papers for the people who raised him to become his adoptive parents. That was the essential difference in our stories and who we both became. I was perpetually searching for what was missing; he had to discern what was false and reject it.

It was difficult for me at first to read her letters he had taken the time to translate for me. Everything I had asked of her, she had willingly offered to him. And that is also how karma works. She became the outsider wanting into his family as I had once wanted to be part of hers. But then, it was only my family and Glen's family that were joined, and because of so many precarious moments, decisions, interventions.

There might not be a God nor a grand design, but something connects and orders consciousness. It is receptive, sensitive, responsive, and perhaps intelligent. I call it Sticky Karma.

Acknowledgments

With a step or two already into 2022, there really doesn't seem to be an end in sight to this viral madness. But I am done with it. At least done with writing about it.

Back when I thought I might be dying, I reviewed my life and what was left on my bucket list. I was okay with everything but did have one regret. There was a book I had wanted to write, and a story I felt I must tell.

All praise and appreciation begins with Susan. If not for her, I would have quietly bled out of this life. What has been written since has benefited from her insight and inspiration, and from her most excellent proofreading skills.

Without next the confidence of Ira's daughter Logan, trusting her gambler's intuition, Latah Books would have passed on this. Instead, I received inestimable assistance, clarity, and direction from Jon and Kevin, and so now that one missing piece is in place. I am both satisfied and incredibly grateful.

And, finally, I am blessed with talented and generous friends, like Randy Harris and David Fitzsimmons, who have added their artistic magic to this project.

About the Author

Lee Shainen was a Tucson garbageman when, with less than a day to prepare, he found himself in front of a composition class at the University of Arizona. That summer, he was invited to the inaugural Southern Arizona Writing Project, became a research assistant for SAWP, and met many who were reimagining the teaching of writing. He went on to be awarded for teaching excellence.

In search of community, romance, a spiritual path, a subpar round—all while gathering novel material—he traveled extensively, taking on jobs of all sorts, but always returning to teaching, writing, and golf.